Education for the World, Education for All

Quebec Education in the Context of Globalization

Jocelyn Berthelot
Translated by David Clandfield

Part of the *Our Schools/Our Selves* Book Series
in collaboration with Everybody's Schools: An Education Policy Institute
2008

Education for the World, Education for All:
Quebec Education in the Context of Globalization

Part of the *Our Schools / Our Selves* Book Series
In collaboration with Everybody's Schools : An Education Policy Institute
2008

Édition originale : © Jocelyn Berthelot,
Une école pour le monde, une école pour tout le monde, VLB éditeur, 2006.

EXECUTIVE EDITOR
Erika Shaker

ISSUE EDITOR
David Clandfield

Special thanks to Jocelyn Berthelot

EDITORIAL OFFICE
Canadian Centre for Policy Alternatives
Suite 410, 75 Albert Street, Ottawa, ON, K1P 5E7
tel: (613) 563-1341 fax: (613) 233-1458

ISSN 0840-7339
ISBN 978-1-897569-14-6

PRODUCTION
Typesetting and design by Tim Scarth
Cover photograph and design by Nancy Reid (www.nrgrafix.com)
Printed in Canada by Transcontinental

Jocelyn Berthelot began his career as a teacher. From 1977 until his retirement in 2007 he worked as a researcher for the Centrale des syndicats du Québec (CSQ). During this time he participated in all the major educational debates in Quebec including: public funding of private schools, programs for the gifted, and intercultural education. He is the author of numerous articles, and four books in French, several of which propose new paths for democratic education.

David Clandfield is Professor Emeritus of French at the University of Toronto. A founding editor of Our Schools Our Selves, he has written on education politics and translated the writings of progressive pedagogues from France and Quebec. He served as a school trustee in the 1980s and as an adviser to the NDP in Ontario until parting company with them in 1993 over his opposition to standardized testing and the social contract.

Preface to the English Edition

From the Author:

I wrote this book in 2005-2006, while I was still working in the research department of the Centrale des syndicats du Québec (CSQ), a labour federation that notably includes most of the education workers in school boards as well as some of those in cegeps. I want to express my gratitude to the CSQ for their support and for allowing me all the time and freedom I needed to undertake such a task.

I would also like to acknowledge the help I received from many colleagues at the CSQ who generously gave me the benefit of their expertise and their criticisms, the valuable work of the technical assistants at the Resource Centre, and the unflagging support of the secretarial staff. Finally, my thanks are due to my primary reader, Marie Gagnon, who did so much to make this work more of a pleasure to read.

In the two years since the French publication appeared, neo-liberal politics have continued to plague the process of globalization. Despite a few setbacks and temporary retreats, the politics of privatization and liberalization still dominate the public sphere in many countries. Nor have resistance efforts buckled either; the recent failure of WTO talks is ample evidence of that.

In education, the major trends analyzed in this book have not deviated from their course. Privatization, the commercialization of educational activities, the exacerbation of inequality through school choice, and competition between schools have all gathered strength.

Even so, some revisions were necessitated by important events and new policies. So the text has been updated slightly. But it was not possible to give a full account of the research published since the first edition for every topic discussed. However, there is nothing to show that the data underpinning the analysis that follows have been thrown into doubt by the publication of new studies. Quite the reverse; the publications of the last two years seem to confirm the results of earlier work.

To conclude, I wish to thank the whole team at *Our Schools/Our Selves*, Erika Shaker of the CCPA for coordinating the edition, and especially David Clandfield for agreeing to take this on and for providing an excellent translation.

I consider it an honour that through this book I can make a contribution to the CCPA's work in exposing the commodification of all human endeavours, including education.

Jocelyn Berthelot, October 2008

From the Translator·

I want to add my thanks to Erika Shaker for her support, to BCTF for funding this work and to George Martell for rekindling my interest in education politics after the long exile that followed my frustrations with the Rae Government. I particularly thank Jocelyn Berthelot for being such an obliging and attentive author. He gave me a free hand, but even so checked everything in a spirit of solidarity. Thanks to him, I did avoid some embarrassing mistranslations. Needless to say, any that remain are my responsibility alone. Finally my thanks as ever to Sandra for her patience and understanding once more.

David Clandfield, October 2008

From the Executive Editor:

The CCPA is so pleased to have the opportunity to make this excellent book by Jocelyn Berthelot available to our members and to an English-speaking audience through David Clandfield's precise and eloquent translation. Our sincere thanks to the British Columbia Teachers' Federation for their financial assistance, to Larry Kuehn and George Martell for their involvement throughout this process, and to VLB Éditeur.

In addition to marking the 20th anniversary of *Our Schools/ Our Selves*, the release of the English edition of *Education for the World, Education for All: Quebec Education in the Context of Globalization* represents the beginning of an occasional series of books, several of which will be produced in collaboration with Everybody's Schools : An Education Policy Institute. We look forward to the opportunity to augment the work of the CCPA and *Our Schools / Our Selves* through this relationship, and to make the excellent work by internationally-renown authors such as Jocelyn Berthelot even more widely available.

Erika Shaker, October 2008

Introduction

Globalization is still a hot topic. In Quebec, as elsewhere, events conspire to remind us of this every day. The economy, the environment, culture, celebrations of solidarity, all facets of social life are affected by it. Plant closings and relocations, financial crises, efforts to redefine the role of the State and education, the Kyoto protocol, anti-globalization demonstrations, the rapidity and sophistication of communications bear ample witness to this thrust for change.

Some observers are declaring a brave new world, a new era in human history. The current upheavals, they argue, are the broadest since the industrial revolution, or even since the invention of agriculture. For the most optimistic among them, this new era is linked to remarkable advances in democracy, the breakdown of boundaries, an updraft of solidarity. For the first time ever humanity is in a position to provide all this planet's inhabitants access to a decent life.

Others criticize all this "globaloney" and reject the unworldliness all around us.[1] For them, the paeon of praise that greets globalization serves only to mask its hidden agenda. Far from being new, it actually forms part of the hard and fast logic of capitalist development, ever expanding its reach and its grasp. The much vaunted "global village" is turning out to be a "global pillage." Globalization is market-driven, neo-liberal, non-egalitarian.

Sadly we must acknowledge that the current round of globalization is bourne along on a wave of ultraliberalism reminiscent of the 19th century. Market fundamentalism is eroding the democratic gains of recent decades and is increasing inequality among nations and within them. But a very lively alternative globalization movement makes the point that another kind of world is possible. The future, still ours to build, has nothing to do with foreordained fate. To prove it, all that's needed is to look back into the past.

Globalization has ancient roots. It already has a long history that deserves scrutiny. Accordingly, our first chapter begins with a historical review. This review will give us a better picture of the enduring features of this age-old movement, as well as its new directions and sudden breaks.

So the doctrine of laissez-faire and free trade is not new. Nor is the resistance it has met nor are the subsequent swings of the pendulum. On the other hand, the Nation-State is witnessing a radical redefinition of its responsibilities by the proliferation of international bodies and agreements and, for the first time, the very survival of our planet is threatened by unbridled growth.

This review of the history of globalization along with a brief analysis of the high stakes linked with it seemed necessary to us because the tightly woven links between education and society means that they must both face the same challenges.

Just like the State, education too is in upheaval. It is the object of criticism, restructurings and reforms. Even the words being used to describe it are changing. Concepts of performance, competition and marketing are being borrowed from the corporate world. School culture is becoming a business culture; educational systems are getting to be more and more alike; national differences are being ironed out under the weight of a "new educational world order." The second chapter takes stock of the new educational model that is gradually taking root.

In effect, international economic organizations are imposing their own discourse and philosophy. The General Agreement on Trade in Services (GATS) could even place limits on national specificity in education. The changes under way almost everywhere have a familiar feel: decentralization, competitiveness, performance review, meeting the demands of business. Shrinking the State means that education is being deprived of urgently needed resources. Even so, in every society, despite these broad trends, historical and social considerations along with struggles to hang on to democratic gains have brought about resistance and have forced compromises.

So where is Quebec in all this? Where do the current changes in education fit into this new educational model? What were the results of the resistance and social struggles that they provoked? What lessons can be learnt from experiences elsewhere and the research about them? Quebec will emerge as a society that has retained some distinctness; but the "Quebec model" is treading water, as it is being eroded by utilitarian discourses and practices.

And yet, the last few decades have seen public education contribute significantly to the development of Quebec society and to the advancement of democracy. Every effort must be made to prevent education from being reduced to a mere consumer product. Education must stand strong and reject the discourse of inevitability. It must once more become a collective project dedicated to equity and social justice. That is the purpose of the third chapter, which advocates maintaining the link between education and the common good.

The proposals in this last chapter affect all levels of education. They favour an internationalization of education that emphasizes cooperation and solidarity; they promote global awareness in preparation for the challenges that humanity is facing; they give full weight to increasing diversity and pluralism; and they respond as fully as possible to the demands of a new sense of citizenship. Driven by the need to strive for educational equity unrelentingly, they will be based on experiments that have proved their worth elsewhere in the world and on the revealing results of international research. They call for the equitable distribution of students among schools and among classes, support for the most vulnerable groups in early childhood, and improved school participation rates for both young and adult populations.

This is meant as a starting point for reflection and debate and aims to reach first and foremost the men and women who make education their daily practice. These proposals are put forward in a spirit of the total respect that their work deserves.

The sheer scope of the task, as it is clear, has not allowed every subject to receive full attention. The urgent need for a synthesis led to pruning and choosing only the most relevant data. In order to maintain a good flow, references are all grouped together at the end of the book for each of the subsections of the chapters; endnotes will be found after each chapter. Readers can subsequently satisfy their curiosity or even check the accuracy of the related facts in the bibliography.

Notes

1. The term "globaloney" has apparently been around since 1943 when it was first coined by Republican Clare Boothe Luce in her maiden speech to the U.S. House of Representatives. More recently it has re-surfaced in Michael Veseth's *Globaloney: Unraveling the Myths of Globalization* (Lanham, MD: Rowman and Littlefield, 2006). I use it to translate Berthelot's *globalivernes,* a more recent coining he attributes to Paul Ariès writing in *Relations* (March 2005). The use of unwordliness here is a lamer attempt to capture the punning neologism *immondialisation* also quoted by Berthelot from Ariès. [DC]

CHAPTER ONE

Changing Times

Every era is marked by one particular issue that serves as a lightning rod for every debate and every struggle. The issue today is economic globalization. Its market-driven logic is draining off all the resources of the planet, all societies, all cultures and all aspects of life.

Jacques Gélinas, *La globalisation du monde*

The use of the word globalization is quite recent, first gaining currency in English in 1962[1]. Its French equivalent, *la mondialisation*, preceded it in 1960, according to *Le Petit Robert* dictionary. It quickly caught on to denote the multiple changes affecting national societies and the world. It has now entered the everyday speech of both its supporters and its detractors.

As often happens in the humanities and social sciences, the expression does not have a single meaning. The interpretation of it varies with the discipline and political stripe of the speaker. Economists generally emphasize markets and international trade. Anthropologists tend to focus on changes affecting different cultures. As for the stresses on the Nation-State, they are the central concern of political scientists. And finally, issues of equity and historical cycles are of interest to sociologists and historians alike[2].

Some people prefer to use the plural. There are several globalizations at work. In its hegemonic forms, globalization gets its impetus from global capitalism, with its winners and losers. Opposing these forms are those that embrace a more counter-hegemonic approach, giving weight to a cosmopolitanism based on human rights and engaging in the defence of a common heritage of humanity.

One final distinction has to do with the historical nature of the phenomenon. The world-system theorists are most insistent: in the long term there is nothing new under the sun. What is happening is a quantitative expansion of long-term trends going back to the origins of capitalism.

To discuss this, the U.S. sociologist Giovanni Arrighi goes back to the beginnings of our era by emphasizing the transformation of this "long twentieth century." In his view, the latter consists of three phases: a financial expansion which, at the end of the 19th century, broke up the British domination of old, a material expansion which then lasted until the 1970s, and a second financial expansion which presages the decline of U.S. domination. This decline is a logical conclusion to the analysis of successive hegemonies going back to the 12th century. If we take this as true, then the question is: what's next? Shall we witness the consolidation of a new financial hegemony in and around China, for example, or shall we see the birth of a new form of domination based on supra-national entities?

In her book *The First Globalization: Lessons from the French*, Suzanne Berger tries to learn the lessons from a period of globalization similar to our own today and which happened over a hundred years ago. Almost the entire globe was part of a world economy dominated by Britain. Not only did goods and services circulate as freely as they do today, but the same was true of people.

The critics of world-system theory feel that the insistence on the long view interferes with our ability to notice what is new about the current period and masks the global nature of the process that is unfolding. For this view, globalization is a radically new phenomenon going back only a few decades. It is essential to grasp its specific characteristics, because we are witnessing a veritable revolution. Social relations are less closely linked to territories, frontiers are being breached, and human geography is being transformed as a result.

A final group of observers, including this writer, draws attention to the fact that the current phase of globalization is accompanied by neoliberal ideology whose thesis is that all societies should be governed by the rules of trade and analyzed solely through the prism of economics. If the dominant ideology emphasizes the private sector rather than the public sector for the totality of social functions and activities, its opponents remind us that this choice is not self-evident.

Beyond these academic quarrels, there is everything to be gained by borrowing from various disciplines and by harnessing a variety of approaches to get a better handle on the current round of globalization. This is what we have set out to do in this first chapter. Of course, crossing disciplinary boundaries carries certain risks. The hope is that the experts will forgive the occasional errors or omissions that have slipped in.

The first part of the chapter is given over to a brief historical retrospective. The present has both old and new elements contained within it. There is continuity and discontinuity. The continuity observed over centuries goes along with the significant transformations of the last thirty years. From the conquest of America to the Washington Consensus, by way of *pax Britannica*, the New Deal and the Thirty Glorious Years, a short journey back in time will allow us to take another look at the apparent inevitability of neo-liberal globalization.

The second part will consider the nature of the changes currently transforming the world. All facets of our lives are affected by them. Political, economic and cultural life, national and international institutions, production, social relations and the natural world are being influenced in different degrees. New forms of resistance are erupting and projecting the vision of a better world. This thematic analysis will also go back in history. It will help us distinguish the old from the new and put a gag on the mantra of inevitability. We shall catch our first glimpse of the issues being raised for education by these transformations, issues that will be dealt with in the following chapters.

As the essayist John [Ralston] Saul has written: "The belief that we do not have choices is a fantasy, and an unfortunate indulgence in abdication" (2005, p.15). Globalization stands for the limits of both our hopes and our fears. Peoples and institutions are the products of past events and their choices are based on the sense that they can make of these events. The future is still a construction that belongs to all human beings, whatever the context for their activism. This is the conviction that serves as a rock for the thoughts that follow.

GLOBALIZATION, A LONG HISTORY

Globalization has been built up in stages. As summarized by Arrighi (1994), it goes like this: the Genoese discovered the world, the British conquered it and the U.S. has, until recently, been consolidating this conquest. An ever-expanding integration of the globe has been taking place, despite periods of decline and wars.

*   *   *

The conquest of America marked the beginning of the first true globalization, "the beginning of the planetary era," to quote Edgar Morin. The realization that the earth was round opened the way to the great oceanic expeditions. Europeans launched caravels to India both westwards and eastwards. Christopher Columbus reached the American continent in 1492 and Vasco da Gama rounded the Cape of Good Hope at the southern tip of Africa in 1497.

Venice and Florence controlled the land trade routes to China and India. No sovereign, no city state was in any position to rid them of this monopoly. So others had to bypass the "Italian" route. That was the ambition of the monarchs of the Iberian peninsula with the support of Genoese capital.

The route to India actually led to America and Africa. From the Caribbean islands, colonization extended to the whole American continent, first to the south and then to the north. Trading posts and colonies were gradually established along the Indian Ocean's coastline of Africa. The European powers shared the booty amongst themselves. Gold, silver, precious gems and spices flooded the markets.

The upshot was a globalization of trade. The Americas provided maize, potatoes, manioc, pimentos, groundnuts, tomatoes, cocoa beans and tropical fruit. Europe introduced wheat, alfalfa, onions, sugar cane, vines and rice, as well as domestic animals, tools and new technologies.

These intercontinental movements exposed populations to new diseases. Smallpox, influenza and pneumonia killed off about 90% of the population in the Americas. The population declined from more than 50 million at the time of the Conquest to fewer than 5 million by the beginning of the 17th century. In Quebec, the aboriginal populations that consisted of some 25,000 souls when the colony was founded were reduced to a few thousand by about 1660. This globalization of disease was made worse by inhuman treatment. As Denys

Delâge has put it, the settlers came to a land that was not virgin so much as widowed.

The exploitation of natural resources was accompanied by cash crop cultivation on a massive scale, notably sugar cane and cotton. The cultivation of sugar cane was probably the first economic enterprise to be globalized. European plantation owners forced African slaves to produce a grass brought from Asia into the American tropics for European consumers. This led to the birth of the infamous "trade triangle."

It is estimated that between 1500 and 1888, the year that marked the end of slavery in America, more than nine million Africans were kidnapped and sent to the New World on slave ships that plied the "ebony trade" in inhuman conditions. Thus was solved the problem of the massive labour needs of the great plantations.

The Colonial Pact forced colonies to restrict their imports to products coming from the metropole and to export all their raw materials back there. As a protest against this injustice, British settlers threw a highly valuable cargo of raw tea into the Boston Harbour. The gesture passed into the historical record as the Boston Tea Party. The Crown reacted with an escalating series of repressive measures. The revolutionaries reacted with the Declaration of Independence and a war of liberation.

This first independence struggle was eventually taken up in the vast majority of the Americas. Liberation movements put an end to European colonial domination. New nations were born. It was essentially only in Lower Canada (Quebec) and Upper Canada (Ontario) that revolt, by the Patriots of 1836-1837, was crushed.

The trade triangle of the 18th century destroyed the social fabric of a good part of Western Africa, established slavery in North America and the Caribbean, and secured the accumulation of capital in Western Europe. By this means, colonial wealth and slavery contributed heavily to the development of Europe and to the acceleration of the British Industrial Revolution. Improvements in productivity thus achieved brought hardly any gains at all to the indigenous populations of the Americas.

An Empire under the Sun

The country which emerged victorious from the rival European powers was Great Britain. It successfully beat out the United Provinces (centred in Holland) several times when the latter were the dominant force on the seas and in financial markets. It conquered France and gave itself the lion's share of the spoils with the Treaty of Paris in 1763[3]. It secured its own domination of the seas after the defeat of Napoleon in 1815. It then exercised its own supremacy through international trade and its naval strength until World War I.

The Industrial Revolution began in England at the end of the 18th century. It was founded on a new mechanized system of production and a new organization of work. The workshops of peasant-artisans gave way to the new manufactories. The steam engine, the mechanical loom and the steamship, later joined by the locomotive and the telegraph, laid the foundations of this new style of revolution. Transportation and communications became faster and more profitable than they had been in the time of horses and sail. All this paved the way for a new world market of capital.

Colonial expansion continued, particularly in Asia and Africa. The metropoles needed more and more raw materials and a market for their manufactured goods. The Colonial Pact was once again imposed by means of unequal treaties and warfare. Japan was forced to open up to international trade. China was subjected to the aggressive incursions of Britain and France, in the course of two so-called Opium Wars, which, in the mid-19th century, sought an outlet for opium produced in India in exchange for the commodities that they needed. Trade had no place for morality.

To cap this, India, which had been a major textile producer before European domination, was forced to knuckle under. It was made to export its raw cotton to England and to import fabric produced in the metropole[4]. The colonies abandoned subsistence farming in order to concentrate on cash crops for export such as cotton, jute, indigo and tea. Deindustrialization and devastating famines were the lot of the subjugated countries.

While the Western states owned 35% of the surface of the Earth in 1848, this proportion rose to 67% in 1878 and 85% in 1914. These numbers give a good idea of the colonial thrust that accompanied the development of Western Europe. And Britain owned the lion's share. Hence the expression so dear to Queen Victoria's heart: "the empire on which the sun never sets."

In the metropole, the first phase of the Industrial Revolution with its hellish factories destroyed its workers. Industrialization caused a massive exodus from the countryside, accelerated by the Enclosures Acts that expelled peasants from the lands they lived on and cultivated. In the industrial cities, the new workers were crammed together in inhuman slums. Children, sometimes as young as four years old, were made to go to work in the factories. Hunger was the fate of the masses. A number of writers and poets have described the horrors of this world.

In the mid-19th century, Great Britain was the unchallenged leader of industrial production and trade. The City of London was the centre of world finance. It was well placed to impose everywhere a liberalization of which it now controlled the levers. And so it proceeded to abolish all the protectionist laws that had once contributed to its supremacy.

The Quebec economy was then integrated into the system of international commerce, mainly through trade with the British metropole. It exported wood, cereals and ships and imported manufactured products. Between 1854 and 1866, the Reciprocity Treaty with the United States opened the border to the south. But it was not until the 1880s that Quebec truly entered the industrial era.

The "great Victorian boom" (1850-1873) signified a great leap forward for the world economy. Commerce broke with its warrior past, peopled with traffickers, pirates and privateers. It was henceforth tied to peace. Free trade became a constituent part of the British national identity. It was to remain so until the Great Depression of the 1930s, although it began losing ground with the serious agricultural crisis that struck in 1873.

This latter crisis and the subsequent depression, which spared neither Quebec nor Canada, shook people's confidence in the capacity of the economy to cure its own ills. Protectionist policies made their appearance, notably in the form of customs tariffs and welfare legislation. The U.S. and Germany were now positioned to become the successors of an empire that had already peaked.

Reduced costs of transportation and rapid long-distance travel favoured trade. Freedom of movement applied equally well to people who did not need passports to travel at that time. Huge population movements occurred. More than 55 million Europeans and 5 million Asians emigrated between 1870 and World War I, mainly to the U.S., but also to Latin America, Australia and Canada. Between Confederation in 1867 and the end of the century, Canada welcomed almost 1.8 million new citizens. The same period, though, saw more than 2.5 million Canadians leave for the United States.

In Europe, the workers' movement generally approved of opening borders to capital, goods and labour. It was seen as a powerful tool of international solidarity. That acceptance was not shared in the New World where protectionism was popular. Xenophobia did not take long to rear its head.

In *The First Globalization*, Suzanne Berger gives several examples of the transformations that occurred within a century or so. At the time of the American Revolution, Benjamin Franklin needed 42 days to cross the Atlantic; in 1912, he would have needed only five and a half. In 1815, the Rothschilds had to use messenger pigeons in order to discover the outcome of the Battle of Waterloo, on which depended the success of one of their great financial coups. Before 1860, information took three weeks to get from New York to London. All that changed dramatically with the telephone and the telegraph.

A very popular British book, published in 1910 and subsequently translated into 25 languages, sums up the spirit of the times in the West. It referred to the increase in interdependence, "the result of daily use of those contrivances of civilization which date from yesterday--the rapid post, the instantaneous dissemination of financial and commercial information by means of telegraphy, and generally the incredible increase in the rapidity of communication which has put the half-dozen chief capitals of Christendom in closer contact financially, and has rendered them more dependent the one upon the other than were the chief cities of Great Britain less than a hundred years ago" (quoted by Berger, p. 108). The famous British economist John Maynard Keynes wrote more or less the same thing in 1919. So it would be wrong to claim that the situation today is altogether new.

The clash over the imperial succession took the form of ferocious struggles among the great powers in order to expand their markets.

These changes did not all come about without some bust-ups. Disciples of Ned Ludd, famous for sabotaging mechanical looms, began destroying machines; the Luddites were active between 1810 and 1816. Discontented citizens rose up on several occasions. In 1848, rebellions shook much of Europe; the spark of revolution, ignited in Paris, spread through many European cities. The bone of contention was the domination of capital. Out of this revolt came the workers' movement, trade unions, and new political parties of the left (Socialist, Communist and Labour).

As Karl Polanyi reminds us in *The Great Transformation*, two philosophies were in conflict. Economic liberalism sought to establish a self-regulating market using strategies such as laissez-faire and free trade. The other philosophy emphasized social welfare and had the tool of legislation. These institutional tensions went along with class conflicts between capitalists and workers. We shall have more to say on this below.

The clash over the imperial succession took the form of ferocious struggles among the great powers in order to expand their markets.

British capital abandoned production to speculation. Germany, for its part, gradually rose to become a world power. Paralleling these events, the United States, after conquering part of Mexico (1848) and winning the West[5] and the end of its civil war (1865), could make the most of an impressive domestic market. Protectionist policies aimed to reinforce this competitive advantage. The first wave of industrial and financial concentration made its appearance. The time of Big Business had come. This was the Age of Titans, the empire builders, and the "robber barons." The Rockefellers, Ford, Carnegie and company amassed huge fortunes[6].

The mood of confrontation among the European powers, "the clash of ambitions and overweening nationalist sentiments" (Manzagol, 2003, p.13), led to the greatest armed conflict that humanity had ever known. National passion was strong enough to send millions of men to war. The defeat of Germany left the way free for U.S. domination.

Two Great Wars and their Aftermath

The Age of Catastrophe, to use Eric Hobsbawm's term, began with the First World War and ended only in 1945. The "long thirty years war" caused more than sixty million deaths and deeply scarred human memory with the barbarity of the Holocaust. It drained Europe of its vitality and put an end to the British Empire. It allowed the United States to emerge as the new masters of the world.

On the other hand, the Bolshevik Revolution of 1917 caused a worldwide shock and transformed the pre-existing relations among nations. It engendered a struggle to the death between two antagonistic social systems. Fears that the "Red Plague" would spread had a profound influence on social struggles and policies.

As for the Great Depression of the 1930s, Hobsbawm has called it the "largest global earthquake ever to be measured on the economic historians' Richter scale" (1994, p. 86). It quickly went global; world trade fell by 60% between 1929 and 1932. One result was a profound change in public opinion about the respective roles of government and private enterprise. In its course it swept away the institutions that had been the glory of the 19th century. And it tolled the knell of British domination.

Two opposing philosophies vied for popular support, both representing a break with the earlier liberal order. One advocated greater social justice. The other was based on the values of order and authority. They engendered popular fronts and the New Deal on the one hand, and fascism and Nazism on the other.

In several countries, including Spain, Italy and Germany, the liberal State was replaced, after deadly social struggles, by implacable dictatorships. The fascist solution was an authoritarian reform of the market economy. Anti-capitalist demagogy, contempt for democracy and a brutal repression tore at the fabric of existing economic and social institutions.

The New Deal, for its part, offered a new social compromise between the State, capital and labour. It had its origins in Scandinavian social democracy and its theoretical basis in the thought, revolutionary for its times, of the British economist John Maynard Keynes. According to Keynes, the market left to itself was incapable of ensuring full employment or a fair distribution of income. It was up to the State to remedy these deficiencies, to provide a framework for competition and to intervene to maintain purchasing power.

The west experienced a shift from faith in individual responsibility and laissez-faire economics to faith in social responsibility and the virtues of powerful interventionist governments. The Depression had revealed the vicissitudes of the market and the general consensus was that the liberal approach had once and for all been consigned to the ashcan of history.

In the United States, reform was spearheaded by Franklin D. Roosevelt who came to power in 1933. In his inaugural address he asserted : "The moneychangers have fled from their high seats in the temple of our civilization" (quoted by Friedman and Friedman, p. 93). He was scathing in his analysis of the crisis: "life was no longer free; liberty no longer real; men could no longer follow the pursuit of happiness" (quoted by Foner, p.196).

The New Deal consisted of three major interventions. It brought in a fairly broad social welfare system including unemployment insurance, a pension scheme for the elderly, and assistance for needy adults and children. For labour, it set a minimum wage, limited the number of hours of work in the week, and supported unionism by recognizing collective bargaining rights. And finally, it gave government a major role in the regulation of the economy.

The welfare state was born. These policies favoured increases in the salaries and purchasing power of wage-earners. It achieved on a grand scale Henry Ford's maxim calling for wages in his own business that would allow his employees to buy his cars. Similar policies were adopted in Britain a few years later, and in France under the Popular Front. The supporters of liberalism did not fail to chant their mantra of the threats to liberty; but theirs was a voice in the wilderness. They returned to the forefront only with the conservative revolution of the 1980s.

In Canada, a New Deal bill was brought to the House of Commons in 1935. It called for unemployment insurance, a minimum wage and a 48-hour work week. But it was adjudged unconstitutional, because it encroached upon the jurisdictional powers of the provinces. It wasn't until after the election of the Godbout government that Quebec agreed to a constitutional amendment allowing the bill to be put into effect. At this time, Quebec began flirting with the temptations of strong-arm government. In 1937, the government of Maurice Duplessis had enacted the Padlock Law, aiming to protect the province from "communist propaganda" by giving the government the right to padlock the doors of any establishment suspected of engaging in such activities.

World War II put the brakes on the social momentum. But the wartime economy required even more vigorous government intervention, thereby proving its ability to manage the economic system more efficiently. The New Deal got its second wind at the beginning of the 1960s, with medical insurance schemes, which varied in their degree of universality from country to country, and with the growth of public education.

At the end of the War, the United States was the unchallenged dominant power. It was now responsible for almost two thirds of the world's industrial production. The average annual economic growth rate there hovered around 10%. A new economic and political order was established. At the outset, Roosevelt had been hoping to broaden the New Deal to encompass the whole planet. But under Truman's presidency, *Pax Americana* became the new order of the free world. Containment of the USSR became the mainspring of U.S. hegemony.

The new economic order was built around two new public financial institutions mandated to ensure economic stability and to prevent another worldwide depression. They were set up at the Bretton Woods Conference in 1944, and with them world domination by the U.S. was complete. The International Bank for Reconstruction and Development (later to become the World Bank) and the International Monetary Fund (IMF), sometimes called the Keynesian twins, were an integral part of a progressive program. The job of the former was to get a shattered Europe back on its feet again and to support decolonization. The latter was to ensure the stability of countries encountering temporary difficulties in their balance of payments. The dollar became a genuine world currency, the only one pegged to the gold standard. The Marshall Plan, on the other hand, was intended as a massive reconstruction enterprise for Europe; it proved itself by making a decisive contribution to the expansion of world trade and production.

But the idea of an international trade organization mandated to sustain international trade was voted down by the U.S. Congress. The preferred alternative was the establishment of a new free trade order with countries opting in to a general agreement on tariffs and trade (GATT). The economy was subordinated to politics. "Trade took directions from the flag."

On the political front, the idea of a world government cropped up for the first time. The defunct League of Nations had never really existed. The United Nations Organization and UNESCO were created. The International Labour Organization (ILO) was resuscitated. The right of the self-determination of peoples was recognized and a Declaration of Human Rights was adopted.

A wave of decolonization swept through what came to be called the Third World. The weakening of Europe provided favourable conditions for a challenge to the colonial order. China, India, Indonesia were followed by other African and Asian countries in the move to independence. Britain did not resist, unlike France and to a lesser extent the Netherlands whose resistance led to bloody liberation struggles.

A new world order, inspired by the logic of universality, was now under construction. It ushered in a golden age that lasted for thirty years. The exploitation of inventions facilitated by the combustion engine, electricity and chemistry gave sustenance to the economic upsurge. A new model of growth, based on mass consumption, the expansion of the labour force and trade unionization as well as the social state combined to provide a steady rise in the standard of living and a social safety net and contributed to the euphoria of these "Thirty Glorious Years."

All over the West, progress was making strides in rights and democracy. There were major advances in civil rights throughout the fifties and sixties. The women's movement, the peace movement and the civil rights movement became social forces to be reckoned with. Social protest shattered the complacency of the powerful, most notably with opposition to the Vietnam War and the student movements of May 1968.

From the 1970s on, however, the institutions of the new world order gave rise to more and more criticism. The U.S. decision to impose wage and price controls[7] and to take the dollar off the gold standard in 1971 caused important financial disruptions. The rise in the cost of raw materials, especially of oil where the price rose 400%, weakened economies that had been undergoing a sustained period of growth.

This was the spark for a new offensive from the supporters of free trade and competition. Among them were Hayek who, in 1974, received the Sveriges Riksbank Prize in Economic Sciences, now called the Nobel Prize for Economics, and his colleague Milton Friedman who went on to win it in 1976.

Liberalism's New Clothes

Since the crisis of the 1970s, the economic domination of the U.S. has no longer been as absolute as it was in the post-war years. Europe, Japan and China have become serious competitors. What's more, the movement from a production economy to a speculation economy is not unlike the decline of the British Empire. Some experts maintain that the world is going through a transitional period, a shifting of tectonic plates between two long historical eras. This period is characterized by the undivided reign of big finance and the domination of giant corporations.

Economic restructuring has proceeded hand in hand with neo-liberal policies and a massive offensive to transform the world into a single market. When Margaret Thatcher came to power in 1979 and Ronald Reagan in 1981, they unleashed the beginning of a conservative revolution. "The State," said the latter, "is not the solution to our problems. It is the cause." Privatization, deregulation and free trade were the main axes of a political ideology that soon dominated. The compromise between capital and labour that had been mediated by governments since the end of World War II was now over. In the United States, strong-arm tactics used against the unions led to the firings of the air controllers. In Britain, the miners' unions bore the brunt of the assault.

Reagan became the champion of hard-line politics and displays of force. His crusade against "the axis of evil" was at the heart of his international policy. The fall of the Berlin Wall and the collapse of the Soviet Union nevertheless brought this final episode of the Cold War to an end.

On the economic front, tax cuts were trumpeted as the keys to freedom. They mainly worked to undermine the social safety net[8]. The State remained strong, however. It was restructured, notably with a massive increase in military expenditures. Despite assertions of the contrary, the conservative revolution did not shrink government; under Reagan, the budgetary deficit reached historic heights.

Aggressive competition to attract "petrodollars" and the priority given to the fight against inflation caused the U.S. government to raise its interest rates astronomically. Bankruptcies occurred in droves. Many developing countries that had been encouraged to borrow in the 1970s found it impossible to meet their commitments.

In Latin America, the situation was dramatic[9]. In 1982, Mexico defaulted on its payments. The debt crisis extended to the whole of the southern continent. The International Monetary Fund intervened to save the western banks, which had made risky loans but refused to bear the consequences. The new loans were conditional on structural adjustments that deprived states of much of their economic sovereignty.

The Reagan doctrine was imposed with what has come to be called the "Washington Consensus." This refers to a tacit agreement between the political decision-makers on two Washington streets housing the U.S. Treasury and the head offices of the World Bank and the International Monetary Fund. The Ten Commandments of structural adjustment included most notably the growth of exports of raw materials and agricultural produce, free circulation of capital, tax cuts for businesses and the wealthy, privatization of public institutions, flexible labour markets and a reduction in social security benefits. All this would allow countries in debt to increase revenues sharply to repay their creditors and to benefit multi-national corporations.

In the course of the 1990s, deregulation extended to financial services, public services and banking services. A sequence of financial crises affected Mexico, Brazil, Thailand and Russia. These crises spread like wildfire, cascading through neighbouring countries and whole continents. Countries that applied IMF policies sank deeper into trouble. Those that refused came out with their honour intact, especially China and Malaysia.

The neo-liberal policies imposed by adjustment programs led to bloody riots, particularly in Argentina, Indonesia and Bolivia. The IMF riots, as they were called, were predictable. In the face of dramatic increases in the price of staples such as rice, flour, oils, etc., people gave vent to their anger on the streets.

The theory that making the wealthy even richer would provide an overflow benefit to the poorest people did not prove to be true. The rising tide did not cause all boats to rise, as the slogan had said they would; the wealth of the most affluent did not trickle down to the poorest of the poor. The foreign debt of developing countries grew by more than 400% between 1980 and 2001. Africa now gives four times more money to servicing the interests on its debt than it invests in health services. It is hardly surprising that infant mortality remains high and that both famine and curable diseases continue to cost millions of lives.

Joseph Stiglitz, the vice president and chief economist at the World Bank for three years, has criticized the role of this institution most roundly and, more especially, the role of the IMF in the crises that have racked the world economy. From the 1980s on, he wrote in *Globalization and its discontents*, "the change in mandate and objectives [of the IMF]...was hardly subtle: from serving global *economic* interests to serving the interests of global *finance*" (2002, p. 207).

What the IMF imposed upon the countries of the South, the OECD proposed to the countries of the North. Balancing the budget became a new dogma. Quebec yielded to it at the first summit called by Lucien Bouchard's PQ government. The Clinton government resisted. Joseph Stiglitz, who was then on the Council of Economic Advisers, considers this to have been one of the greatest successes of the democratic presidency.

Deregulation turned into a frenzy, as detailed in another book by Stiglitz, the *Roaring Nineties*. It led to a new Gold Rush, particularly in the telecommunications and energy sectors. This all too often turned into a "rush to the bottom" (2003, p.93). "Corporate scandals dethroned the high priests of American capitalism" (*ibid.*, p.x). The same can be said for other countries but the scandals at Worldcom and Enron have acquired mythical status. Accounting firms such as Arthur Andersen and the quasi-totality of U.S. banks were implicated. The problems at Nortel, Vivendi, Cinar, Norbourg and many others are so many more examples of the new business ethics.

The collapse of Enron, the biggest of all time, exposed "all the vices" of the roaring nineties. Enron was the jewel in the crown of deregulation. As an energy broker, it manipulated the deregulated California market by causing shortages and huge tariff increases. Any tactic was considered acceptable to bring about scarcity: offshore sales of energy, reductions in the flow rate of pipelines to the power stations, influence peddling, and so on. It cost the government $45 billion. Once regulation was reinstated, the shortages disappeared.

As for the scandal at Worldcom, the U.S.'s second largest long distance service provider and the number one internet access provider, it provoked the loss of almost half a million jobs and several billion dollars on the stock market, and caused turbulence throughout that economic sector. While its leaders were lying about the financial situation of their company in order to maximize their own holdings and to cash them with substantial profits, they urged their employees to tighten their belts and to invest their pension funds in company shares. The employees were taken in by this and lost hundreds of millions.

The remuneration of directors by means of stock options encouraged them to boost the tradable value of their corporations, even if it meant lying to do so. They pontificated about government waste, but their free market "had wasted more money than most governments could have imagined in their wildest dreams" (Stiglitz, 2003, p.168). In this way, "while market values soared, human values eroded" (*ibid.*, p.138) [10].

These scandals and the scathing criticisms leveled against structural adjustment programs, notably in the wake of the 1997 Asian crisis, shook confidence in the neo-liberal agenda. For some observers, the intellectual basis for laissez-faire economics had been reduced to tatters by events. Even so, there was no sign of a change of heart. The appointment of the very conservative Paul Wolfowitz as head of the World Bank was not a good sign. But Wolfowitz was forced to resign in 2007 following his implication in a nepotism scandal. He was replaced by Robert Zoellick, another Bush loyalist. The Global Framework for Development that replaced the IMF's adjustment policies was more of a cosmetic fix than a change of direction.

From the beginning of the 1990s, the proliferation of trade agreements has opened a new free-trade era. The Free-Trade Agreement between the U.S. and Canada was broadened to include Mexico in the North American Free Trade Agreement (NAFTA) and in 1995 the World Trade Organization (WTO) was set up. The first summit of the Americas was held at the same time and was supposed to lead to the creation of a Free-Trade Area of the Americas (FTAA) by 2005. These agreements have encountered significant opposition.

On the production side, there was a structural transformation of the economy in favour of computing, biotechnologies and information processing. A new international division of labour came into existence. Mass production with its assembly lines of workers was replaced with flexible production and automation. The old forms of industrial production (textiles, shoes, etc.) gradually moved to low-wage zones, throwing thousands out of work and turning the old industrial centres into "rust belts."

With information technologies came a real global revolution in finance. Colossal sums of money are now transferred around the world every day. Currency transactions have overtaken world trade in importance in what is now really a "casino economy." Mergers and acquisitions have created behemoths of production and finance and have turned multinational corporations into top players in the process of globalization. More and more they are defying state frontiers and powers. They play governments off against one another in order to turn the world into one giant market.

While this was going on, others were trying to set up a new international order. The Kyoto accord, the International Criminal Court, the global Education for All movement, and United Nations reform were all efforts to shore up the defence of rights on a worldwide scale. Their success was relative.

Finally, globalization has taken on many other facets. The events of 9/11 came to remind us of this: Al-Qaeda is also linked to globalization. Since that event, we have been witnessing the dominance of security issues, to the detriment of democratic rights and liberties, and a return to hawkishness and unilateral warfare with a vengeance, sometimes even at the expense of trade.

As the 21st century dawns, the United States still wields massive military superiority. But the decision of President George W. Bush to cut taxes, while increasing military expenditures, has led to the biggest budget deficit in their history, even queening Reagan's pawn. Government revenues dropped by $600 billion between 2001 and 2004, while the budget deficit, coupled with a mind-boggling deficit in the balance of trade, was reaching $412 billion, thus threatening the stability of the world economy.

> *As the 21st century dawns, the United States still wields massive military superiority. But the decision of President George W. Bush to cut taxes, while increasing military expenditures, has led to the biggest budget deficit in their history.*

The U.S.'s position as a political world leader is also strongly contested. Its economic domination is no longer as absolute as it had been. Europe is consolidating its position as a new regional economic and political leader. China is growing at such a breakneck speed that in July 2004 the *New York Times* was wondering whether the 21st century would turn out to be the Chinese century.

In addition, neo-liberal theories are going nowhere. After thirty years experience, the results are catastrophic. Developing countries are combining forces to defend their interests against big corporations and major governments. The negotiation of trade agreements is not keeping to the original schedule, in the face of the rebelliousness of some countries and a mobilization of the people.

Philip Golub sees a parallel between the current situation and the circumstances that ended the international order previously dominated by Britain; numerous wars, rising waves of nationalism, intensified trade conflicts, and social upheavals are all features common to both periods. The famous Canadian essayist John Ralston Saul has even announced the collapse of globalism. The ideology of neo-liberalism has run out of steam, it seems, and the world is undergoing a transition characterized by contradictory trends. This is a period of doubting and making choices.

It would take a clever observer to predict what will happen next. But we can at least identify these contradictory trends and the choices that humanity must face on a number of questions that will stay on the agenda for a long time to come.

FUTURE ISSUES

The future is under construction. In the words of Riccardo Petrella, there are elements of chance, of necessity, but above all of will. Forecasting is closer to reading tealeaves than to social science. The contemporary successors of Nostradamus had not predicted the severity of the 1930s Depression, nor the women's liberation movement, nor the collapse of the Soviet Union. It is nevertheless worth stopping for a moment to consider the major issues that will play out in this coming world.

Putting the Market in its Place

Neo-liberalism is the current ideology of globalization. The two are closely linked. They complement each other and are proceeding in tandem. It is hardly surprising that the concept of "neo-liberal globalization" has now become so widespread. And yet, this return of ultra-liberalism with a vengeance is not a product of either chance or necessity. It was the subject of one of the most important intellectual battles of the 20th century. And it still is.

1944 saw the publication of two works staking out the ground for this important debate. The first, *The Great Transformation* by Karl Polanyi, was the inspiration for social democracy. The second, *The Road to Serfdom* by Friedrich von Hayek became the manifesto of neo-liberalism with Hayek as its intellectual guru.

The great transformation Polanyi talks about is the break with the economic liberalism that dominated the world throughout most of the 19th century. Polanyi was convinced that humanity had had its fill of this model of civilization from the previous century and had consigned it to the ash-cans of history. "The idea of a self-adjusting market implies a stark utopia. Such an institution could not exist for any length of time without annihilating the human and natural substance of society. It would have physically destroyed man and transformed his surroundings into a wilderness" (p. 3).

He lambasted this old-hat liberalism, which divided society into an economic sphere and a political sphere and subordinated the latter to the former. Such a society was based on one guiding principle alone: profit. And it set in motion a mechanism whose effects were comparable "to the most violent outbursts of religious fervor in history. Within a generation, the whole human world was subjected to its undiluted influence" (p. 31). The free market became a doctrine swept along by a crusading spirit. As another thinker of the period wrote without subtlety, there were only two choices: "liberty, inequality, survival of the fittest; non-liberty, equality and the survival of the unfittest" (Sumner ... quoted in Foner, 1998, p.121-122).

For Polanyi, laissez-faire was absolutely not natural. It was planned. The free market could never have seen the light of day if things had been left to themselves. Its imposition had required a huge growth in the administrative functions of the State to respond to the heightened need for guidance, regulation and intervention. The main problem, according to Polanyi, was not the existence of markets, but the fact that the economy was based exclusively on personal interest.

The Great Depression of the 1930s turned the situation on its head and imposed the incorporation of the economic domain into society. The free market was rejected by an America in crisis. What was needed was a conscious, well-directed administration of world markets. We should remember that, after World War II, conservatives were not popular; they were readily identified with the anti-Semitism and biological determinism that had wrought havoc and still haunted everybody.

How can we explain the sudden forceful return of ultra-liberalism in the 1980s? One of Hayek's celebrated disciples, Milton Friedman gives an explanation in the second edition of his famous work *Capitalism and Freedom*. He reminds us that for several decades the critics of Keynesianism were in a minority, thought of as eccentrics by most thinkers. Seven years after its publication in 1962, his masterwork had still not received a review in any national publications. Friedman's conclusion from this was that "only a crisis — actual or perceived-produces real change. When that crisis occurs, the actions that are taken depend on the ideas that are lying around" (p. IX). Alternatives to existing policies must be developed and kept "alive and available until the politically impossible becomes politically inevitable."

These alternatives were kept alive throughout the 1950s and 1960s by Hayek's disciples. For Hayek, any questioning of economic liberalism would trigger a collectivist spiral paving the way to serfdom. On the contrary, what was needed was deregulation, privatization, cuts in social programs and curbs on the power of the unions.

His disciples, among them Friedman, were even more radical. They formed study circles and came together in what became the Chicago School. The "Chicago boys" got a lot of attention in the early 1970s when they assumed the role of economic advisors to General

Pinochet's government in Chile, following the overthrow of Salvador Allende's democratically elected government. For the Chicago boys, property rights were sacred and nothing was worse than State intervention, not even the Pinochet dictatorship .

The Pinochet government provided the first example of the implementation of fundamental liberalism. As Serge Halimi remembers it, "it was a celebration of the market and the machine-gun (...) It was in Santiago and not London, in blood and not the ballot-box, that the road to serfdom came to its checkpoint" (2004, p. 356)

For Hayek, as for Friedman, the pursuit of personal interest was for human nature what universal gravity was for physical bodies. It was the only universal rational behaviour. The same could not be said of altruism, co-operation, or the pursuit of the common good, which are only subjective and irrational feelings. The market, as the Scottish economist Adam Smith had already maintained, had the virtue of turning the sum of particular interests into the general interest. Thus, the individual who pursued only his own gain would be "led by an invisible hand to promote an end which was no part of his intention. (...).By pursuing his own interest he frequently promotes that of society more effectually than when he really intends to promote it" (quoted by Friedman and Friedman, p. 2).

Hayek did much to enable the right to take up the torch of freedom again. Being free would mean being free of the State. As the Friedmans said "a society that puts freedom first will, as a happy by-product, end up with both greater freedom and greater equality" (ibid. p. 148). The market would be conducive to this greater liberty, because it would allow people to choose what they wanted. It would be a sort of daily referendum in which the consumer would be at leisure to exercise the franchise by buying a commodity or not.

According to these "market internationalists," assembled today in an international group of think tanks that includes the Montreal Economic Institute and the Fraser Institute, the free market is the most efficient way to distribute goods and services, the most equitable and the most democratic, because it reacts rapidly to the wishes of its clients and maximizes freedom of choice. Every activity should be evaluated in cost/benefit terms, without any other considerations. The principle of competition should henceforth be applied to nations, regions, institutions and people.

All aspects of life are transformed into economic issues, if not into commodities. Anything not commercialized before is now getting greedy looks. A culture of individualism and consumption is taking over to the detriment of collective responsibility and the pursuit of the common good. The market seems now to be reaching a new level; it is becoming global.

This has had consequences for education. According to the doctrine, there was no reason why the principles of profitability and competition could not carry the same weight where schools were concerned. Indeed, Friedman was one of the main promoters of the voucher system. For him, the only role for government in education was quality control, using minimal evaluation schemes comparable to health inspections in restaurants. We shall return to this question in the next chapter.

In fewer than fifty years, a theory that had no credibility and whose advocates were voices in the wilderness had imposed itself as the ideological salvation of globalization. As Susan George of the AT-TAC[11] movement reminds us, "So, from a small, unpopular sect with virtually no influence, neo-liberalism has become the major world religion with its dogmatic doctrine, its priesthood, its law-giving institutions and perhaps most important of all, its hell for heathen and sinners who dare to contest the revealed truth." (1999, p.3).

According to Joseph Stiglitz, the United States "pushed a market fundamentalist set of reforms, in any way we could, paying little attention to how what we did undermined democratic processes" (2003, p.25). In Latin America, for example, the triumph of neo-liberalism cannot be separated from the ferocious dictatorships propped up by the United States.

But the evidence against neo-liberalism is mounting. Critics have not been slow to point out emphatically that the social dimension of humanity is being completely eliminated, that unregulated capitalism is increasing inequality, and that there is no natural rebalancing mechanism to make redistribution possible. Structural adjustment programs are bankrupt, deregulation has been scandalous, inequalities have multiplied. The pursuit of personal profit has led to the worst ever frauds in history and the scandals have shaken the Mecca of high finance. Sadly, blind faith has no need of evidence and shuts its mind to any contrary view.

The level of wealth concentration is such that the dollar worth of the 475 billionaires in the world is equivalent to the combined income of half of humanity. Everywhere, inequalities are on the increase. In 2002, 2.8 billion people lived on less than two dollars a day, and of those 1.8 billion on less than a dollar a day. The share of the poorest 20% in global income has fallen from 2.3% to 1.4% between 1989 and 1998. In front of the head office of the World Bank in Washington, there is a clock that counts the number of children dying every day as a result of poverty. One child is added to this death count every three seconds.

And yet, according to the United Nations Development Program, it would cost only $40 billion a year over ten years to guarantee the world's population universal access to basic education, food, health services, and safe drinking water. Unfortunately, at the current rate of aid, it calculates in its 2002 annual report, it would take one hundred and thirty years to put an end to hunger in the world.

We are not setting the State against the market as if it were a question of good and evil. Market relations are not all the same. But deregulation as a universal principle, competitivity in all areas of social life, and gung-ho privatization are all eating away at the social gains of recent decades and only serve the wealthiest among us.

The challenge is to put the market back in its place then, to allow competition to occur in those sectors where it leads to an improvement in production and greater ease of access for consumer. But the market at all costs is something else. As is gung-ho free trade.

Civilizing Free Trade

Free trade is to the international scene what the free market is to the national scene. It is inspired by the same orthodoxy. It is presented as the key to economic prosperity. It is associated with worldwide trade agreements and various forms of regionalization, some of them strictly limited to free trade, such as NAFTA, others more political like the European Union.

The problem is not intrinsically connected with the liberalization of commercial transactions. The problem arises when the liberalization of international commerce is placed above all other political objectives and when it seeks to convert the whole world into one vast market. At that point it becomes a "great destroyer" leading to "governance without government," a politics of the powerful to ensure their domination of the world. History is rich in lessons on this subject.

Imagine the following situation. You are visiting a developing country. It has the highest customs duties in the world. It is doing exactly the opposite of what is recommended by the IMF and the World Bank. Its public finances are in a precarious state and defaults on its payments are making its creditors edgy. It does not recognize foreign intellectual property rights. There is no law to favour competition. Should we declare a disaster zone? You be the judge: this country is called the United States of America and the time is the 1880s.

The South Korean Ha-Joon Chang, from whom this example is taken, has clearly shown that when today's developed countries were still at the developing stage almost none of them followed the free trade path. This is particularly true of Britain, Germany and the United States. The first of these only began supporting free trade in the middle of the 19th century when it already dominated the world economy; when deemed necessary, the policy was imposed by means of colonialism.

As for Germany, following the severe recession of 1873, Bismarck's regime introduced important social legislation and imposed customs tariffs on foreign agricultural products that broke with British imperial policy. As a German economist remarked at the time, Britain kicked away the ladder that had allowed it to get to the top, thus depriving other countries of the possibility of developing themselves[12].

For their part, the U.S. was protectionist until the end of the Second World War. The U.S. Civil War was as much about the defence of protectionism as it was about the abolition of slavery. The South, a great producer of raw materials, consisted of free-traders while the North sought to consolidate its industrial development by means of tariff barriers.

It was only when its supremacy was secure that the U.S. became the ardent defender of relatively free trade.

It was only when its supremacy was secure that the U.S. became the ardent defender of relatively free trade. Congress opposed the creation of an international trade organization at the end of the 1940s. Only when they felt such a body would be to the advantage of U.S. multinational corporations did they become the main promoters of the World Trade Organization.

In the same way, with the exception of Hong Kong, the Asian dragons first took the route of protectionism and state intervention to achieve reconstruction after World War II. In Japan, everything was orchestrated by the very powerful Ministry of International Trade and Industry, the famous MITI.

This is not a rant against any form of free trade. But it must be recognized that it is up to each country to choose the policies most likely to bring about its development rather than to see itself forced to open its borders unconditionally by international organizations or the almighty U.S.

But this is precisely the problem. Trade agreements are "seen as unbalanced, [and] trade liberalization as a new way in which the rich and powerful [can] exploit the weak and poor" (Stiglitz, 2003, p.205). The developed countries, particularly the U.S., have forced markets to be opened up in sectors where the U.S. was strong, but resisted any reciprocity. This allowed the big banks to swallow up those in developing countries and to channel savings towards multi-nationals, thereby depriving those countries of an important development tool.

These agreements are crafted to include clauses opening the door to the continued liberalization of trade. "Like a bottomless pit, each liberalization always imposes further liberalizations" (Halimi, 2004, p.398). Multinational corporations and their pressure groups such as the European Round Table of Industrialists and the U.S. Coalition of Service Industries exercise enormous power in trade negotiations. What we are witnessing is a consolidation of the rights of corporations to the detriment of the rights of peoples. So-called social clauses and rules aiming to guarantee environmental protection are generally excluded.

The WTO, founded in 1995, has the responsibility of monitoring the implementation of a whole series of trade agreements, which all specify that national frameworks should work to achieve the least restrictive effect on trade. The Dispute Settlement Body can strike down any measure considered to be "an unnecessary obstacle" or "more restrictive than necessary." The country at fault must then abrogate the law in question, or pay compensation, without which it exposes itself to trade sanctions. Thus might makes right.

In the framework of the agreement on Trade-Related aspects of Intellectual Property Rights (TRIPS), contrary to the principals of free trade, a 20-year protection period has been imposed for patents, and these have been extended to include living organisms. Accordingly, patents have been issued for traditional medicines and foodstuffs and this has led to charges being levied upon countries that had always considered them to be theirs. This was notably the case of basmati rice, which had been cultivated for centuries by Asian peasants. Similarly, patents have been issued for genetic sequences identified as the source of certain cancers, genetically modified seeds, etc. Some people are saying that the giant corporation Monsanto has become Monsatan.

The debate over medications to treat HIV is probably the one that scandalized world opinion the most. Patents were depriving poor countries of the capacity to produce generic drugs that could save thousands of lives. Even the Council of Economic Advisers, under President Clinton, was aware of the death sentence that this agreement could mean for countless inhabitants in poor countries. That did not stop giant pharmaceutical industries from pressing charges against Brazil, India and South Africa, which had decided to bypass the new rules of international trade. The intransigence of these drug companies, who came charging back after an initial compromise, has contributed to the death of thousands of people.

Time and time again, the Dispute Settlement Body has taken decisions that ride roughshod over national prerogatives and show scant respect for laws designed to protect the environment. It came down on the U.S.'s side in the "banana war", forcing the European Union to end preferential purchasing policies that benefited the poor countries of Africa and the Caribbean, an important element of European foreign development policy. It similarly sided with Japan by abolishing regulations intended to protect sea turtles and dolphins from fishing practices threatening their survival.

The European Union's ban on imports of beef fed with growth hormones, considered carcinogenic, led the United States to take countervailing measures against symbolic products such as foie gras and Roquefort cheese. People responded by ransacking a McDonald's eatery in France. In addition, the demand for a moratorium on genetically modified organisms (GMO), arising from concerns about health risks and biodiversity, is still under discussion. But health and safety reasons have also been invoked to impose the will of the powerful. Products from Argentina were left to rot in the ports on the east coast of the U.S., because of alleged safety risks. Mexican avocados were kept out, because of the alleged presence of a small fly, although no trace of one could be found by inspectors sent to check it out. Only the threat of a countervail against corn put an end to U.S. bad faith.

On the agricultural front, the rich countries continue to provide generous subsidies to their producers. Our neighbours to the south grant $14 billion annually to dairy producers, almost 40% of their total revenue. Every head of cattle in the U.S. and Europe gets a subsidy of about two dollars a day. Subsidies to U.S. cotton producers exceed the value of the product and are ruining African peasants; the subsidies amount to three times the total sum of U.S. aid to Africa. The same thing is happening with the rice flooding the Haitian market. But at the same time, cash crop production for export is imposed upon countries of the South at the expense of subsistence agriculture. "Export and die" has become a grim reality.

The hypocrisy is flagrant. Developing countries are forced to open their markets while the wealthy countries maintain high customs barriers and big subsidies. The laws of the market trump any other aspect of international law[13], but the rules are far from being applied equitably.

This situation led to the failure of the 1999 WTO meeting in Seattle when the developing countries refused to sign the proposed agreement. The same thing happened again in Cancun in the summer of

2003, in Hong Kong in 2005 and in Geneva in 2008. With Brazil and India at the centre, a group of twenty countries, the G-20, demanded the end of agricultural subsidies by the rich countries in exchange for opening their markets. They got nowhere.

The General Agreement on Trade in Services (GATS) is a framework agreement for a series of negotiations for "the early achievement of progressively higher levels of liberalization of trade in services." Any liberalization of a sector amounts to what is effectively a life sentence. The objective is to open all services to international competition, including public services such as health and education. There will be more on this in the next chapter.

The "millennium round" that was re-launched in Doha in 2001 is spinning its wheels on several fronts. The ministerial meeting in Hong Kong did not come up with the expected results and the December 2005 deadline has had to be put back. The latest round of negotiations at Geneva in the summer of 2008 ended again in failure, largely as a consequence of disagreements about mechanisms designed to protect farmers in the poorest countries. India's Trade Minister declared on this occasion "I'm not risking the livelihood of million of farmers."

As Jacques Parizeau pointed out in an interview with the daily *Le Devoir*, the WTO is probably here for good. The number of members is constantly growing and no-one is threatening to quit. A mechanism for monitoring international trade is necessary, but it has to lose its imperial character and become accountable to parliaments and peoples.

On the regional agreements front, NAFTA has had significant consequences for national policies, particularly in Mexico and Canada. One of the conditions of the agreement was an amendment to the Mexican Constitution that prohibited the sale of indigenous common lands, the *ejidos*. This triggered the Zapatista uprising on the day that NAFTA went into effect, January 1, 1994.

NAFTA has also led to the abrogation of a grab-bag of regulations on foreign investment, export quotas, national preference in procurement, etc. It has put downward pressure on Canadian social programs, particularly in the field of employment insurance. Opening markets to U.S. agricultural products in January 2004 spelt ruin for millions of small peasant corn producers in Mexico. These then migrated to big cities and the North. Today, the militant defenders of the homeland are now hunting down illegals on the southern border of the U.S.

The highly controversial Chapter XI allows businesses to require financial compensation if a government makes a move that could hinder their chances of making a profit. Famous cases have been heard or settled out of court. For instance, the Canadian government agreed to rescind a ban on a gasoline additive produced by Ethyl Corp, to pay $19 million in compensation, and to declare publicly that this posed no health risk, against the advice of the experts of Health Canada. The little municipality of Guadalcazar in Mexico was sentenced to pay $20 million to Metalclad, a major U.S. corporation, for denying it permission for a toxic waste disposal site, out of fear that its source of drinking water would be contaminated.

Canadians are all aware of the case of softwood lumber where a duty of almost 30% was levied on the grounds that Canada was making hidden subsidies to logging businesses. Despite a decision in favour of Canada from the NAFTA tribunal, the United States has kept dragging its feet for years before a tentative settlement was reached in 2006.

The current process aiming to extend this agreement to a North-American agreement on security and prosperity, also known as NAFTA Plus, along with the negotiations for Free Trade Area of the Americas (FTAA) is discouraging. But here, as elsewhere, resistance is being organized. At the meeting of Heads of State of the Americas at Mar del Plata in November 2005, the United States, for the first time, did not get its own way. The combined opposition of Argentina, Brazil, Venezuela, Uruguay and Paraguay provoked the collapse of the negotiations, which caused President Hugo Chavez to say that FTAA was well and truly "buried." To be continued.

The United States is trying to work around this resistance and to isolate the objectors by signing a series of bilateral agreements. This has happened particularly in Central America and Ecuador, where popular resistance keeps mounting. The strategy consists in consolidating earlier gains and bringing forward new files, thereby broadening the extent of matters covered by each agreement.

Elsewhere, on the initiative of Brazil, a South American Community of Nations came into being in December 2004, later renamed the Union of South American Nations. It intends the progressive integration of the 12 countries in the south of the continent to form a counterweight to the United States and the European Union. For its part, Venezuela's counter-project to implement the Bolivarian Alternative for the People of Our America (ALBA in Spanish) is promoting a plan for continent-wide cooperation focusing on the fight against poverty and social exclusion.

Civilizing free trade, then, has become a major issue. Otherwise, we could witness nationalist retrenchment, even new trade wars whose consequences are always hard to predict. Some observers are even announcing a return of protectionism with a vengeance, at the very least in certain strategic sectors.

Reinforcing Democratic Institutions

The growing space occupied by the market and the expanded role for international organizations and trade agreements are raising questions about the future of the Nation-State. Some people refer to its erosion, even its disappearance, and are using this as a pretext for dismantling democratic structures in favour of giant private entities. Others are referring to a redefinition rather and pointing out the weakness of its contribution to the process of globalization.

There is no doubt that nation-states have abdicated part of their sovereignty to the benefit of worldwide and regional authorities. And that applies not only in economic affairs. The International Criminal Court, the Kyoto Tribunal, and various treaties or political pacts have each established rules that serve to limit nation-states' freedom of action. But those institutions and treaties are far from exercising the constraints imposed by trade agreements.

In other respects, the increased power of big corporations is disturbing. Of the top 100 economic powers in the world in terms of annual turnover, more than half are multinationals. They are trying to impose their will and to bypass political power. They play governments off against one another, seeking out the best conditions to increase their profits. Their ideal would be a world where national political bodies are content to protect private property, enforce social order, and maintain infrastructure.

This combined influence of international agreements and major corporations has helped with the homogenization of policies and discourses in many areas. To conclude from this that a new "empire" is governing the world, that the State has been vanquished, and that the structural process is now irreversible is a big stretch. Even if globalization is shaking the age-old order of nations, we are far from such a cataclysm.

It has to be said that national policies, by allowing the market to take over, have in turn subjugated the State to its rules; social relations are less dependent on frontiers, and there are tensions between the transnational, global nature of the economy and the national character of nation-states. It is nonetheless true that national realities are still very divergent, both in the economic sector and in the social sector. National institutions still have a decisive influence. The nation is still the context in which democracy and solidarity among community members can find a voice. While globalization is conceived globally, it is being enacted locally. The diversity of nations leaves no room for doubt about this. Even if nation-states have given up some aspects of their sovereignty, we are far from uniformity.

In the same vein, a comparison of the fiscal policies of OECD countries reveals the continuation of considerable divergences in rates of taxation. The same is true of education policies, as we shall see in the next chapter. As Suzanne Berger has pointed out in *The First Globalization*, research studies on this agree. There is "far greater room for national policy autonomy and the implementation of national preferences today than the conventional understandings of globalization suggest" (2003, pp.98-99). The range of these possibilities has a lot more to do with political will and planning.

Globalization is modifying the role of nation-states rather than weakening them. Even large corporations need the State. Their development rests on solid national infrastructure. Markets still depend on government regulations, from the justice system to labour relations, including the education system.

If nation-states have abandoned some of their responsibilities, they have sometimes compensated for this by expanding into other domains. In some cases, their role has even grown stronger. Thus the events of 9/11 caused them to increase their security functions and repressive measures along with tighter control over movements of capital they consider "illegitimate."

The transformations also affect the existing international order. The legitimacy of international organizations is put in question. To respond to criticisms, efforts were made to reform UN institutions to make them more democratic albeit with scant success. According to the report of the World Commission on the Social Dimension of Globalization, created on the initiative of the ILO in 2002, international institutions must be able to monitor the current round of globalization in order to give it an ethical framework. This would require a strengthening of the UN, an improvement of the protection of rights, and the creation of new sites for global dialogue.

On the other hand, globalization, with its accompanying destruction of cultures and traditions, is creating backlash. Christian, Hindu and Islamic fundamentalisms are questioning the founding principles of the Enlightenment. Contemporary fundamentalism is an offspring of globalization, uses it and responds to it. A certain level of ethno-cultural fragmentation is occurring as a reaction against cultural homogenization.

In the face of the risks of homogenization and the WTO's domination of all aspects of social life, an international movement has come to the defence of the common heritage of humanity represented by cultural diversity. After two years of bitter negotiations, the General Assembly of UNESCO adopted the Convention on the Protection and Promotion of the Diversity of Cultural Expressions in the fall of 2005. Despite their fierce opposition, the United States could win no support except that of Israel. The Convention allows countries to adopt measures they consider necessary to preserve cultural diversity, whether by means of subsidies, quotas, or tax measures. It is not subordinated to other international treaties, but there are fears that its effectiveness is blunted by the fact that the dispute settlement mechanism has no teeth.

Opening up to the world is still a challenge. The rise of the Nation-States was generally accompanied by a closing of frontiers. Today, there is less freedom of movement than was a century ago; the proportion of immigrants in the world's population then stood at 5%; now it is only 3%. But globalization, with its "global village," should make for greater mobility in the coming years, despite the tensions that could be exacerbated by the growing appeal of security and creeping xenophobia.

More and more corporations are spreading their activities across several countries. They are trying to attract more skilled labour, well-trained students, even academics. This has consequences for developing countries, which as a consequence lose qualified people whom they helped train with their own meager resources.

Seasonal migrant workers are also more numerous, such as the Mexican workers who are "imported" for fruit-picking in the Montreal region. These make up the cheap labour that is sent back to its country of origin after use year over year. A more transparent reception policy for a more diversified workforce is needed, as much in the interest of the receiving country as of the country of origin.

So we can expect a growth in immigration in the coming years. Already, Canada is trying to make itself more welcoming. The demographic situation characterized by low birth rate and by the relative ageing of the population is an incentive for this move. Given the specific cultural situation in Quebec, a rise in immigration will need to be handled carefully, particularly with respect to citizenship and integration. This question will be dealt with in the last chapter.

Democracy has suffered at the hands of globalization. It is threatened by cynicism and apathy[14]. The growing conviction that it is no longer possible to influence governments is undermining it. But since governments are the ones who made up the rules in the first place, they can equally reshape them in order to make up the obvious democratic deficit.

Globalization brings with it a challenge to renew democracy. It must give consideration to the interests of nations. It must respect rights and freedoms, the environment, and cultural heritage. It opens new possibilities for democratic influence over shared global issues. It has stimulated a new planetary consciousness. The popular movement calling for culture and education to be excluded from trade negotiations has scored points.

There is no contradiction between the reinforcement of national democratic institutions and a greater democratization of world government. In the current context, this dual requirement can be seen as two sides of the same coin.

Controlling Economic Restructuring

The globalization of the economy has major consequences for production and labour. It is characterized by an increased internationalization of production and trade, by the transition from mechanized industry to automated industry and the growth of the service sector. The corollary of flexible production is flexible labour and a more marked polarization of jobs as relocations lead to a new international division of labour.

The model of labour regulation that has prevailed since the New Deal was based on a recognition of the role of unions and the sharing of productivity gains between capital and labour. The rationalization of work devised by F.W. Taylor, who separated the understanding of work from its execution, and the generalization of the assembly line introduced by Henry Ford, led to a system of production and mass consumption. Division of work and rising wages characterized what came to be called the Fordist model of production.

Today, a new model called flexible production is in place. This has a dual character: external flexibility based on outsourcing, just-in-time production, inter-firm cooperation, and relocations, along with internal flexibility based on part-time employment, self-employment and teamwork.

The international labour market has not known such a shake-up since the industrial revolution. A new planet-wide factory has been created. The act of production is fragmented around the globe, reorganizing itself into a long chain of suppliers and sub-contractors distributed across numerous countries. The great multi-nationals can function as globalized entities on a planet-wide basis, thanks to the potential opened up by new technologies. Information and knowledge are becoming the new tools of production.

And so the assembly of a twin-engined jet by Bombardier in Montreal uses sections and parts from several cities and countries. The stabilizer fin is made by a Spanish company, the rear of the fuselage by Mitsubishi in Japan, the engine by General Electric in the U.S., the central fuselage by Bombardier in Belfast, and so on.

Corporations can also move from one part of the world to another, according to the costs or training levels of the labour force, tax breaks, labour legislation, etc. In five years, Nike has closed 20 factories and opened 35 elsewhere, sometimes thousands of kilometers away. The Mexican maquiladoras use raw materials from the U.S. that they transform and then re-export to the U.S.; the working conditions are difficult, labour laws are not respected, and unions are not allowed on site. That has not prevented several of these corporations from moving to other places with climates even more favourable to capital.

The end of quotas in the textile sector in January 2005 and the entry of China into the WTO have caused much gnashing of the teeth in the rich countries. In a few months, the imports of Chinese products have taken an alarming leap in Canada, the U.S. and Europe. The Quebec industry has been hard hit. The city of Huntingdon has become its symbol: at the end of 2004, we learned that six textile factories were closing and 850 jobs were being lost. Overall, 25,000 jobs were lost to this industry between June 2004 and the end of 2005. The Quebec Federation of Labour (QFL) was quick to demand that the federal government enact special legislation to ensure the survival of the threatened production sectors. Under combined pressure from the West, China has finally decided to grow its market share in a more measured way, even though it had been scrupulously following the rules of the WTO.

Generally speaking, the cost of restructuring is being borne entirely by the most vulnerable groups in society.

Generally speaking, the cost of restructuring is being borne entirely by the most vulnerable groups in society. According to the World Commission set up by the ILO, the brunt was borne by unskilled labourers, small producers, the poor, women and native peoples. Even as these massive layoffs are going on, corporate profits and CEO salaries are going through the roof. If the industrial wages in the U.S. had gone up at the same rate as the remuneration of the bosses between 1990 and 1998, the minimum wage would be close to $30 an hour and an average employee would be earning more than $100,000 a year.

This new international division of labour is no longer being limited to traditional manufacturing. China is getting into automotive and aeronautic production; its economic growth is nudging an annual rate of 10%. For its part, India is supplying experts in computing and finance to numerous multinational corporations; 100 of the top 500 firms use Indian software services. Swiss Airlines has its accounting services there and Air Canada its booking system. China is on the way to becoming the world's workshop and India a world centre for business services.

Labour flexibility on the other hand is usually synonymous with lower wages and the dismantling of union protection. In fact we are in the presence of a new segmentation of the labour market. The spread of part-time work, moonlighting, and self-employment has created downward pressure both on wages and on unionization. There are many examples of major corporations threatening closures or the scaling back of production if workers do not make concessions on working conditions.

This goes along with government willingness to slash the protections provided by labour legislation. Britain has transformed one of the strongest systems of union protection into one of the weakest. Just about everywhere, deregulation is now the rule. In Quebec, the laws passed by the Charest government since it came to power are another case in point[15].

And so unions have to face a concerted and sustained attack from business, government and neo-liberal thinkers. They are viewed as barriers to the free trade of labour. In many countries the decline of unionization rates is alarming[16]. In Quebec the trade union movement is not affected to the same extent; union membership levels remained relatively stable between 1997 and 2004 at 40%, the highest in North America. But the union movement is pushing back by strengthening international organizations; we shall return to this below.

So how will employment evolve in the coming years? According to Robert Reich, the former Secretary of Labour in the Clinton administration, workers will be spread across a series of boats from now on, "one sinking rapidly, one sinking more slowly, and the third rising steadily" (quoted in Robinson, 2000, p.12). The first boat contains the unskilled or semi-skilled workers affected by relocations, the second has the support staff experiencing layoffs as plants close, while the third holds the new managers of production and consumption who operate in the global economy.

According to other experts, we are witnessing a simultaneous increase in highly skilled employment and low-skilled employment. But, in the long term, what is expected is a gradual rise in the occupational hierarchy, with jobs requiring higher levels of education growing more rapidly than others.

This evolution of the labour market and the erosion of social protection are leading to a greater polarization of society into the included and the excluded. The gendered division of labour continues unabated and poverty is being feminized, especially with the increase of single-parent families. Exclusion can lead to violence and antisocial behaviour.

There is no doubt that an extended quality education and retraining programs will be assets in dealing with this transformation of the economy and employment, both for individuals and societies. This is because educational level is more than ever an important part of social and economic development. But at the same time, it would be a mistake to cave in to corporate requirements. There is too much at stake.

Protecting our Planet

When commercial considerations become the be-all and end-all, the viability of our planet is threatened. In recent decades, the destructive impact of economic activity on the planetary ecosystem and its natural resources has increased to dangerous levels. Humanity is now capable of disturbing the very foundations of its ecosystem, but it is also in a position to protect it. Along these lines, the multilateral agreements, however fragile, on the environment with respect to climate, diversity and desertification that emerged at the Earth Summit of 1992, and the protocols that followed, indicate a desire to confront the risks.

If predictions of catastrophe occasion some skepticism, indeed even denial from the big corporations, it is still the case that the vast majority of scientists believe that in the absence of concerted action, the threats are serious. According to the respected Quebec astrophysicist Hubert Reeves, the upheavals could be comparable to the great extinctions that accompanied transitions between geological eras.

Warnings about the dangers our planet faces occasionally take on an apocalyptic air. Global warming, the shrinking ozone layer, the pollution of soil, air and water, the depletion of natural resources, and the accumulation of toxic waste are all indicators of a planet in poor shape. Human beings are now the main threat to their own survival.

Global warming is undoubtedly the most alarming phenomenon. Recent research by a team of scientists from a dozen or so countries into the Antarctic ice-cap have confirmed the full extent of climate change associated with pollutants emitted by human activity. We are witnessing a veritable "global fever" due mainly to methane and carbon gas emissions. Scientists characterize this rise as brutal and alarming; its progress is unprecedented.

Since the beginning of the twentieth century, the average global temperature has risen by 1°C . The ten hottest years since 1867 have occurred since 1980. If the current trend continues, it is estimated that by the end of the 21st century the average temperature will have gone up by an amount varying according to different calculations from 1.4°C to 5.8 °C. This is a giant leap. According to the Arctic Climate Impact Assessment report that came out in the fall of 2004, this region is undergoing a warming rate twice as rapid as anywhere else on earth. This is threatening the traditional way of life of indigenous peoples and is making sovereignty over the eventual North-West passage a significant issue. The Arctic could actually be free of ice in summer a few decades from now and be open to commercial shipping, realizing a dream that cost the life of Sir John Franklin and his crew in the 19th century.

Generally speaking, the effects of the rise in global temperature are well known and in some cases already perceptible. Greater desertification, the melting of the great glaciers and the polar ice-cap, a rise in sea-level, an increase in climatic catastrophes and the disappearance of species are all changes, which, if not controlled, could even threaten the survival of the human species. While sea levels have risen by some fifteen centimeters in the course of the twentieth century, experts calculate that this rise could reach a metre in the course of the new century. In twenty years, according to the World Health Organization, the number of people affected by desertification will have doubled to reach 1.8 billion.

The increasingly ominous situation finally convinced a sufficient number of countries to implement the Kyoto protocol on greenhouse gas emissions (GGE) in the April of 2005. This agreement anticipates a GGE reduction by 2012 of 6% of their 1990 levels. For Canada this would mean a target of 30% from current levels, since they had risen by 24% since 1990.

Following up on its commitment, the federal government released its national plan to combat climate change in April 2005. It was a huge disappointment. According to Louis-Gilles Francoeur, a columnist at the daily newspaper *Le Devoir*, the plan was like "an enormous open bar." The targets for the big sources of GGEs, the oil industry, the automotive industry and the thermal power stations, were very low. The major corporations would have had to absorb only 15%

of the effort expected of Canada. The essential burden would have been borne by the individual taxpayers themselves. This modest plan was dropped by the conservative government of Stephen Harper that came to power at the beginning of 2006. The Harper government has persisted in rejecting the Kyoto protocol, preferring a voluntary program based on a reduction in emission rates over a reduction in emissions overall.

Other things are now threatening the natural resources that had until now been thought of as inexhaustible. It is estimated that hydrocarbon resources will be exhausted within thirty years. Deforestation is continuing at a rate of two football pitches per second. Groundwater pollution means a depletion of drinking water that some are already calling "blue gold;" it is estimated that a growing percentage of the world's population will experience water shortages. Biodiversity is declining at an unprecedented rate.

In Quebec, the revelations in *L'erreur boréale*, a sensational documentary by Richard Desjardins and Robert Monderie, concerning the state of Quebec's "plundered" forests, were confirmed by a parliamentary committee. The government had no choice but to acknowledge the over-exploitation of the forests and to impose an immediate 20% cut in coniferous logging. But that did not go far enough. "Aux arbres, citoyens!" cried the environmental groups[17], calling on Quebec to give itself a genuine land protection policy in order to reach the 8% coverage recommended by the Convention on Biological Diversity.

All these threats are leading to a new round of global consciousness-raising. Ecological coalitions of all kinds are making their voice heard. Infinite growth is not possible in a finite world, they insist; we must stop thinking that some seven billion human beings on the planet can consume as much as the West is doing today and survive. A broad-based movement is coming to the defence of the world's commons — air, water, forests and the climate — and a universal right to the vital necessities of life.

International bodies such as the United Nations Development Program and the World Health Organization are putting forward solutions to make sure that all of humanity will have access to sufficient food and drinking water. Only strict controls and sustained government intervention will allow us to confront the risk. Humanity can mobilize to stave off the extinction that some are predicting. Education has a major role to play in this matter.

Globalizing Solidarity

History teaches us that every new form of domination and exploitation engenders new forms of resistance. Today's issues are reminiscent of others in the past. Just as at other times, a new awareness of global issues is appearing. Solidarity is being constructed internationally. New social movements are organizing all over the world as unions gradually resume their former internationalism.

In the face of this resistance, the arguments or threats used to counter it also have a *déjà vu* feel to them. Old demands as elementary as limits on work hours have come under attack on the grounds that they will harm the competitiveness of companies or lead to the flight of capital. In the same way, the abolition of slavery, women's right to vote, universal education and the end of colonialism were all thought of as utopian in their time. That didn't stop the adoption of laws to transform societies progressively.

Thus, the workers' movement was born as a reaction against the harsh exploitation that came with the industrial revolution. It was developed outside of the law and met with brutal repression. The six-day week, the ten-hour day (later eight hours), job security, and the gradual outlawing of child labour were all gains made after bitter struggles. The international symbol of the union movement, May 1st, owes its origin to a strike for the eight-hour day. In 1888, Chicago workers began a general strike that was brutally suppressed. Its leaders were hanged. It was not uncommon at that time for strikes to result in numerous fatalities.

The ban on union organizing led British workers to become the first to form Friendly Societies at the beginning of the nineteenth century. The early proponents of utopian socialism took the initiative to form agricultural and consumer cooperatives; today's co-ops are their descendants.

At its inception, trade unionism was synonymous with the workers' movement; it grew hand in hand with socialism. The association took different forms in different societies. In France, trade unionism came from political organization; in England, the trade unions created the Labour Party at the beginning of the 20th century. Unionism thus acted as vehicle for a whole range of political demands that gave birth to the first steps towards the social state at the end of the 19th century.

Internationalism was at the core of union and socialist action as early as the middle of the 19th century. The first international organizations brought craft unions together; later they extended to industries and specific sectors. Two Workers' Internationals followed one another before World War I. "Workers of the world" united to change the world. Even if they were predominantly European in character, the idea was no less than the bulwark of a global workers' front against the new forces of international capital.

In Europe, the internationalism of the unions generally led them to defend positions favouring the free movement of labour. They saw to it that the collective interests of an expanding working class took precedence over national interests. This partly explains their opposition to the First War. But national interests eventually prevailed. As a consequence, worker internationalism splintered along lines separating the political and corporatist emphases, the West and the East.

In Quebec too, the first strikes that greeted the construction of the Lachine canal were bloody affairs. It was only after 1872 that association for the purposes of negotiating working conditions was no longer viewed by the courts as a coalition creating obstacles to free trade. In the 1880s, the Knights of Labor were advocates for a range of political demands including universal suffrage and compulsory school attendance. Moreover, in Quebec, international unionism meant mergers between Quebec organizations with U.S. unions at a time when frontiers were still wide open.

As for democratic demands, it took a civil war for the U.S. to end slavery. That has not prevented institutional discrimination from being the target of struggles throughout the 20th century. Similarly, the women's movement took off in the 1960s. Its demands led almost everywhere to profound transformations of social life, both in human rights and in private life.

Colonial domination, for its part, provoked resistance movements that were able to take advantage of the great powers that had been weakened by the Second War. These liberation struggles, highly varied in nature, marked the second half of the last century and left a toll of death and suffering in their wake.

The current round of globalization is bringing new forms of struggle, a new internationalism, expanded this time to take in the whole planet. Unions are closing ranks globally, both generally and by sector. They are trying to strengthen their capacity for action and to pool their experiences in the face of increasingly globalized policies. The old division into West and East or on the basis of ideologies is yielding to new planetary common front.

We are witnessing a fusion of great organizations like the International Confederation of Free Trade Unions (ICFTU) and the World Confederation of Labour (WCL) as well as the creation of new sectoral internationals, such as Education International, which is also seeking to bring all education workers together. More and more international professional secretariats are being formed. International federations of unions from the same sector or in the same multinational corporation are also trying to respond with one voice to the issues that affect them collectively. International framework agreements include a growing number of corporations; there are now some 40 such agreements, of which more than 30 have been signed since 2000[18]; these agreements are applied locally and usually contain procedures for monitoring and settling grievances.

Groups are mobilizing to enforce respect for international labour laws by major corporations that outsource production. Thus, Nike and The Gap have been the targets of boycotts protesting against worker and child exploitation in their outsourced companies. In April 2005, Nike, following the example of the Gap, published the list of its suppliers and revealed the results of an internal inquiry into their compliance with labour laws. The Quebec Coalition against Sweatshops, which is working to denounce barefaced exploitation in countries of the South, welcomed this initiative; but much more needs to be done.

The current round of globalization is bringing new forms of struggle, a new internationalism, expanded this time to take in the whole planet.

As for social movements, the moment is ripe for globalization there too. It has two facets. On the one hand, mobilization is becoming more and more a feature at each of the great international meetings where free trade and the commodification of the world are on the agenda. On the other hand, globally coordinated actions are being engaged simultaneously around the planet.

The parallel Earth Summit at Rio in 1992 was probably the first event to herald a worldwide social movement. The 1995 conference held in parallel with the UN's Fourth International Conference on Women in Beijing followed suit. But it was the engineered collapse of the Multilateral Agreement on Investments (MAI) in 1998 and of the new "millennium round" of the WTO in Seattle in November 1999 that really caught the imagination of the anti-globalization movement.

The "coalition of turtles and teamsters," as it was then called, inflicted a humiliating defeat on the champions of the control of the world economy by the great multinational corporations. The nickname refers to the alliance of ecologists in defence of turtles threatened by industrial fishing methods and traditional unions identified with the Teamsters. A new alliance had come into being between the union movement and a social movement.

Since then, this alliance has been reformed on a number of occasions, coinciding with regional summits and significant meetings of heads of state or international institutions of finance. Quebec, Genoa, Cancun, Hong Kong are all so many cities which, in recent years, have seen a succession of people's summits that have cemented new bonds of solidarity.

On another level, since 2001, the World Social Forum (WSF) has become the counterweight of the Economic Forum of Davos, a meeting of the world's mighty. A decentralized alliance of diverse organizations, the WSF has regionalized. European, Asian, African and American social forums as well as many national social forums have been held in recent years. Some people worry about the burnout from such a proliferation of events. Others see this simply as the "high mass" of the left where sermons follow sermons. However, there can be no denying the pivotal role of social forums in the development of anti-globalization theory and strategy. They have consolidated a genuine global movement and breathed hope into current struggles, something needed now more than ever.

Other movements, while having global objectives, are more clearly anchored in national activism. This is notably the case of the World March of Women initiated by the Quebec Federation of Women that has met with worldwide success. ATTAC, "an action-oriented people's education movement," was established in 1998; by 2003, it existed in 51 countries. Its first objective: the Tobin tax on financial markets and multinational corporations in order to redistribute income globally. Since then, its scope has broadened; ATTAC notably launched a campaign to encourage cities to declare themselves symbolically "GATS-free zones"; Montreal is one of them.

Finally we should not forget the ecological and peace movements. February 15, 2003 signaled another step in this globalization of resistance. For the first time in history, dozens of millions of people took to the streets of the world's capital cities in a coordinated manner to protest against the invasion of Iraq by a coalition under U.S. command. In Montreal, despite -20° temperatures, more than 250,000 joined in.

And so social movements are well on the way to developing a new kind of internationalism. A new alliance with the union movement and the development of concerted actions at the local, national, regional or global levels give grounds for hope. Citizens the world over are finding new horizons of meaning. It is no longer Utopian to say that "another world is possible." Another form of education is also possible and an international dimension based on solidarity should have its place within it.

*   *   *

It is true that we are now living in a more globally conscious world. The connections between what is happening here and what is happening thousands of kilometres away are many and daily. Reports of events are passed on instantly. Global businesses are planetary manufactures. The drop in the cost of communications and transportation is bringing ordinary people together, even if this cost is still beyond the reach of many.

Such changes could allow humanity to take giant steps towards greater equality and provide all inhabitants of the planet with access to basic common needs. Instead, however, we are seeing increases in inequality and a proliferation of the abandoned and the rejected in both South and North. The fact is that the dominant form of globalization is the prerogative of the powerful and the merchants, and spells freedom for the wealthy. It is borne along by the giant corporations and the institutions running it are operating beyond democratic control.

But as in other moments in history, this globalization of the powerful has generated a counter-movement that is advancing new strategies and proposals for a better world. The construction of this planetary humanity is humanity's business.

These changes and issues affect the full range of social institutions. The effects vary considerably according to the situation, the history and the resistance in each country. Education is no different. In fact, what is happening in other spheres of activity has a direct bearing on patterns in education; the commodification of the world is also happening in education and resistance to one is as valid as resistance to the other. Moreover, education needs a vision: it is a transmission of the world and a preparation for the future; while it must account for the world as it is, it must refuse to submit to it. The following two chapters will allow us to take stock of all its ramifications.

Notes

1. It came into regular currency with Theodore Levitt's influential article "The Globalisation of Markets" (*Harvard Business Review*, 1 May 1983). But, the *Oxford English Dictionary* has traced its first use back to an article in *The Spectator* (C. A. Cerami, "The U.S. Eyes Greater Europe', *The Spectator*, 5 October 1962)

2. Translator's note: The French version points out that the French use two words: *la mondialisation* and only more recently *la globalisation.* "The latter word is adopted by those who find that it resonates well with the family of words to which it belongs. The noun *globe* suggests its planetary significance; the adjective *global*, its all-embracing quality. The distinction between *mondialisation* and *globalisation* is helpful because *mondialisation* (based on *monde* or "world") can be taken to have beneficial effects, which are not associated in French with the word *globalisation*." (DC)

3. This put an end to New France and began the British domination of the French-speaking populations of North America.

4. Almost a century later, Gandhi would make the return to traditional textile production one of the symbolic elements of the struggle against British domination and for the independence of India.

5. Thousands of native people were displaced and exterminated and their land usurped to make space for increasing levels of immigration.

6. Anti-trust laws, like the Sherman Anti-Trust Act adopted in 1890, attempted to break these new monopolies. It wasn't until 1911 that the monopoly of the Standard Oil Trust was broken up into ten companies, among them Exxon, Mobil and Chevron. They are now in the process of merging together again.

7. In order to wrestle inflation to the ground in Canada, the Trudeau government also passed a wage and price control law, but only the former were kept under control.

8. Joseph Stiglitz shows that, in opposition to the claims of the defenders of "voodoo economics," tax cuts are not self-financed through offsetting rises in consumption and employment. He suspects that the Reaganites were well aware of this and that that was why they did it.

9. In Quebec, the Lévesque government was caught in a panic as interest rates soared. He imposed a 20% wage reduction on public and parapublic sector employees for a period of several months and tried to "break the unions" with a package of special laws.

10. The subprime mortgage crisis of 2008, with its mortgage-backed securities and collateralized debt obligation, is the latest example of the "creativity" of the market with all its negative consequences.

11. Association pour la Taxation des Transactions pour l'Aide aux Citoyens (Association for the Taxation of Financial Transactions for the Aid of Citizens); an organization based in France originally simply promoting the Tobin tax but now broadening its focus to confront the neo-liberal version of globalization. It favours globalization only in a framework of social justice and sustainability.

12. It happens that *Kicking Away the Ladder* is the book title used by Chang to describe the real history of free trade.

13. It should be remembered that this did not stop the United States from imposing sanctions or embargos on countries whose politics it doesn't approve of. Thus, the Helms-Burton law, adopted in 1996, hardened trade sanctions against Cuba, even targeting third party countries that "traffic" with the island.

14. A decline in the popular vote is visible almost everywhere in the West. In Canada, participation went from an average of 77% in the sixties to 73% in the seventies and eighties to reach a 66% plateau in the nineties.

15. Jean-Marcel Lapierre (2005) has well described the "deterioration of collective working rights under the Charest government". The changes to article 45 of the Labour Code

in favour of sub-contracting and the ban on the right to unionize for family childcare providers and intermediate health resources are two examples.

16. Between 1995 and 2003, the rate of unionization has gone from 34.1% to 30.4% in Great Britain, from 29.2% to 23.2% in Germany, from 24% to 19.6% in Japan, from 14.3% to 12.9% in the United States and from 35% to 30.4% in Canada (Labrosse, 2005).

17. The slogan mimics the revolutionary cry *Aux armes, citoyens!* in the La Marseillaise, the national anthem of France.

18. They involve such large corporations as Renault, Volkswagen, Bosch, Danone and Telefónica.

CHAPTER TWO

Business Goes to School

Education (...) can no longer escape the hurricane that is sweeping the planet, imposing far and wide not only the law of the market in general, but a well-orchestrated commodification of the world.

Sanuel Joshua. *Une autre école est possible!*
Manifeste pour une éducation émancipatrice

When the purposes of education become narrowed to economic advantages, ... an easy next step is to regard schooling as a consumer good rather than a common good.

David Tyack and Larry Cuban,
Tinkering Toward Utopia: a Century of Public School Reform

Historically, public education has been at the core of the policies that marked the birth and development of the social state. It was closely associated with the protection of children's rights and the pursuit of greater equality. It made a major contribution to economic development. It also served to consolidate nation-states, by providing a way to share a common national history and by promoting a common language and set of values, sometimes to the detriment of minority groups. From its inception, and throughout the twentieth century, education and nationhood were indivisible.

At the end of the nineteenth century, compulsory school attendance took its place in the movement to shore up liberal democracies. The corollary of universal suffrage was compulsory universal education to guarantee an enlightened citizenry. It was claimed by the workers' movement, who saw it as a sure route to emancipation. It was necessary for the integration of millions of immigrants. It was even advocated by some employers who were looking for a better-trained labour force to meet the requirements of industrialization and who wanted to avoid the shameful competition of child labour. Sweden was at the forefront, instigating compulsory school attendance in 1842 while Quebec dragged its feet right up to the mid-1940s, twelve years after Vatican City had introduced it.

Different societies have built education systems with different structures, thus reflecting the diversity of national political cultures. And while all children were required to attend school, the education system was highly compartmentalized. The children of the bigwigs and the small fry did not share benches in the same schools.

After World War II, public education went through a major expansion. Economic revival required a general boost in education levels. Universal Declaration of Human Rights forcefully reaffirmed the right to education. Equality of opportunity gradually took its place on the agenda. The former two-track structure began yielding to a more open school, better attuned to the new emphasis on democratic life. Even so, some characteristics of the Taylorist industrial model did make their way into schools, most notably the fragmentation of learning into a multiplicity of objectives.

The post-war educational policies shared common goals until the 1980s, even if their first loyalties were to national cultures and economies. Almost everywhere, the same challenges were identified and tackled: enrolling ever more pupils for ever more years, delaying selection, compensatory interventions in poor neighbourhoods, the integration of children with special needs, improvement of pre-service training, and the elaboration of professional development.

In Britain, Sweden, France, Quebec and elsewhere, new comprehensive schools[1] were established in order to broaden and diversify pupils' experiences in preparation for the exercise of democracy as well as to instill tolerance and mutual understanding. They also aimed to promote greater educational justice while responding to the new demands of the labour market. There were some who criticized this social mixing while others pointed out the persistence of the inequalities that were supposed to be lessened; in fact, the opening of the public school to a more diverse population did not succeed in achiev ing the desired social blend and equality.

Throughout its development, public education was a subject of conflict and struggle. Finding the right balance between freedom and equality, centralization and decentralization, individual development and preparation for the labour force, maintaining school autonomy and meeting the needs of business, all of these tensions characterized this "long century" in education.

These issues today are taking on a new sharpness. Education is having to submit to the globalization of its principles and rules, and these are challenging the initial foundations of public education and are dislocating the respective places of the public and private spheres.

Since the early eighties, the welfare state has been on the firing line. The Nation-State is being redefined. These two pillars in the development of public education are being shaken. The merchants have taken the school by storm. The notions of competition, productivity, performance, clients, and consumers are gradually replacing the humanist discourse that had been characteristic of education.

The school is being rethought, restructured, reformed. The educational policies being introduced almost everywhere are all taken from the same source. This is not the fruit of pure chance. Many analysts are pointing out that a new educational paradigm is at work. A new model, a new ambition on a worldwide scale, this is what explains this spreading "ambient sound," these "recurrent concepts," these similar analyses that are seeping through national frontiers. To take the title of a research report coming out of the Research Institute of the *Fédération syndicale unitaire* (FSU, France), we are witnessing the emergence of a "new world order in education."

According to this new paradigm, the sum of the self-interests of every individual should take the place of educational policy. Competition among individuals, schools and nations is expected to guarantee a new efficiency and a return to educational quality. Education is to become a product like any other, with the parents and pupils becoming the new clients of this school market. The management paradigm of big business, which thrives on output and performance, is to be emulated.

The consequences of this are already being felt. The educational mission is increasingly being reduced to its economic dimension alone. Some parents have more choices than others and the losers must be content to be bystanders. Business is invading and investing in education. It is exercising pressure upon the educational mission and is advocating a utilitarian vision centred on the production of "human capital" so valuable in the game of global competition. It wants to intervene in curriculum content and on the provision of training; and it is trying to blast its way into this last bastion of public power by finding new markets to "exploit."

Regardless of what the official speeches may say, the humanist objectives of emancipation, fulfillment and the acquisition of culture are giving way to productivity and value-added processes. Education is being seen in quantitative terms, reduced to what is measurable.

The global nature of the neo-liberal educational paradigm involves a genuine break with the past. Nowadays, even if education is still a field where states can affirm their sovereignty, educational policy is more and more being developed along international lines and being implemented in a well-orchestrated manner. International economic bodies are coordinating the introduction of reforms, when they are not actually imposing them willy-nilly.

Thus, the World Bank has imposed on many countries of the South, in the wake of structural adjustment policies, a framework for educational reforms fully in tune with the Washington Consensus. For developed countries, the Organization for Economic Cooperation and Development (OECD) is the main coordinator of policy development based on the same objectives, all in favour of the growth of the "education industry". Just about everywhere, education spending cuts, school choice, expansion of the private sector, accountability for outcomes, and merit pay constitute together the gamut of measures accompanying the decline of public education.

The purpose of this chapter is to identify the main principles underpinning this new education paradigm and its consequences for Quebec.

The first part will deal with the claims that the laws of the marketplace are a necessary solution and that the way to improve education can be found in the "imperative to compete," with its corollaries of school choice, decentralization and accountability for outcomes.

The second part will dwell upon more direct forays into education by business. Business is seeking a variety of ways to get into our schools, and to change the curriculum and the mission. Here as elsewhere, public-private partnerships and the commercialization of education are the order of the day. Most ominously, a sword of Damocles is dangling over higher education; the current negotiations on the General Agreement on Trade in Services (GATS) brazenly aim to make education a commodity, subject to the rules of international trade.

For each topic discussed, a similar sequence will be followed. First, the situation in several European and Anglo-Saxon countries will be described then analyzed in the light of a synthesis of research findings. The description of the realities in Quebec follows, thus enabling these to be understood in the international context.

Two points need to be made here and borne in mind in what follows. In the first place, despite the indisputable spread of the neo-liberal education paradigm, it does not pervade all education policies, and that is all to the good. While there is indeed something that Dorval Brunelle calls "a constituent doctrine," we are not dealing with a single doctrine here and the game is not over. Education is still a focal point of social struggle and resistance is not in vain.

On the other hand, some of the changes brought about by the current phase of globalization have inevitable consequences for education, whether it is the increasingly apparent need for a citizenry *open to the world*, the restructuring of the labour force, or the threats to the future of our planet. And it is precisely the possible educational response to these challenges, as part of a democratic plan that keeps its emphasis on accessibility and the pursuit of greater equity, that will be the subject of the third chapter.

THE MARKET AS SOLUTION

The neo-liberal education paradigm is based on a premise that is certainly not obvious, whatever the twisted reasoning of its advocates might lead us to believe. That premise states that the introduction of competition between a range of educational services in a free market is the best guarantee of equality, efficiency and excellence. Parents are envisaged as choosing from a broad variety of schools whose survival depends on their ability to satisfy their "clients." The role of the State is then limited to quality control.

The market is taken to be the solution to what ails our schools. Bureaucratic control of public bodies and the negative role of special interest groups, including teachers' unions, are said to be contributing to the inefficacy that is under attack. The alleged superiority of private schools, whose characteristic is precisely that of having evolved in a market environment, is advanced as the proof. To be successful, schools will have to find a niche by targeting specific values, disciplines, or special groups.

This was Milton Friedman's thesis from the fifties on and it has since been picked up by numerous conservative academics and think tanks. In the United States, John Chubb and Terry Moe published their famous work *Politics, Markets and American Schools* in 1990. In it they tried to confer a scientific veneer to this ideological enterprise[2]. Characterized as "a polemic wrapped in numbers," it unleashed a storm of criticism.

Obviously, the leaders of the big corporations did not take long to get into the act. The chairman-CEO of IBM and one of his former colleagues from Nabisco wrote a highly popular book in which they went on at length about the need to "reinvent education by supporting entrepreneurship in schools." In their view, the discipline of the market was the last hope for public schools.

Under Milton Friedman's inspiration, Chile led the way in the 1970s. They decentralized to the municipal level, introduced the voucher system, built a private network, banned the national union and replaced it with a professional association. These reforms were brought in under Pinochet's dictatorship.

The Anglo-Saxon countries followed suit, albeit more democratically. In the United States, the second wave of reforms in the 1980s, called "school restructuring", was characterized by decentralization, school choice, and accountability. In Britain, under Thatcher, an assault on the power of local authorities and unions was added to this policy mix. The same model was adopted by right wing governments in countries whose education system was performing well and had occasioned little criticism, as happened in Sweden.

But education, especially basic education, cannot easily be reduced to a commodity susceptible to the rules of the classic free market. Education benefits the individual, the family and society all at the same time. Its providers have to work under a significant amount of state control. The "clients" are under an obligation to consume and for a long time (compulsory school attendance), and the act of choosing can transform the product (the school). These are all reasons why sociologists and political scientists have adopted the concept of "quasi-market" to describe the recent neo-liberal shift in education.

This notion is a good description of the model that is being introduced throughout the world. It has important features redolent of markets: choice, a varied supply, competition to attract the consumer, independence. But for all that, education is still a public service: it meets certain social needs and the State still has a large role to play.

If we return to the basic premise of this paradigm, results from research studies in numerous countries invalidate the claims that the introduction of competition improves the quality of education and reduces social inequality. One example was a longitudinal study in New Zealand that aimed to verify the statements of both the defenders and detractors of the application of market laws in education. In it, David Hughes and his colleagues agreed with the latter and concluded that the market is neither effective nor efficient. The myth that as soon as education was freed from the "shackles of the State," it would flourish and improve does not stand up to scrutiny. Their report was called *Trading in Futures* because "in effect education markets trade off the opportunities of less privileged children to those already privileged" (p.2).

Michael Apple's synthesis (2001) takes the same tack; it is clear that the existence of a quasi-market model in education has led, almost everywhere in the world, to worsening class and race divisions and to an increase in cultural apartheid. After examining the situation in various countries, Helen Ladd (2003) also concluded that the data show that competitive regimes were sources of inequality, because they exacerbate the problems of schools with poor results, successful pupils moving away from them leaving disadvantaged and struggling pupils in an even higher proportion.

Philippe Meirieu, who has recently taken up his pen in defence of the public school, goes even further with this cry from the heart. "I have reached the point where I view the current spirit of competition among all schools, both private and public, as a lethal blow to the future of our democracy" (2005a, p.9). In fact, in a system where everyone is looking out for number one, we are entitled to wonder how the school system can contribute to the common good and social stability, how it can promote a more egalitarian society and how it can pass on the values of citizenship and solidarity.

In Quebec, this market thesis has, since the end of the 1980s, found defenders in Jean-Luc Migué and Richard Marceau with their assault upon "the public monopoly of education." They have subsequently become distinguished founders of the Montreal Economic Institute (MEI), which serves as an echo chamber for neo-liberal ideas[3], and Marceau went on to be one of the instigators of the annually published ranking of Quebec high schools, the clone of a Fraser Institute initiative.

When parents are torn between their duty as citizens and their duty as parents, they normally give priority to the latter. The result is a diminution of our ability to improve education for all by collective action.

The introduction of the market model into education needs to satisfy three conditions. It is worth spending some time looking at them. Firstly, competition between a diverse range of educational services requires that consumers of these services can actually choose their child's school. Secondly, schools will need greater autonomy so that there can be a wide range to choose from. Thirdly, in such a context, the State's role would be to control quality and provide the necessary information about the value of the products on offer in the marketplace.

School Choice: Failure to remain at the scene

Not so long ago, in the vast majority of countries, the primary or secondary school that a prospective student attended was mainly determined by the catchment area in which the student lived. The boundaries of these areas were set by the State or a local education authority. This catchment scheme made it difficult for students to attend any school other than the one to which they were assigned. The diversity or uniformity of the social mix in the school depended on the social mix in the school neighbourhood and, given the relative sizes of the catchment areas, there was more homogeneity at the primary level than at the secondary. Even so, various kinds of choice did exist, depending on local traditions and social patterns. In some cases, available choices varied by language of instruction, by religious de-nomination, or by sector (public or private).

Today, the vast majority of educational systems have to deal with parents' ability to choose and the consequences of that. So there is a move away from a system where all the schools are similar in na-ture while catering to a diverse student population to a system where there is choice among a diverse range of schools each catering to a special clientele whose members are similar in nature. In this com-petitive climate, pupils' performance becomes a marketable product in its own right. Schools vie with one another for the best students, those who cost least to educate, those who are seen as adding val-ue to the school's appeal, while trying to avoid pupils with so-called 'negative value.'

The defenders of free choice argue that this is a fundamental right, that parents and pupils have preferences they should be able to ex-ercise, that this would be the best way to improve the quality of ed-ucation, and that this would allow the most disadvantaged ones to escape from their "ghettos" and to have access to better schools. "If people can and must have the choice of food, clothing and housing for their children, why can't they choose their school?", write two Que-bec advocates for free choice and competition with the private sector (Migué and Marceau, 1989, p.87).

Their opponents have been quick to retort that education is not a simple consumer product, but a common good; that the choices made by some have negative effects on the schooling of others; that the better off and the better informed members of society will be best placed to choose; and that this will reinforce school segregation and inequality.

Freedom of school choice does, however, command a fairly large measure of support. On the one hand, it does cater to the identity con-cerns of diverse groups in our society. On the other hand, those who have given up on the promised hopes for equity, especially the black population and the poor, see in choice a last chance to escape from the vicious circle of exclusion. When parents are torn between their duty as citizens and their duty as parents, they normally give prior-ity to the latter, in any context where diversity of choice is a practi-cal proposition. The result is a diminution of our ability to improve education for all by collective action.

*   *   *

The U.S., with its charter schools, its vouchers debate and its home schooling boom, provide a good example of the changes under way.

What is happening in other countries is equally revealing. Taken together, they help us understand realities in Quebec.

The development of charter schools is rooted in a profoundly anti-government feeling popular among neo-liberals. The charter school is an autonomous school governed by a charter that defines its mission and its objectives. This contract with the local school board usually specifies the test results that the school must achieve by a set deadline, to avoid having the charter cancelled. The school is subject to a minimum of regulation and receives public funding at the same rate as other public schools. Arrangements for student selection and the freedom to raise additional funds vary from state to state.

Since the first charter school was opened in Minnesota in 1991, the model has expanded phenomenally. By 2003-2004, legislation enabling the creation of such schools had been adopted by 41 states, the District of Columbia and Puerto Rico. There were more than 3,000 charters with an enrolment of close to one million. And the phenomenon is booming; since the year 2000, the number of charter schools has increased by 50%[4]. Several observers however, condemned the fact that many of the schools were choosing their pupils, that they were not reaching their stated objectives, and that some of them were not even reporting their test results, an obligation usually stipulated in the contract.

Governments have had to amend some of their legislation in response to these criticisms. Accordingly, in seven states, selective admission is now prohibited, and, in a third of the cases, the school's enrolment must respect racial balance. Apart from a few exceptions, the costs of transportation are borne by the parents. On the other hand, 18 legislatures have been authorizing private for-profit companies to finance schools, and almost all have allowed the contracting out of cleaning, curriculum development and teaching. These arrangements have spurred the growth of private for-profit companies specializing in the management of schools. It is estimated that one in five charter schools is managed privately. The 2004 bankruptcy of one of the biggest private companies managing charter schools, the California Charter Academy, locking out almost 6,000 pupils, led to second thoughts about the sparsity of government regulation in this sector.

As students went back to school in 2004, The American Federation of Teachers (AFT) published a study that burst like a bombshell in neo-liberal circles and hit the front page of the *New York Times*. The study revealed that charter schools were obtaining lower test scores than comparable public schools. Drawing on the analysis of the 2003 National Assessment of Educational Progress (NAEP) test scores, the AFT researchers showed that the pupils in charter schools were about half a year behind the pupils in public schools in reading and math, in both the fourth and eighth grades.

Despite a rush to the barricades by conservatives who paid for full-page advertisements in several major dailies to refute the allegations, everything seems to confirm these findings[5]. Another study conducted by the U.S. Department of Education in five states and published in November 2004 concluded that on the whole charter schools were less successful than public schools with comparable demographic profiles[6].

As for vouchers, they are still as controversial as ever among our southern neighbours. A voucher is a sum of money that parents can use to educate their children in the school of their choice, public or private. The goal of its promoters is to give private education greater access to public funding.

In the U.S., private schools are overwhelmingly religious in nature and the First Amendment of the federal Constitution concerning the separation of Church and State prohibits the use of public funds to support programs or institutions with religious purposes. So this is an attempt to get around the constitutional constraints by providing money in the form of vouchers to the parents rather than the school. It is hardly surprising that these schemes are fought all the way to the Supreme Court and are frequently subjected to referendums.

Such schemes are few in number, despite pressure from the Bush administration. In November 2000, voters in California and Michigan voted almost 70% against the introduction of vouchers in their state. In 2004 alone, voucher proposals were defeated in twenty-six States. The U.S. Supreme Court nevertheless breached the dam in June 2002, by acknowledging the constitutionality of a project under way in Cleveland to provide poor families with vouchers, allowing them to choose a private school, either secular or religious. On the other hand, in 2004, the Supreme Court in Colorado declared a similar project unconstitutional.

Financial support for vouchers is not coming from reformers. It has nothing to do with the desire to help poor families. Its support comes from free market advocates associated with the religious right. Milton Friedman himself, through his Foundation, has obtained the major portion of the funding for pro-voucher campaigns; it is also financing the Black Alliance for Educational Options, which is promoting vouchers in the black community. In the words of a well-known journalist, it is "about breaking up the public school system in pursuit of profit or in pursuit of permission to teach the Bible in classrooms." (Lewis, 2003, p.564).

The 2003 Quebec election campaign put this issue back on the agenda. Action Démocratique du Québec (ADQ) made it one of the main planks of its education platform. There was no shortage of controversy as the ADQ's proposal provoked a hostile reaction from education circles generally[7].

But the big boom in the U.S. is in home schooling. While it was still illegal in several states fifteen or so years ago, it is now growing annually by almost 20%. In 2003, more than a million U.S. children (about 2.2%) were being schooled at home. The most powerful and numerous group is from the Christian right. They hold the view that the moral and spiritual needs of their children are not being met by public schools. A second group, in the minority, is made up of a variety of movements all seeking greater autonomy through partnerships with public schools.

This is a new demonstration of the consumer mentality in education. It is assumed that education is the sole responsibility of parents who should be able to provide the educational environment they want for their children and get the means to do this through the curriculum materials market. William Bennett, a former Secretary of Education in the Reagan administration, has actually founded a private company, K12 Inc., which aims to supply all the material necessary for these new educators, while at the same time developing the concept of online schools. More than 40% of the pupils in home schooling are using distance education in one way or another.

For its critics, home schooling is endangering the notion of citizenship. The school is in fact one of the rare institutions where a high degree of social diversity may be found and where children can assimilate a stock of common values. The exercise of freedom, it is recalled, presupposes the freedom to make up one's own mind, the opportunity to hear a variety of points of view, and the possibility to question one's own beliefs and preferences from time to time. This hardly seems feasible in the context of schooling under the strict supervision of parents with highly inflexible ideas.

In Quebec, the Ministry of Education estimated the number of children in home schooling to be about 400 in the 2003-2004 year. For the Quebec Association for Home Based Education, whose goal is to encourage and support this practice, the actual number lies between 2,500 and 5,000. As a rule, the school board is supposed to monitor the quality of the schooling being provided[8], but this does not seem to be happening, judging from the uncertainty over the number of children involved. The movement could soon pick up and grow, if we are to judge by media interest, the creation of promotional groups, and the popularity of home schooling among our neighbours.

Finally, school choice has led in the U.S., as elsewhere, to the proliferation of specialized public schools, notably the magnet schools, and the use of promotional strategies not unlike commercial advertising. Secondary school fairs, glossy flyers, etc. are now being used to publicize this range of products. The resultant choice is not inconsequential. "Typical white" families are leaving their neighbourhood schools at a rate three times higher than "typical black" families.

*   *   *

In New Zealand, Australia, Britain, Sweden and France, school choice is also a topic of debate. Thus, at the beginning of the 1990s, the Labour government of New Zealand granted the right to school choice, while still retaining priority for parents in their local school. When the right came to power, they brushed aside all the standards intended to guarantee a measure of social equity. A charter now regulates the relationship between each school and the State. Parents evidently tend to believe that schools with a high proportion of pupils who are white and successful are better than schools with pupils who are from minority groups or struggling. The results were not long in coming: the secondary school exam scores went up in the schools in demand and fell in the schools with declining enrolments. The rankings only served to add "shame and blame" to schools already on a downward spiral. Competition had negative effects on the totality of school life and this could even end up affecting the appeal of teaching as a profession.

As New Zealand had often been a reference point for neo-liberals on the lookout for reforms, the team of David Hughes and his colleagues went looking for empirical evidence in support of the claims made by the defenders of free choice. Their conclusions are unequivocal. Choice has worked to the benefit of the more affluent; characterized by the flight of middle-class Whites, it has led to a concentration of pupils at risk in some schools; the children from privileged backgrounds are three times more likely to have a chance to attend top schools than those from poor backgrounds.

In Australia, as in Canada, education is the responsibility of each state. The same trends are observable there even so. First, special schools were developed for children identified as gifted and talented in order to avoid the flight of successful students to private schools, and then little by little choice was extended to more and more schools. In Australia, the conservative government elected in 1996 has constantly trumpeted parents' right to choose their children's schools.

In Britain, the model put in place by the Thatcher government in the 1980s has undergone only a few modifications by the succeeding New Labour government. The possibility of public financial aid to allow low-income families to attend private schools (the Assisted Places Scheme) has been abolished. At the same time, the possibility for schools to opt out of local education authorities' jurisdiction and become autonomous has been maintained. These grant-maintained schools have control of admissions, budget and school staffing. This autonomy is linked to free choice with the aim of making schools more accountable to their "clients".

After a comprehensive analysis of the situation in Britain, the team of Geoff Whitty and his collaborators observed that choice particularly disadvantaged those least able to compete in the market and that it heightened differences between schools, reinforcing a "vertical hierarchy of schooling types rather than producing the promised horizontal diversity" (1998, p.42).

More recently, the labour government has made secondary school diversification one of the major features of its education policy. Schools are invited to find sponsors to pay a portion of the additional costs incurred by specialization. Projects may vary. In this way, there have been schools established for ethnic or religious communities and even schools reserved for black students[9]. A school backed by an automotive millionaire is offering a curriculum designed to meet the requirements of Christian fundamentalists; it was rated excellent by the Office of Standards in Education (Ofsted), the body charged with evaluating schools. Other denominations have also taken advantage of this opening to sponsor their own schools.

In the winter of 2006, the Blair government confirmed its intention of pursuing choice-driven education. But its plan ran into stiff opposition within the Labour Party itself. Faced with a revolt by fifty or so Labour MPs, the government had to rely on the support of the conservatives to pass a bill giving more autonomy to schools and broadening the possibilities of funding from private groups.

In France, the traditional school catchment areas may now be breached more easily. Parents can generally indicate their choice of three schools to the regional superintendent (*inspecteur d'académie*). The government has given into pressure from those wanting their children taught in streamed classes and has increased the number of international or bilingual classes available so as to avoid having private schools occupy this niche alone.

Even if only a little more than 10% of pupils benefit from being allowed to attend school out of area, there are consequences. In the Bordeaux region, the effect has been to double the percentage of students from immigrant backgrounds in some schools. Agnès Van Zanten, in a study of *collèges* (middle schools) in the suburbs outside Paris, con-

cludes hat the trend towards "social, ethnic and program differentia
tion among school populations has grown since the 1980s" (2001, p.5).
There are now so-called "peripheral schools" characterized by a level
of social, cultural and economic marginalization that flatly contra-
dicts the fundamental ideals of democratic societies. If the new directions announced by the right-wing government of President Sarkozy
go into effect, all school catchment areas will have disappeared by
the beginning of the school year in 2010, with a predictable exacerbation of the differentiation already observed.

The same vicious circle can be observed on both sides of the English
Channel. The top schools are becoming even more selective to the extent that they will only admit students who will help them raise their
score in the rankings. Other schools are fighting to keep their best
pupils, while trying to get rid of their struggling pupils into still other schools. The avoidance of schools in poor neighbourhoods is leading to a deterioration in the teaching and learning conditions, which
in turn leads to the proliferation of avoidance strategies. This "downward spiral" can only be stopped by strong public intervention.

As Philippe Meirieu has rightly described it, "we are now having
to deal with two competing systems(...); the competition between private and public schools inevitably re-emerges inside the public system itself, which feels obliged to adopt the same behaviour as the
private sector in order to maintain market share" (2005a, p. 13). We
are seeing a much bigger gap opening up between affluent schools
and "'dumping-ground schools' complete with metal detectors and
surveillance cameras (...) for those whom we have given up trying
to teach" (p. 68).

In Belgium and Holland, where school choice has been around for
a long time, there is noticeably profound social and ethnic stratification. In Holland, this free choice was apparently used as a way to
"flee schools attended by black pupils, while at the same time Moslem
groups are doing their utmost to have their own schools supported by
public funds"(Duru-Bellat & Murat, 2001, p. 212).

The same kind of situation exists in Sweden where the "free choice
revolution" started by the right in 1991 was marked by the introduction of public funding for private schools, the development of specialized schools, and the elimination in many municipalities of catchment
areas. Ethnicity and the level of parental education have had the biggest influence in the exercise of choice, with some schools doubling
the percentage of minority pupils enrolled within the space of a few
years. Holber Daun (2002) has remarked that the most sought-after
schools had not experienced a rise in enrolment. Rather they had become more selective, thus increasing social segregation. This reduc-

tion in the diversity of pupils within any one school and the growth of diversity among schools has led to a polarization that threatens even the principle of equality so dear to the hearts of Swedes.

*   *   *

In Quebec the reforms of the 1960s maintained a level of choice between public schools and private schools generously funded by the public purse, especially at the secondary level. Competition between these two systems, along with the integration of pupils with special needs into regular classes and the disappearance of streaming in the secondary school, provided both explicit and implicit motivations for the diversification of the "range of programs on offer" that got under way at the beginning of the 1980s. Schools boards then decided to "take on the challenge of competition" and began to worry about "marketing" in a war for customers with the burgeoning private school system.

The movement supporting special programs for gifted and talented pupils has contributed significantly to the stratification of public schools. Special schools and classes in the various "talent domains" have sprung up: the arts, music, science, and sport. 1987 saw the first international schools, those "private" schools inside the public system, as they were styled at the time.

The situation became so alarming that the Commission for the Estates General on Education[10] declared that the top priority for Quebec education should be to "reestablish the principle of equal opportunity." The Commission did not mince its words. "Gradually, and almost imperceptibly, schools have become stratified, adopting selection practices based on performance and creating a small group of elect students and a contingent of excluded ones (...) A large number of students (...) often from the most socially and educationally advantaged backgrounds, no longer attend regular schools, a phenomenon that is having alarming results. Regular classes in public schools now shoulder the crushing pedagogical burden imposed by our social choices in education (...)". (1996, p.9).

The Commission recommended the phasing out of public funding for private education and measures to encourage common school attendance by pupils of diverse social backgrounds and academic achievement. Unfortunately, the recommendations fell on deaf ears. While still maintaining school choice that had been introduced in 1989, the amended Education Act of 1997 nevertheless did give some priority to the local school and allowed schools exclusively dedicated to specialized programs only in exceptional circumstances. After that, streaming into special programs inside regular schools took over from streaming into special schools.

The school choice movement was bolstered by the publication in the magazine *L'actualité* of the rankings of secondary schools as compiled by the MIE. The rankings directly contributed to a boost in private school enrolments, and as a corollary, a proliferation of selective programs in the public schools. This is not a co-incidence, when we know the ideological bent of their authors. The consequences for inequality are predictable.

A study by Pierre Dubuc of the average income of parents in schools at both the top and bottom of the 2002 rankings shed light on the gap separating families in these two school categories. The parental income in the top 50 schools was above the provincial average in all but two of the cases. At the other end of the ladder were the schools with the lowest parental incomes. In other words, the rankings were a pretty good guide to schools' ranking by parental socio-economic status.

Today, almost one in every five secondary students is enrolled in a private school, and that proportion rises to one in four in the big urban centres. The number of public schools offering special programs with selective admission procedures

The movement supporting special programs for gifted and talented pupils has contributed significantly to the stratification of public schools.

is estimated at more than 700, that is more than a quarter of all public schools. On the secondary side, more than half the schools offer such programs. And the phenomenon is on the rise. In the context of declining enrolments, resulting from the declining birth rate, the competition between the public and private systems and among public schools is likely to become more pronounced.

While there is no robust research data allowing us to calculate the level of stratification in the Quebec school system, we nevertheless do know that a disproportionately higher number of the pupils attending private schools and selective public schools are from privileged family backgrounds. According to a 2005 study commissioned by the Quebec Federation of Private Schools (FEEP), 32.3% of the pupils in their network were from families with an annual income in excess of $110,000 and 28% from families with less than $60,000 a year[11]. The social basis of selection becomes clearer when we compare these figures with the income distribution of all families in the province; in 2003, fewer than 15% of Quebec families had an annual income above $110,000, while almost 60% had an income below $60,000.

On the public side, only one indicator is available: almost half the pupils attending the international stream of a school in the region of Quebec City had parents with university degrees as opposed to somewhat fewer than one tenth in the regular stream.

Everything, then, indicates that the situation in Quebec is similar to that in other societies where the field of education has changed into a vast zone of competition in which families vie with one another to get their children into the schools thought to be best. Foreign research makes things quite clear. It shows that affluent, well-educated families are the ones who take advantage of choice. They seek out a more homogeneous educational setting for their children and avoid schools with a high proportion of pupils from visible minorities or in difficulty. They are in a better position to visit schools and to take on the added costs of special programs and transportation. And so school segregation complements residential segregation.

These research studies also show that having schools compete with one another does not improve the general quality of education and that parental choice has quickly evolved into the school's choice of its students. Families make their decisions on the basis of their own interests, without considering the consequences of their choice on the fate of others. So the resulting homogenization of school settings has significant consequences on school life, and on the attitudes and performance of the students. The concentration of poor or struggling students in a few schools clearly has the effect of depriving them of a right that is supposed to be universal. We shall return to this in the following chapter.

To sum up, the extension of school choice, in a context of exacerbated competition, has very definitely set Quebec schools back where equal opportunity is concerned. A finer balance has to be found between individual interests and collective interests, between liberty and equality.

The Paradox of School Autonomy

The level of centralization varies considerably from society to society. Republican regimes traditionally favour centralization and delegate some of their responsibilities to administrative regions. Regimes in the British parliamentary tradition, on the other hand, place responsibility for education first and foremost with local authorities in partnership with the central State, or with provinces in federal regimes. There are usually provisions in the constitution that specify the jurisdiction for education, as they do in Canada.

Now, despite this broad range of approaches, a noticeable trend is gathering momentum in many societies. Important responsibilities are being devolved to the school level all over the place. What is more, centralized states are getting excited about devolution to local areas, while in the decentralized systems, higher levels of government are arrogating new powers for themselves.

Public school autonomy is one of the main features of the current round of reform; it is a necessary condition to ensure the range of alternative educational programs desired by the market model. In such a context, the central State, increasingly beset by the complex phenomenon of global competition, has the duty to provide a seal of approval, a single guarantee of the worth of an academic product. Greater autonomy is thus accompanied by the centralization of curriculum, prescribed methods and examinations: hence the paradoxical nature, to say the least, of a devolution of responsibilities to schools along with a redefinition of the powers of central and local authorities, all of which is leading to greater uniformity among educational systems.

But market arguments are not the only ones calling for decentralization. In stark opposition to market-driven arguments, there is the logic of the community school rooted in participatory democracy. Both lines of argument serve as inspiration for school-based decentralization, conceived either as a better way of exercising local democracy or as the imitation of a business model based on optimizing client satisfaction.

All things considered, a lot is being asked of decentralization. It is being called upon to facilitate quicker, better decisions, reduce bureaucracy, encourage collaboration, contribute to academic success, and better reflect the needs and interests of the local population.

*　　　*　　　*

While the process began in the Anglo-Saxon countries, there are few educational systems that it has spared. In Europe, for example, there is not one country where school autonomy has been reduced in recent years. In Canada and the U.S., the vast majority of provinces and States have introduced school-based governance and administration. But everywhere, central controls have been installed where none had existed before.

Models vary with the relative importance given to market ideology or democracy. Variations occur mainly in the make-up of school councils, their responsibilities as well as the central controls over them. For example, members of the school council may or may not include teachers and other staff, may or may not give the power to the parents or the community. The role of the principal can be that of a business manager or of a facilitator. Powers can be limited or extend to the totality of decision-making, from personnel management to complete control over the school budget.

In the U.S., the School-Based Management movement, which became popular in the 1980s, is where decentralization took off. Given the great diversity of education there, almost all possible models can be found, right up to charter schools that have almost total autonomy in exchange for accountability for test results.

In Britain, Local Management of Schools was introduced in 1988 and gave schools control of their budgets, hiring and wages, even if the Local Education Authorities (LEAs) were still the employers. The establishment of the Office for Standards in Education (Ofsted) in 1992 added the control counterpart to local autonomy. New legislation from the Labour Government in the winter of 2006 brought in the possibility of autonomous schools run by "trusts," non-profit organizations that could appoint the members of the board of governors.

The same is true in New Zealand, where school councils have been given the responsibility of allocating funds, hiring and firing staff, and pupil achievement. The Education Review Office has a mandate to monitor and report publicly on school performance. The same division of responsibilities exists in Australia and in Canada. In Ontario the establishment of school councils with parental, community and business representation was followed by the creation of the Education Quality and Accountability Office.

In France, however, decentralization ran into stiff resistance in the spring of 2003. The plan to download more than 100,000 education jobs from the central government to local authorities had to be shelved after massive opposition to what was perceived as an "attempt to dismantle the public education system." This was viewed as a disguised form of privatization, since local authorities did not have the means to make up the gap in government funding after cuts in grants.

Everything suggests that this enthusiasm for decentralizing policies is not due to their ability to improve pupil achievement so much as to their political usefulness as a way of managing conflict. Indeed, no correlation has been observed between school autonomy and 14-year-old reading levels in 12 countries of the OECD. Other research confirms these findings, that there is no evidence that local autonomy improves achievement. But there is no doubt that it downloads controversial decision-making to the schools themselves.

*   *   *

In Quebec, schools were given a certain amount of autonomy in 1989 with the creation of steering committees. These committees, made up of parent reps, staff members, and, in secondary schools, students, were primarily advisory but took on an important responsibility concerning the school's educational plan.

A few years later, to follow up on the report of the Commission for the Estates General on Education, the Ministry of Education proposed making the school the "pivot of the education system," notably by bringing in school councils of which half the members were to be parents. The Ministry plan conferred many powers upon these administrative bodies, notably the choice of teaching methods, learning assessment tools, and so on. Teachers mounted a vigorous opposition.

The mobilization led to the adoption of an act providing for a balance between parental and staff representatives and a division of powers that took better account of their respective roles. In some quarters, this outcome was seen as a half-hearted decentralization and there were regrets that the schools had not acquired an autonomous judicial status nor the means to wield true financial independence. In other quarters, however, there were condemnations of the inequalities that could arise from the freedom of school councils to raise funds privately and to determine the amount of time different subjects could occupy in the timetable.

Even so, all the stakeholders agreed to put their backs into making the reform work. An important study in the spring of 2001 concluded that implementation had on the whole been a success[12]. Respondents to the survey reported that the atmosphere at the school councils was good and that they were having a positive effect by opening schools up to their communities, improving relations between teachers and parents, and enabling innovation.

Nevertheless, major divergences of opinion were uncovered. While 45% of the parents in francophone schools believed that schools should be evaluated on the basis of student results, one of the abiding features of the market-oriented school, fewer than 10% of the teachers shared this point of view. In addition, far more parents wanted local powers extended, including the management of human resources, while a major proportion of the teachers felt that the legislation was already conferring too many powers upon school councils, something that could accentuate differences between schools.

As far as representation was concerned, it was noticed that far more affluent parents were involved. While 29% of Quebec families had an annual income under $30,000, this group accounted for only 12% of school council members; at the other end of the spectrum, families earning more than $80,000 counted for 15% of the population at large, but 28% of the council members.

Among administrators, there was happiness over the more harmonious relations and the greater freedom of action, but there were complaints about the increased burden of work, the amount of time consumed in administrative work to the detriment of pedagogical counseling, and the suffocating pressure of constant accountability. Teachers, for their part, found a major irritant in the fact that, for most of them, participation in school councils was not included in their workload.

The model of school councils adopted in Quebec has so far avoided the trends observed in other countries, notably with respect to employment relations and total budget control. But the balance is a fine one; some powers granted or imposed are in direct line with the market model and results-based management that are transforming Quebec education. In fact, there is much local pressure in support of plans that introduce selectivity, and higher levels of government can now wash their hands of such decisions. On the other hand, such autonomy is sometimes only a façade, since the State has hardly abandoned top-down government at all.

The autonomy wave has not spared the *cégeps* either. In 1993, College Renewal recognized *cégeps* as institutions of higher learning, thereby justifying their increased powers, notably with respect to curriculum. At the same time, measures were put in place to monitor results and to establish a more rigorous assessment mechanism: the *Commission d'évaluation de l'enseignement collégial*.[13] Several measures are preparing the way for greater decentralization, as advocated by the *Fédération des Cégeps*, whether for specific admission regulations, the possibility of curriculum review or development, and the power to grant interim certificates.

*   *   *

The paradoxical side of this decentralization process is clearly visible in decentralized states, especially federal states. In Britain, Australia and New Zealand, the introduction of a national curriculum stands in stark contrast to their traditions of decentralized education. In the United States, the imposition of conditions on States seeking access to federal funding is the biggest and the most damaging intrusion by the federal government into local constitutional responsibilities.

In Canada, ever since the first National Consultation on Education was held in Montreal in 1994, centralizing tendencies have taken off at an alarming rate. While the idea of a Pan-Canadian curriculum was unanimously rejected, it is interesting to note that the Maritimes and the Western Provinces have since come together to develop a core curriculum aligned with the School Achievement Indicators Program (SAIP) first introduced by the Council of Ministers of Education in Canada (CMEC) back in 1993. A Common Framework of Science Learning Outcomes (K-12) for use by curriculum developers has also been proposed by CMEC and another similar framework is under way on educating for citizenship.

As for the federal government, the fact that education is a fundamental part of economic development and international competitiveness serves as an argument for a level of interference that threatens the constitutional jurisdiction of the provinces. The creation of the new Canadian Council on Learning, which "is committed to improving learning across the country and across all walks of life," is certainly a gateway into provincial responsibilities as defined by the constitution. Every region, except Quebec, will see the establishment of a knowledge centre dedicated to a particular population: early childhood (0-6 years), adults, Aboriginal peoples, and the labour force.

In September 2005, the Canadian Prime Minister stated that it was necessary to see in his "pan-Canadian approach to early learning, a project of nation-building," which would be a landmark in the country's history; a little further on he added that the national interest had to come ahead of provincial prerogatives. Several federal initiatives in the field of higher education point in the same direction, in particular the Canadian Research Chairs program launched in 2001 and the controversial Millennium Scholarships.

The almost unanimous opposition in Quebec to these centralizing initiatives goes beyond anything seen in other federal countries. It is deeply rooted in the history of a nation whose language and culture are defended and promoted first and foremost through education.

Briefly, then, although Quebec has avoided certain tendencies of decentralization, the issue is not dead. The full extent of the autonomy granted to schools endangers equality of opportunity and encourages the development of a spirit of competition that must be fought. In other respects, the combined interventions of the federal government will continue to be a concern for Quebec society at the highest level. The route to the maintenance of a "distinct society" lies first and foremost through education and it is to be expected that this will have an impact on debates concerning the political future of Quebec.

Punishments and Rewards

At the end of the 19th century, at a time when every effort was being made to measure everything, Sir Francis Galton, one of the fathers of the IQ test, stated: "Wherever you can, count." In our wiser moments, we might say conversely, in the spirit of a slogan that Einstein pinned up in his Princeton office, "Not everything that counts can be counted, and not everything that can be counted counts." The first of these sayings is the one that seems to be the inspiration for educational policies all round the world, while the second is deeply embedded in teachers' practices. This explains the stiff resistance to the new control mechanisms being forced into education.

The State was looking to "shift the blame" for the failure of its own policies down to the local level, by making schools and teachers responsible for reaching objectives over which they have little control.

Once the new regulatory procedures are in place, they take on a two-faced appearance. On one side, they meet the requirements of a new public management model based on accountability, specifically by introducing rewards and sanctions for schools and teachers, linked to responsibility for outcomes and "turnaround" interventions. On the other side, it sets up an assessment system based on quantitative data for publication to meet school consumers' demands for comparable results, like league tables.

For the neo-liberals, who were more and more inclined to think of schools as being on the same footing as commercial businesses, the same practices could be applied and the quality of the educational product could be reduced to a set of figures. In accordance with results-based accountability, numeric indicators could become proxies for primary references and be used as a yardstick for measuring each school on the basis of pre-established targets.

The State was looking to "shift the blame" for the failure of its own policies down to the local level, by making schools and teachers responsible for reaching objectives over which they have little control. This new form of governance is introducing the principle of "remote control," which frequently gives the impression "it is blame for failure, rather than the freedom to succeed, that has been devolved" (Whitty et al., p.12).

Britain provides a first example of the imposition of this new model. In 1988, the introduction of a national system of evaluation for pupils aged seven, 11, 14 and 16 was accompanied by the publication of performance league tables. The whole thing was intended to provide more complete information to parents and to judge the quality of schools and teachers.

Every school must now table a development plan, approved by the school's authorities, which fixes three-year targets subject to annual review. Teams of private-sector inspectors co-ordinated by Ofsted provide follow-up. Schools may be designated as being *"subject to special measures,"* or *"failing,"* whereupon they can be put on the block so that private contractors can bid to take them over.

Similar situations have been introduced in several other jurisdictions. In New Zealand, the Education Review Office investigates school performance and produces a public report. In Ontario, the introduction of tests for the totality of pupils in Grades 3, 6, 9, 10, and 11, at an annual cost of more than $50 million, was accompanied by the establishment of the Education Quality and Accountability Office. The latter annually publishes a list of schools on the basis of their performance. In British Columbia, a school accreditation scheme has been set up that works from detailed school plans for improved achievement.

Many Children Left Behind

But it is above all the U.S. legislation *No Child Left Behind* (NCLB) that has most recently attracted the attention of all the experts. This program was adopted under President Bush's administration.[14] It is intended to improve pupil performance and to reduce the gaps that separate different social groups. In an official document, the text reads: "No student should be trapped in an underperforming school" and NCLB represents "a crucial step in addressing the achievement gaps that plague our nation."

While there was a warm welcome from disadvantaged groups who were being recognized for the first time and the amounts of funds allocated by the Federal Government were well-received in the poorest areas, there has been no shortage of critics. "Smokescreen", "rhetoric", "weapon of mass destruction [targeting] the public schools," "neo-liberal education program" are just some of the epithets used to condemn the new policy. The State of Wisconsin has even decided to challenge the jurisdictional power of Washington to impose obligations on States without any guarantees of adequate funding. The fierce opposition of the biggest education union, the National Education Association, caused that body to be labeled a "terrorist organization" by then-U.S. Secretary of Education, Rod Paige.

The plan places a set of conditions on states wanting to benefit from federal subsidies for low-performing students or students from economically disadvantaged backgrounds. Each state must make sure that the relevant schools are making progress annually towards the 2014 target of raising all its students' achievement above the current average on standardized tests. This annual rate of progress must be checked for each of the sub-groups identified by race, socio-economic status, gender, mother tongue and disability, so that no group will be left behind.

A school needs only to miss out on the targeted annual rate of progress for a single sub-group to be subject to penalties. In such a situation, the more diversified a school population is or the lower its base average score, the more the school is at risk of falling short. The sanctions are graduated over a period of five years, from providing the option for students to transfer to another school or charter school to a complete restructuring by the government or a private corporation, including the replacement of the principal and all of the teaching staff. The fact that pupils can choose to opt out of a school experiencing difficulties does nothing to help the situation, quite the reverse.

Schools identified as "needing improvement" must make available 20% of the federal government funds to help in transfers to other schools and to maintain private tutoring services for pupils who stay at the school. For their part, the States must publish a list of the schools, including a table of indicators for each of the targeted sub-groups.

For many, the 2014 target and the annual progress stipulated seem quite simply out of reach. In 2002-2003, it happened that 26,000 of 91,000 public schools in the U.S. had not made sufficient progress. If the trend of recent years continues, it would take 61 years to reach the target for Grade 4, 66 years for Grade 6 and 166 years for Grade 12. According to the projections for some states, more than 90% of its schools would not reach their targets. Some fear that the use of so much numerical data has the long-term goal of advancing the privatization of education, since accountability for outcomes is the concomitant of privatized school management.

For the time being, the states are still responsible for choosing tests, fixing the passing grades and other criteria that have an impact on the statistical significance of the data. In most cases, the tests are produced by major private publishing corporations.

This plan is inspired by the practices in several states, which were already publishing a report on their schools, with a list of those adjudged ineffective and a system of rewards and sanctions. This was particularly the case in Texas and Florida, two states so dear to President Bush's heart. But in both cases, researchers have not been slow to challenge the claims of improvements in pupil achievement. The

Texan miracle has even become the Texan scandal. The improvements reported on local tests were far from being confirmed by national test results, since dropouts and struggling pupils were being kept under wraps. As for Florida, as one analyst slyly remarked, this is a state that specializes in "creative counting," something not limited to votes in presidential elections.

Almost everywhere, research into results-based accountability schemes has yielded similar conclusions. Schools engage in highly questionable practices in order to boost their test scores. There is wholesale trickery. For example, more pupils are made to repeat a year rather than risk them dragging the following year's results down; the weaker ones are shunted off into adult education or General Education Diploma (GED) courses, since that group is left out of the count in the U.S.; there is cheating to avoid school closures, statistics are manipulated, and so on.

Thus, in Florida, the number of pupils enrolled in the GED rose by 50% between 2003 and 2004. In Dallas, more than 400 schools are suspected of cheating on the tests. In Britain, a scandal broke in the summer of 2000: the marks of almost 20,000 students were inflated in order to avoid criticisms of a drop in achievement. We could probably add the case of Charlemagne school in Quebec, convicted of cheating to maintain its place in the top echelons of *L'actualité*'s rankings.

There has been massive documentation of the statistical tricks used to keep schools off the black list as U.S. federal policies were implemented. As one author of a piece about this issue has recalled: "If you torture the data long enough, they will confess to anything." Some observers have no hesitation in speaking of rigging to describe the numerous devices used to make the scores seem better.

Moreover, several surveys, including one by the National Board on Testing and Public Policy at Boston College that canvassed more than 42,000 U.S. teachers in 47 states, have revealed alarming trends in teacher training programs and pedagogical practices. Teachers report that they are increasingly teaching to the tests, spending more time prepping the pupils for tests, dumbing down the material being taught and cutting back on subjects that are not tested[15]. Some try to avoid teaching grades where tests are scheduled as well as in schools thought to be underperforming. All of this is profoundly affecting the work that teachers do.

There is a clear and present threat to the solidarity and cooperation necessary for effective teaching. Where school plans are required, there are complaints about the amount of time they take on paperwork to the detriment of education. It should not come as a surprise to learn that, by and large, teachers are opposed to these policies. Their view is that this approach contributes nothing to the improvement of learning, that the consequences for their work are negative, and that they are imbuing education with an accounting model that has no place there.

At the same time, however, it is clear that teachers are not opposed to some form of accountability. While they do object to a narrow perspective based on test results, school rankings and competition, they tend to favour a perspective that takes into account the relationship between public schools and their communities, as part of an approach that helps support teaching and learning for all pupils.

Many critics have drawn attention to the downward slide to inequality that comes from results-based accountability. Its negative effects are felt most of all in schools serving poor neighbourhoods, depriving students who need it most of a quality education. In addition, it has been observed that the decision in some countries to contract out the development of standardized tests to major publishing houses gives the latter *de facto* control over curriculum content.

Testing Mania: A Pandemic

These testing regimes are heavily influenced by the desire for international comparisons, the *raison d'être* of the Program for International Student Assessment (PISA). This program has occasioned serious criticism alongside praise for the diversity of the information it analyses. With PISA, educational systems are no longer analyzed according their own stated objectives, but according to skills thought to be of immediate use in everyday life. Some see this as a good thing within the prevailing doctrine of utilitarianism and efforts to create an adaptable labour force. Others protest against cultural biases, some of the statistical concepts, and the use that is made of the results.

The creation of PISA came about following pressure from Britain and the U.S., who wanted an instrument to allow comparisons between educational systems. When UNESCO refused to get involved in such a process, they turned to the OECD. France and Germany were reticent at first, but came on board when the instigators threatened to withdraw from the OECD's Education Directorate. The model is based on the U.S.'s NAEP, but has retained only some of its features. For example, while NAEP assesses reading under three rubrics ('literary experience', 'information', and 'to perform a task'), PISA has limited itself to the third rubric.

Governments came to believe that PISA was genuinely able to shed light on the strengths and weaknesses of educational systems and could influence the capacity of countries to compete globally. This explains the use of these data to establish a ranking of countries that is virtually meaningless. That doesn't stop it from bringing pressure to bear for a homogenization of curricula, with a clear emphasis on learning judged useful in real life situations. And yet other far more relevant information about the organization of these systems is barely considered, especially when it comes into conflict with the dominant educational model. We shall return to this in the next chapter.

This mania for testing and assessment is not limited to students[16]; it is also being extended to teachers. Such features as merit pay, re-certification, and Colleges of Teachers are cropping up all over the place. It is claimed that teachers will work harder to get their hands on the promised rewards, that economic gain is the main motivator for their work, and that a new morality based on personal interest is preferable to one based on collective well-being.

Britain, Australia and more than 15 states in the U.S. have adopted a merit pay scheme introducing a new form of hierarchy into the profession and this has occasioned much debate along the way. The idea is not a new one. Merit pay was tried out several times in the course of the 20th century and was dropped each time following studies that demonstrated its ineffectiveness.

Generally speaking, teachers have no confidence in the capacity of those given the job of defining merit and do not agree with the criteria being used to define a "good teacher." The judges thoroughly misunderstand what inspires teachers to do good work. They are trying to steer teachers' work by instrumental and financial considerations. This has nothing to do with the intrinsic motivations that guide teachers' work: the desire to see pupils make progress and be successful. As for competition among colleagues, it is disastrous because it encourages individualism and threatens the collective enterprise that is at the heart of the profession.

Unions are also being excoriated. They are accused of hanging on to working conditions that are rigid and out of date, and thus standing in the way of desirable flexibility. The industrial collective bargaining model, that has inspired labour relations between teachers and the government, is being decried and transformed. This accompanies the many steps intended to weaken union membership. Organizational models are being proposed or imposed that give priority to individualism, such as Colleges of Teachers.

This has happened in Ontario and British Columbia. In the first case, the government's constraints on the College of Teachers, particularly the requirement of recertification after five years that involved a Professional Learning Program consisting of 14 courses, ran into massive opposition. The Liberal government elected in 2003 abandoned the move. In British Columbia, when the College refused to follow certain ministerial directives, the government dismissed the board of governors and appointed administrators who would carry out its orders. In the face of this show of strength, the members of the College refused to pay their fees, thereby putting the whole body at risk, until the government decided to put an end to its trusteeship.

In Quebec, an Effective Resistance

In Quebec, the idea of setting up a College of Teachers, as proposed by the Conseil pédagogique interdisciplinaire du Québec (CPIQ) with the support of a majority of Education Science academics, came to nothing. The Office of the professions of Quebec whose mandate is to advise the government on matters concerning frameworks for the professions, took the view that the creation of such a body was unnecessary and acknowledged the professional role of teachers unions. But the Liberal government had included it in their election platform, and it took more than 90% of the members of Fédération des syndicats de l'enseignement (FSE-CSQ) to express their opposition clearly in a referendum before the project was finally dropped. It remains to be seen what other tricks the government may have up its sleeve to gain control of the teaching profession.

This struggle is something of a repeat of what happened with results-based accountability. Following the Quebec Youth Summit in 2000, the Minister of Education launched a Success Plans scheme for schools and cégeps, "the school equivalent of a business plan," to use his term, and announced the negotiation of performance contracts with the universities. The minister asked each school to set three-year goals for graduation rates, with strict annual targets and the means for measuring outcomes. He strongly recommended that a success plan should include an annual improvement of about 2% in graduation rates and "grade promotion." The same direction was suggested for cégeps.

When the list of 470 schools "under investigation" was published and the ministry sent plans back to school boards that it considered inconsistent with ministry requirements, the fat was in the fire. The education sector howled its opposition to this behaviour. While there was general agreement to analyze the situation and to identify appropriate steps for improving achievement, there was outright refusal to set graduation targets and compare schools. There was condemnation of the sorcery implied by thinking that setting numerical goals would improve learning, as if by magic.

The minister's retort was to table bills[17] imposing a cascading chain of targets from the provincial level down to local schools. These bills visibly reinstated the logic of centralization. They aimed to imbue the entire education system with the principles of accountability from the Public Administration Act of 2000, broadly inspired by the principles of "new public management"[18].

Faced with the fierce opposition of the stakeholders, the government had to beat a retreat, at least where the schools were concerned. The new amended regulations make the development of a school plan mandatory, along with the circulation and evaluation of its execution; but success is now understood as referring to the mission of the school as a whole. The choice of ways to do this must be respectful of the prerogatives of teachers and the school council, but should also take into account the philosophy and goals of the school plan. Each school has the responsibility to define its own goals. The School Board is under an obligation to make its own strategic plan consistent with that of the Ministry of Education.

As for cégeps, the government refused to amend its original bill. Colleges now have to set annual targets and make known the outcomes of the agreed graduation rates. In universities, after the antagonism occasioned by performance contracts, these became "agreements for optimal development" to be negotiated with each university. Fears remain nonetheless for the precarious future of university autonomy and over the sidelining of quality criteria in favour of criteria based on efficiency and performance.

In fact, wherever such contracts have been set up, there is an observable emphasis on research aiming to increase university revenues, a shift to more "productive" activities, a ranking of disciplines and tasks, and, in some cases, a consideration of the amount of public research funding achieved.

Results-based accountability will continue to be a hot topic. In the face of the totality of international data being collected, there have been protests against the fundamentally "amoral character" of these policies with their negative effects on curriculum and teaching. It is not acceptable to go to any lengths to put the bravest face on the scores and statistics. There are also doubts about the technocratic process used to produce numbers that are supposed to have something to do with the quality of education, when they do nothing of the sort.

Quebec has managed to avoid some of the pitfalls in the new policies to control pupil achievement and teachers' work thanks to the resistance put up by educational organizations. But there is no reason to think that the debate is over, whether it is about results-based accountability or central control mechanisms.[19]

ALL-TERRAIN BUSINESSES

Competition among schools, free choice for school consumers, and a management style that mimics big business have all made a profound difference on what it means to educate. But that's not all. Buoyed by their attacks on public education institutions, and profiting from the budget shortages to which the latter have been subjected, and intoxicated by the belief and hype wanting them to be the very best, businesses are forcing down the doors of teaching institutions and trying to convert education to commerce.

Stigmatized and weakened, schools are more vulnerable now. Just about everywhere, the social wall that protected the school and its pupils from external interference is now breached on all sides. The freedom of the university community that was the foundation of higher education is caving in. The private sector is becoming generous, to be sure, but in order to secure greater control.

There is no shortage of prophets predicting a new multi-billion dollar industry: "The education industry." Some are already salivating at the promised profits, even if the flood is slow to materialize. The masters of globalization are getting into the act and demanding that education too be subject to the rules of international trade. And once educational services are reduced to the status of merchandise, they can become the object of a flourishing trade. Happily, the education world is refusing to be enticed, but the tug of war is on.

This will be our topic in the second half of this chapter.

He Who Pays the Piper...

Philanthropy is the love of humankind. A philanthropist is someone who is dedicated to improving the lot of fellow humans, who acts altruistically, and who seeks no gain, as numerous dictionary definitions remind us. Nowadays, in education, there are few philanthropists. Gifts are thinner on the ground than investments. The so-called generous donors are often the same ones who are pressuring governments to reduce education budgets, and who avoid any call on their profits as much as possible. And they expect gratitude in the form of support for their ideology and their brand names.

Almost everywhere, school space is under commercial pressure. Neither basic education, nor higher learning, nor research are immune to it, despite furious widespread resistance. Even the school itself has become vulnerable. It needs cash. Sponsorships and sole supplier contracts, consumer inducements, teaching kits, advertising, fund-raising, are all ways that are used to feed school coffers. Some tactics utterly undermine the civic function and values embodied in the public school.

For some businesses, schools are looked upon simply as marketplaces, advertising locations teeming with consumers and endless potential, an add-on to the exponential development of marketing directed at young people, as can be seen all over the West. There is no need for sophisticated measures of audience ratings: all children are required by law to attend school. And some large companies are engaged in a war to see their brand winning the game.

The Consuming School

In North America especially, sole supplier contracts with the giant soft drink corporations have long been the fuel for a "cola war." Sales tactics are sometimes quite scandalous. In 1998, a major U.S. daily paper published a memorandum from the director of a school board to the school principals that really put the cat among the pigeons. It established sales targets for a particular beverage product and suggested ways to get youngsters to consume it, most notably by increasing the number of vending machines and making them more readily accessible.

Competition among schools, free choice for school consumers, and a management style that mimics big business have all made a profound difference on what it means to educate.

In Canada, a survey conducted in 2004 by the Canadian Centre for Policy Alternatives (CCPA), the Canadian Teachers Federation (CTF) and Fédération des syndicats de l'enseignement (FSE) revealed that more than 19% of the elementary schools and 56% of the secondary schools had sole supplier contracts with either one of the two major players. In Quebec, this was true for about 5% of the schools. Promotional tactics don't vary much. In 2003, a daily paper in Vancouver revealed that Pepsi was offering bonuses to schools that could get their pupils to purchase more of its products. It was the same story in Ontario, where the persistence of one secondary school student obliged a school board to make public its own sole supplier contract with the multinational company, one that also included consumer incentives.

At the same time, however, in recent years concerns about children's health have dealt a major blow to such agreements. In February 2004, the American Academy of Pediatrics declared that schools were not an appropriate site for the sale of soft drinks. Obesity, type 2 diabetes, calcium deficiency and later weakening of the bones, are all concerns that have forced public authorities to take action. Many states have banned or restricted sales of soft drinks and junk food in schools and several Canadian provinces are getting ready to do the same thing[20].

Not that it makes a difference. The ogre just turns into Tom Thumb. In the winter of 2004, Refreshments Canada, an umbrella organization for the soft drink industry, announced its intention to withdraw its products from vending machines in elementary schools. This measure, an attempt to save face for a badly scarred industry, did not affect secondary schools, however, nor any of the other products high in sugar and calories with which they are tempting the students.

Pepsi has set up a program called Balance First, which encourages pupils to eat 100 calories fewer per day and to walk more to use up calories. There is nothing yet that acknowledges the harmful nature of the multinational's products. Keep drinking Pepsi and walk more, that's the message.

Coke did not want to be left behind, and so it is sponsoring sports activities after school. McDonald's is doing the same thing by offering a physical fitness program that comes with money for schools to purchase sports equipment. Its mascot has been disguised as a "health ambassador," and visits schools to promote physical fitness and a balanced diet. One wag has gone to the trouble of calculating that it would take a ten-year-old more than fifteen hours to walk off the calorie intake from one of that famous chain's servings of hamburger, fries and coke.

Corporations are very ingenious in their choice of tactics to get schools to promote their products. Reward and fidelity programs designed for adults are copied. One of the most popular examples is Campbell's Labels for Education program, first launched in the U.S. in 1973, and then imported into Canada in 1998. General Mills used the same approach with its "Box Tops for Education." In both cases, families and neighbours are encouraged to purchase the product in question to get a corporate donation to their school. According to the survey mentioned above, more than one third of the schools in Canada, mainly elementary schools, have joined in such programs[21].

As for teaching kits, they vary considerably and are worming their way into the curriculum in many countries. An international survey of commercial production for schools showed that the greatest polluters in the steelmaking, chemicals, paper and petroleum industries were the main producers of teaching materials about the environment. Credit card companies offer tools to help develop bud-

geting skills, overlooking the fact that their own campaigns directed at young adults are one of the major reasons for their debt problems. In France, Vivendi, the giant multinational specializing in the
privatized supply of drinking water, puts out a teaching kit suggest-
ing experiments on the theme of water for pupils in municipalities
served by the company.

There are numerous contradictions between the flaunted virtues
in what they are providing to schools and the commercial practices
of such companies. This is not about providing fair and full information to the pupils. This is about boosting the product, defending their
practices and promoting their values.

What is more, commercial advertising is all over the façades of
buildings, in the corridors and the cafeterias. School buses, diaries
and textbooks are not immune to their invasiveness. A school in Auck-
land, New Zealand, even sold the right to name each of its classrooms
for the modest sum of $3,000 per year, with the sponsors thereby
gaining exclusive rights to advertising in the school[22]. In New Jer-
sey, these rights were auctioned off on eBay. More astutely, a school
board in British Columbia envisaged selling advertising space on the
rooftops of its schools; the advertisements would not upset the sensi-
tivities of the local population, since they would only be visible from
aircraft flying over the nearby airport.

In France, too, there have been protests against allowing the outside walls of school buildings to be used for billboards. Not so long
ago, a teacher complained (*Le Monde de l'éducation*, October 2005)
that the textbook adopted by the school principal for the teaching of
English included two whole chapters about McDonald's and that other brand names were heavily represented in the exercises.

According to the CCPA-CTF-FSE study mentioned above, commercial advertising is widespread in Canadian schools. 54% of the secondary schools reported the presence of advertisements, either in the
buildings or on the grounds of the school, and 22% mentioned that
advertising space had been sold inside the school; the proportions in
elementary schools were 28% and 5% respectively. Both local businesses and major corporations have been involved[23].

But the most scandalous example of the confusion between education and commercial promotion is the U.S. program known as Channel One. Under this, secondary schools receive a daily TV news show
lasting twelve minutes and including two minutes of commercials.
The school has to sign a contract for three to five years guaranteeing
that the students will watch the show. In exchange, the school gets
a satellite dish as well as two VCRs and two TV monitors per class.

As Michael Apple has pointed out, "Students, in essence, are sold as a captive audience to corporations" (2001, p.42).

The show reaches about eight million students. Corporations selling junk food, sportswear, chewing gum and youth products pay as much as $200,000 each to promote their wares. Schools with a high concentration of poor students are twice as likely to use Channel One as more affluent schools. Students exposed to this advertising bombardment are far more supportive of materialist values; far more of them believe that money is the most important thing in life and that owning a fine car is more important than a good education. They are not equipped to distinguish between the news and the commercials and do not regard the latter as a sales pitch.

A Canadian clone of Channel One, the Youth News Network (YNN), has fortunately been less successful. According to the promotional material circulated in the early nineties, the goal was to "create interesting and long-term links between the worlds of education and business." They insisted that "the constant call on taxpayers to increase the resources of the school system is an illusory approach" and that private business sponsorships were therefore becoming a "practical alternative."

Quebec's Minister of Education at the time had found the idea "very interesting." But he had to reconsider his opinion following the outcry that greeted it. YNN had nevertheless managed to worm its way into some Canadian schools. The invasion caused some epic struggles that persuaded several Ministers of Education, such as those in British Columbia, Saskatchewan and the Maritimes to ban YNN in their schools.

The New Philanthropists

Whether or not public schools engage in various business transactions to fill their coffers, they are all on the lookout for private funding. In the U.S., a pronounced change can be observed in the tradition of "educational philanthropy," dominated until quite recently by the Ford, Rockefeller and Carnegie Foundations. In 2002, the two top donors were the Gates Foundation (Microsoft) with a capital of $20 billion and the Walton Foundation (Wal-Mart). They have been stout supporters of school choice, merit pay and results-based accountability. They have unquestionably had an influence on the current round of neo-liberal reforms.

On a more modest scale, the selling of a variety of goods has long served as a way to finance extracurricular activities. In the U.S., what we are seeing now is the increasing use of such funds to defray the cost of needs previously covered by public funding. And once again it is the schools in rich neighbourhoods that are taking on the lion's share.

In Canada, still according to the study mentioned previously, fundraising campaigns have become normal. In line with our southern neighbours, the funds raised are no longer limited to extracurricular activities, but are going also to "programs of study," the purchase of library books and school supplies. On average, schools now raise more than $15,000 a year each. The differences in amounts raised vary enormously between neighbourhoods; so the amounts go from a few hundred dollars to several tens of thousands. The Toronto group People for Education has established that Ontario secondary schools with the highest parental incomes (the top 10%) grab the most, leaving only crumbs for the schools in poorer areas. The story is much the same for elementary schools.

Britain has branched out by opting to involve businesses directly in the financing of schools. A school that wants to get special school status, has to find a sponsor willing to stump up the modest sum of fifty thousand pounds. Big companies anxious to demonstrate their "corporate citizenship" are responding to the challenge. But they are also taking advantage of the opportunity to influence curriculum content, to develop "business and enterprise" programs of study, and even to obtain contracts in the case of software and IT companies.

Still in Britain, the creation of "academies," public schools in poor neighbourhoods that bypass local education authority control, is intended to encourage the involvement of the private sector. In this case, sponsors must provide 20% of the cost of building the new school, which is then owned by the academy. The sponsoring firm is empowered to appoint the majority of governors to the board and thus control the school, including its programs and services. Among the motivating factors underlying such "generosity" is the desire to promote business values, to improve the company's image, to develop a better labour force and to improve its relations with government.

Quebec's Safeguards
Quebec's schools have eluded this business thrust to some extent. In fact, Quebec, along with Sweden, is one of the few jurisdictions to ban all commercial advertising in schools. All the same, the Public Education Act (article 94) has, since 1997, allowed schools to receive gifts and engage in fundraising, as long as the students and their parents are not subjected to any commercial soliciting and are not urged to buy specific products or services. These provisions are in direct line with the Consumer Protection Act, adopted at the end of the 1970s, outlawing any advertising to children under the age of 13[24].

It is up to the school council to decide whether the gifts it receives are commercial or not, but within defining parameters set by the Office de la Protection du Consommateur. Even so, it has needed a constant battle to make sure the law is properly enforced. This legislative framework seems to have been relatively well respected, judging from the results of the CCPA-CTF-FSE survey. In fact, only 1% of Quebec's francophone schools admitted to participating in contests encouraging the purchase of products.

The situation is not so brilliant where advertising is concerned. It was occurring in 21% of the schools (but not on school buses, following almost unanimous opposition from education circles several years ago). The situation surely warrants a more detailed analysis, in order to check out whether these practices are in compliance with the legislation. And this has not prevented Young Liberals from recommending that schools be opened up for advertising and businesses in order to get their share of such generosity.

For example, the owner of a chain of clothing stores some years back proposed to a school in a disadvantaged area a reward system intended to stimulate improvement in academic achievement and student effort. A points award scheme would have allowed the top students to choose a reward among the items in the store's sales catalogue. The school refused and the businessman took offence. He arrogantly believed that his fortune gave him the authority to impose his views on a school in a poor neighbourhood.

Pepsi is subtly trying to get its foot in the school door with a program of "physical health and nutrition education" called "L'équilibre avant tout," adapted from its U.S. "Balance First" program. To get around the law, the program is being distributed by the Canadian Association for Health, Physical Education, Recreation and Dance. Teachers are invited to visit a website to learn more about the concept of energy balance … and about this multinational's products. That physical and heath education specialists should be taken in and believe that such a product can help in health education, as reported in *Le Devoir,* is quite flabbergasting.

The magazine *L'actualité* is also trying to give its image a boost with students. For every ten students who subscribe to a minimum of five issues, the teacher gets a teaching kit. The teacher is even invited to send in student's addresses, if it is felt preferable to have them receive the magazine at home, even though this is confidential information protected by the Access to Information Act.

In the Fall of 2005, the Lucie and André Chagnon Foundation declared that it was ready to invest $400 million over 10 years to combat obesity, overweight, and sedentary lifestyles among the young people of Quebec. This declaration came in the wake of a report published by the working group that came out of the *Forum des générations* of October 2005, of which M. Chagnon, the former cable TV magnate, was a member. This was good news and showed laudable intentions. But there was a snag: the Foundation's gift was conditional on a government match to the same amount. A private body was giving itself the right to dictate social policy to the government, and the Charest government refused to go along with it for that reason.

As for fundraising, the annual Quebec average is around $14,200 per school. As in the rest of Canada, funds raised are used for all kinds of activities, including those that are the essential work of the school. But nothing is known of the resultant inequalities. This needs more work.

According to a survey of parents and teachers on francophone school councils, more than 80% believe that commercial advertising has no place in school. At the same time, parents look favourably on the fact that schools may solicit private funding (62% as opposed to 51% of the teachers), while about 60% of each group want public education to be financed entirely by public funds.

Universities on a War Footing

Institutions of higher learning are also on the lookout for cash. Sole supplier contracts are widespread. At the Université de Montréal, the persistence of a group of students using the Access to Information Act has forced signatories to sole supplier contracts to make the terms public. It was discovered that one such contract anticipated the consumption of 12 million litres of soft drinks over a period of ten years, amounting to an average of 17 litres per person per session. The institution was undertaking to take "every reasonable means" to ensure that targets were met and annual meetings were scheduled to make adjustments to the promotional strategies.

Overall, there is a tightening of the relations between universities and business. To be sure, such relations are nothing new. Industrial development has relied heavily on the contribution made by university research. But there used to be clear boundaries between the responsibilities of universities and those of business.

There is more and more talk of "academic capitalism." Partnerships with business and university entrepreneurship are the new slogans of the OECD and the World Bank. Many large universities have established "commercial wings" aiming to use their "intellectual capital" to generate funds. The "scholars" of yesteryear are becoming "entrepreneurs." Publicly funded research is leading to patents for the purposes of commercialization taken out by researchers who are creating their own businesses.

Pierre Hébert criticizes The New Warrior Universities, referring to the "belligerent attitude" adopted by universities in recent years as they "take on globalization" and bellow forth the "war songs" of their new masters. This new vision is not only among us, it is apparently "part of us" now.

This has all led to a ranking of disciplines and research work; disciplines useful to the market, more readily open to commercialization, are hot while the humanities and social sciences are devalued and basic research is being left for dead.

The current spate of commercialized research is threatening the traditional autonomy of universities. Businesses are providing money or equipment in exchange for priority access to research results and patents; they are negotiating the right to intervene in the conclusions of research work, the publication of findings, the content of degree programs as well as participating in the research committees of departments, even to the extent of designating the key people. This is all undermining the innovative capacity of universities, in both the medium and long terms.

Many large universities have established "commercial wings" aiming to use their "intellectual capital" to generate funds.

By way of example in 2003, Stanford University signed a contract worth $225 million to study climate change over a period of ten years, thereby allowing Exxon and other corporations a say in which projects would be financed. Enron provided fat grants to research centres in Harvard to promote the deregulation of energy in California.

In France, corporate Chairs are booming; corporations such as Axa (insurance), Procter & Gamble, Unilever and many others are intervening directly in teaching and research at the *grandes écoles*. In Canada, Nortel has donated $8 million to create the Nortel Institute for Telecommunications. The agreement signed with the University of Toronto assigns to Nortel the intellectual property of all products arising from research and the occupants of the Chair were selected in consultation with the corporation.

Since the early 1980s, U.S. universities have been authorized to patent their discoveries and to turn a profit from them. The kind of knowledge that was once a common good is now out of the reach of other researchers and the public behind the high barrier of property rights. Even living organisms are not exempt. There has been no shortage of scandals, as we are reminded by journalist Jenny Washburn's brisk account in *University Inc. The Corporate Corruption of American Higher Education.*

Thus, the blocking of access to generic drugs against HIV, discussed in the first chapter, has directly implicated no less an authority than Yale University. Yale had effectively given its exclusive patent rights for stavudine to Bristol-Myers Squidd, which then refused to share the benefits. This is not the standard practice, particularly since the research that went into perfecting this drug had essentially been publicly funded.

At the University of Utah, the discovery of an important gene responsible for breast cancer was not shared with other researchers, even though government funding had contributed almost $5 million towards the initial research. The gene was patented and the exclusive rights to its commercial use sold to Myriad Genetics, a company founded by a professor in the university.

The contract for $25 million between the University of California at Berkeley and Novartis gave the latter priority rights to patents, including for projects that it was not even funding, and two seats on the research committee. Opposition from researchers and students led the Senate of California to launch an inquiry and the famous journal *Nature* to accuse the university of selling its soul to promote GMOs. One of the fiercest critics of the contract, who had published a paper describing the genetic contamination of native corn in Mexico by GMOs, was denied tenure.

In Canada, the Olivieri affair also got a lot of ink. Doctor Nancy Olivieri was working in a research program linking the Hospital for Sick Children, affiliated with the University of Toronto, and the pharmaceutical company Apotex. In the course of her research, she discovered that the drug she was studying as a treatment for a genetic blood disease affecting millions of people was harmful to some patients. She decided to warn her patients and her colleagues, but the company denied her the requisite permission and closed the study down. She disregarded the company and told the people of her findings, with the support of the University's Ethics Committee.

Doctor Olivieri went further and published a paper in a highly respected scientific journal. She was threatened with prosecution by Apotex and was fired from her research post by the university[25]. The *Canadian Medical Association Journal* put forward a very plausible explanation for this cavalier attitude on the part of the university. The latter was soliciting a gift of several million dollars from Apotex and did not want to put this precious godsend at risk. This story pitting ethics against profits had a happy ending. After various grievances and lawsuits, Doctor Olivieri finally won her case.

This saga was a partial inspiration for John Le Carré's novel *The Constant Gardener*, which vehemently condemned the manoeuvrings of major pharmaceutical corporations. Saskatchewan replaced Ontario and tuberculosis replaced the blood disease in question; Africa became the place for these lethal experiments. Like Olivieri, one of Le Carré's characters is fired from Dawes University and the Hospital for Sick Children in Saskatchewan, after informing patients of the dangerous side effects of the drug being tested. Le Carré points the finger at the "profit god" and a fat donation being promised to the university by the corporation.

These close associations have given rise to mushrooming conflicts of interest. In February 2000, the highly respected *New England Journal of Medicine* publicly apologized and acknowledged that almost half of the articles on drugs it had published since 1997 were written by authors with financial links to the manufacturers of those drugs. In 2001, the editors of 12 scientific medical journals announced that they would refuse to publish any paper on new drugs unless the authors would guarantee that they had had access to all the research data and that they alone were responsible for the conclusions of their study. It is estimated that barely 1% of all researchers mention their relationship with the companies funding their work.

Beside the spirit of the age that allows businesses to impose their views on universities like never before, cuts in public funding also help to explain such practices. In many countries, free or low-cost access to university education was based on the fact that it constituted a common good. From now on, insistence is placed on the individual benefits that higher education brings in the labour market to justify raising tuition fees.

Canada's research policies, like those of many provinces, encourage partnerships between businesses and universities. An example is the Canada Foundation for Innovation, created in 1997, which requires that projects lead to direct financial gain for a private partner who must provide half of the required funding[26]. The Foundation is controlled by the private sector. Twenty-three of the 30 Board members come from industry. The same model exists in Ontario with the Ontario Research and Development Challenge Fund, and the Access to Opportunities Program that aimed to increase enrolments in the fields of engineering and computing.

This shift towards the private sector is also reflected in the symbolic gesture of naming university sites. The names of major corporations and industrial magnates are cropping up over and over again, another sign of the gradual takeover of higher education. Sometimes they become a cause for embarrassment: the Center for the Study of

Markets in Transition at Rice University was named after Ken Lay, former CEO of Enron, since convicted of fraud. This phenomenon is on the rise in the U.S. and in Canada is now reaching Quebec.

Throughout Canada, departments, chairs, research laboratories and faculties are being increasingly identified with their generous donors. Ericson, Bell, John Deere, 3M, Maclean Hunter, Nortel and Sony are some of the names associated with Canadian universities, in anticipation of a return on their investment, particularly through privileged access to research work and the best graduates.

In Quebec, the names of historical and cultural figures are gradually losing ground to the great names of industry. If the School of Music at the Université de Montréal is forever associated with the memory of the composers Vincent d'Indy and Claude Champagne, the Faculty of Music at McGill will now be associated with the mining magnate Seymour Schulich. Chairs and buildings carry the names of Jean Coutu (pharmacy), Abitibi-Price (forestry), Rogers and Bombardier (entrepreneurship), Industrielle Alliance (leukemia research), etc. The actual classrooms of Business Schools are named after giant corporations, such as IBM.

Finally, there are the many agreements affecting the supply of equipment in exchange for specific financial or promotional advantages. For example, the Bois-de-Boulogne cégep in Montreal has signed a contract with the network computing company CISCO to develop a training program and commercialize its products. The company provides the hardware and software for use in the training program in exchange for which the college is expected to promote its products.

In the coming years, there is no doubt that the pressure for reductions in the public funding of education will continue. They will encourage a wider search for private funding and a narrower subservience to the dictates of corporations. Basic education in Quebec enjoys certain enviable protections that are keeping commercial advertising at bay. The rights to relatively free education, including higher education, can also rely on broad public support. But the universities are more vulnerable to pressures from business, particularly in research. There are then assets to be defended and protections to be secured.

The Education Industry

The concept may be new but it is flourishing. The advance figures are mind-blowing. There are apparently hundreds of billions of dollars up for grabs. We are being told endlessly that the world of education is estimated to be worth upwards of $2 trillion. The international institutions of finance, the OECD and several conservative governments are promoting this "industry of the future."

There are some who think that this is the driving force behind the educational reforms. According to a U.S. business devoted to this new industry, "educational entrepreneurs will be the real change agents in the twenty-first century." In more and more conferences and forums, the effort is being made to persuade investors of the attractions of doing business in this new market. The financial press has only good things to say about this new breed of educators.

Gone are the days when just a few related services were consigned to the private sector, such as school busing, as was the case in Quebec. Nor are debates limited to the contracting out of cleaning or catering, despite the importance of issues concerning service quality and working conditions. This new round of "industrialization" is now reaching into all aspects of school life. Businesses are specializing in the construction and leasing of school buildings, the total management of schools, test sales, marking and tutoring. Universities, even school boards, are opening "branches" overseas. Private universities are springing up all over the place and are increasingly going online. Foreign students have now become the new revenue stream.

This development of the education market is creating new challenges for educational institutions. While the internationalization of higher education has long been synonymous with cooperation and exchanges as a matter of pride, commercialization is on another plane altogether and raises ethical questions of great significance. No country is being spared. The strategy of the most active countries consists of beginning in the national market and then trying it out overseas.

New Business Opportunities

Here too, the Anglo-Saxon countries are the leaders. In the U.S., with the support of Republican administrations, Educational Management Organizations (EMOs), profit-making businesses that are taking over the total management of schools, have really taken off. In 2003, there were about 60 profit-making companies managing public schools in 25 states. In terms of schools and students, the numbers are small, under 0.5% of the total, but the phenomenon is disturbing especially when viewed in the long term.

It works like this. The company signs three- to five-year contracts with public institutions, which then give it total management of one or several schools. It receives a sum equivalent to the amount spent by the board for the students in the school in question. In exchange it agrees to be bound by results-based accountability, usually as defined by standardized test scores.

To be sure, we can get some joy from the misfortunes of some of these vultures. As of now, the profits are not showing up. Even *Fortune* magazine is dampening its past ardour and in 2002 was expressing doubts about the viability of EMOs. The first of these to come into existence, Education Alternatives Inc. (renamed TesseracT in 2000), has gone bankrupt. Only two companies posted profits in 2004.

Even so, the number of companies quadrupled between 1998-1999 and 2004-2005. According to estimates of Merrill Lynch, 10% of public funds will be channeled into EMOs in the next ten years, which amounts to a market of $30 billion. Some companies are making steady progress but the history of Edison Inc., which runs roughly half of all public schools under private management, suggests that it is too soon to celebrate a victory.

The founder of Edison was not lacking in ambition. His company, as Chris Whittle (also the founder of Channel One, discussed earlier in this chapter) constantly reminds everyone, was named after the inventor of the electric light bulb who, at the end of the 19th century, had not tried to make a better candle, but had invented a new way to make light. Mr. Whittle promised to do the same thing with education, thanks to a new style of education based on "Success For All," the intensive use of new technologies and more time spent in school. The support of the business press and well-known conservative luminaries in the world of education, including the president of Yale University who was hired as Director, gave the company enormous credibility from the get-go.

When it started up in 1991, Edison's business plan aimed to create a network of private schools to take full advantage of the voucher slush bucket promised by President Bush Sr. But Bill Clinton's victory in 1994 forced the company to re-invent itself by turning to public school management. In 1999, it went public on the stock exchange where its shares traded at $18. After some fluctuation, shares shot up to $38 boosted by the enthusiasm of analysts who believed in the promise of the "education industry" and by the sustained promotional efforts of Edison. But then the company's books came under scrutiny of the Security Exchange Commission, the U.S. exchange police. It was discovered that Edison had never made a profit, that it had lost $354 million over twelve years, and that its revenue figures had been inflated. A minor financial scandal played itself out in a number of lawsuits and a drop in share value to 14 cents by the end of 2002.

Whittle then bought back all the shares and took his company private again. And he found a buyer. The story of this sale has all the elements of a Hollywood script. Edison's collapse had left the supporters of privatization and the Republicans red-faced. A New York investment firm, Liberty Partners, part-managers of Florida's public service employees' pension fund, acquired the company in July 2003 for $182 million. Now half of this pension fund consisted of contributions from teachers who were ferociously opposed to Edison.

On the day following the sale, the supervisors of the fund, the Florida State Board of Administration whose members included Governor Jeb Bush, the President's brother, and two of his colleagues, advised Liberty Partners that auditors' reports were showing significant management problems on its side which forced the authorities to limit the maximum sum that the firm was able to invest. If this news had come a day earlier, the sale of Edison would not have gone ahead. There were protests against what had all the appearances of a high-level stratagem to use the teachers' pension fund against the latter's professional and financial interest in order to save the prodigal son of privatization.

Part of the woes of Edison came from its sorry performance in its schools. Schools managed by the company were getting results well below those of comparable public schools. There were criticisms of its treatment of struggling pupils and of its cost-cutting measures, in particular the closing of school libraries. In 2002, Edison lost at least six of its contracts as they expired. In Dallas, the contracts for seven schools were even cancelled before they had come to term; the results were awful and they were costing the school board 10% more.

This did not stop the company from winning its biggest contract in that same year from the Pennsylvania Ministry of Education. Edison had earlier been awarded, without tender, a three million dollar contract to study the needs of the Philadelphia Board of Education. Not surprisingly, it recommended placing the school board in trusteeship and privatizing the management of its schools. A well-known Republican governor, who later went on to lead up national security, Tom Ridge, did everything in his power to make sure this happened.

Edison secured the management of 20 schools, a number below its expectations. The ink had hardly dried on the contract when the company demanded an additional sum of $1,500 per student to recruit and train teachers. That did not stop them from laying off almost 200 staff. Whittle accused his adversaries of having "described the battle as a titanic ideological clash to prevent the intrusion of profit-making into the classroom rather than as a high-accountability partnership with research-tested private-sector entities focused on generating 'achievement by design'"(2005, p.35). To pour oil on troubled waters, he added that Edison was not opposed to public education.

Profit-making educational corporations have recently turned to on-line education. There are now at least four giant corporations running 17 on-line schools in 11 states. The biggest is K12 of the very Republican, very conservative Bill Bennett. Another of them, Sylvan Learning Systems, is also present in Canada. On top of the revenues from selling on-line courses for home schooling, these corporations have benefited from the passage of legislation supportive of online education to rake in funding equivalent to the amount for public schools. Unions do not look kindly upon this development and challenge the right of these corporations to profit from public funds for courses lacking adequate supervision by certified teachers, as the law normally requires.

Educational businesses are also enmeshed in the new business openings in the testing and tutoring industries through measures included in the No Child Left Behind legislation. Standardized testing in the U.S. constitutes an annual market of roughly $2 billion. The principal beneficiary is McGraw-Hill. By a happy coincidence, besides producing the tests, McGraw-Hill also produces curriculum materials preparing for them. This led one respected education critic to say that President Bush's standardized testing scheme was doing for his publishing friends[27] what the war in Iraq was doing for other friends engaged to carry out reconstruction, Halliburton in particular.

Tutoring businesses also have the wind at their back, thanks to the requirement that schools failing to meet their annual targets had to offer this service to their students. By law, these services must be offered by the private sector, as the Board of Education in Chicago found to its cost. In 2004, it spent $53 million to provide tutoring to 80,000 pupils, in partnership with private firms for half of them. The cost came to $1,300 per student on the private side compared to $400 when the services were offered by the board's own staff.

The Federal government called the recalcitrant board to account: since the public schools concerned were failing, they were no longer qualified to offer compensatory education. The Feds then ordered the school board to enroll all eligible pupils in private programs, despite all the additional costs entailed and the many problems that had been documented.

Even though nothing shows that private tutoring helps to improve student achievement, the growth of this industry is clearly part of the policy of the U.S. Federal Government. The American Institute for Social Justice estimates that this market represents somewhere between $20 billion and $30 billion a year for profit-making private businesses. It also points out that huge sums are being spent without any accountability.

Since the U.S. education industry sees Canada as an interesting market, it has already crossed the border here. A U.S. company is currently administering certification tests for Ontario teachers. Tutoring businesses, totally private for the time being, are opening more and more centres and the number of clients is growing rapidly: parents have to spend about $150 a month for these services. In Quebec, Oxford Learning was the first to open a branch in 2000, at Dollard-des-Ormeaux.

In Britain, efforts to develop the "industry education" have not yet achieved the success expected. The role of Local Education Authorities (LEAs) has nevertheless changed; they must now work to open a market for the full range of services and seek out partnerships with the private sector. Schools, for their part, are free to purchases their services wherever they like. New specialized providers are now coming in with a vast array of services. Major private conglomerates have set up branches in the education sector. One example is a contract for about £300 million that has been awarded to a private company to train teachers. A goodly number of companies is working to develop performance evaluation measures for teachers and principals. The Ofsted teams are actually teams of private inspectors. Many schools contract out tutoring and counseling services; auditing, building maintenance, supply teaching, professional psychological and guidance services are increasingly being handed over to the private sector.

But the latter is still not feeling much attraction for the total management of schools, even if the law now requires LEAs to put the management of future schools or of schools classified as failing out to tender. One of the biggest British companies in this area, WS Atkins, has tried its luck by winning a contract worth £100 million over five years to improve a number of struggling schools. After two years, according to an article in *The Guardian* of April 30, 2003, the company wanted to back out, since its profit margins were so poor. Even if the floodgates haven't opened, the management of a handful of LEAs and several schools is already in the hands of private companies.

Ever since 2002, British schools may hold intellectual property rights, reap profits from the sale of their programs of study and act as profitable consultants for other institutions. This is a massive change to the public character of schools, to their place within society and to the relations that they had previously maintained amongst themselves, based on collaboration and exchange.

British Columbia has done the same thing by authorizing school boards to set up profitable companies. These companies expect to make money by selling distance education domestically and elsewhere, by providing programs to international students in private schools, and by selling their programs of study. The Ministry of Education has moreover identified a score or so of private schools that could be managed by the province's school boards or through public-private partnerships in Japan, Taiwan, and China[28]. It is, to say the least, ironic that public institutions are selling private education to the elites of other countries in order to finance their own operation.

B.C. school boards are also authorized to open online schools aimed at students in home schooling. Since 2002-2003, they receive $5,000 per student and can recruit them from anywhere in the province. Competition is fierce and some families get offered subsidies to the tune of several hundred dollars to pay for the teaching resources. The goal: to make profits that will make up for budget cuts, while encouraging home schooling.

As for infrastructure in the U.S., only a few states allow private companies to build and lease schools. When it does happen, it is stressed that the companies in question do their utmost to maximize revenue: metal detectors, video-surveillance cameras, armed guards, fast-food franchises, etc. At the end of the day, it costs school boards far more to open new schools based on educational approaches that are to say the least repressive.

Ever since 2002, British schools may hold intellectual property rights, reap profits from the sale of their programs of study and act as profitable consultants for other Institutions.

In Canada, similar public-private partnerships (PPPs or P3s) are authorized in several provinces. Nova Scotia blazed the trail. To make sure that new school construction costs don't add to the provincial budget deficit, the government decided to resort to PPPs for all of them in 1997. Those in the business had every right to be enthusiastic. The first school to be built in Halifax won first prize from the Canadian Council for Public-Private Partnerships in 1998. No matter that the water was not drinkable and the roof leaked. What miracles are possible through the power of positive thinking!

But no miracles happened in Nova Scotia. Observers found that the sites chosen by the builders fell far short of the real needs of local populations. The sites chosen for new schools tended to be sites that the builders themselves already owned. The government decided not to make the signed contracts public; but eventually it was forced to do so. The cost turned out to be much higher than if the public sector had undertaken new school construction. For thirty or so schools, it was estimated that the costs were $30 million higher.

Over a period of twenty years, private enterprise went on to recoup 89% of the initial costs of construction from leasing fees while still remaining sole proprietor of the buildings and land, from which it could reap further profits, especially outside of school hours. The government on the other hand was responsible for the upkeep and operating costs. To cut a long story short, the profits went to the private partner while the risks were borne by the public partner.

Two years later, the situation became politically untenable. The newly elected conservative government cancelled its predecessor's plan. But local authorities were still grappling with the problems of the schools that had already been built and the long-term contracts that the government could not get out of. In January of 2003, in view of the critical situation afflicting several schools, the government resigned itself to a lawsuit. The court decision confirmed the worst fears of PPP's critics. The owners were in their rights to demand high fees for the evening use of facilities and also to pocket a third of the profits from cafeterias and vending machines. This decision certainly did nothing to end the controversy.

New Brunswick, Prince Edward Island and Alberta have also gone in for PPPs. In New Brunswick, the owners have exclusive use of technological equipment after three in the afternoon and of the whole school after six, with the result that they can put on private classes for both children and adults. In Alberta, the first PPP-built school was in the same building as a supermarket.

Universities for Profit
The education industry has designs, equally if not more so, on higher education. More and more major corporations are creating their own "universities." Private for-profit institutions are sprouting up all over while on-line teaching is a new cash cow for universities starved for revenues. Foreign students are now being considered as imported goods helping the balance of trade and filling institutional coffers.

According to the OECD, the number of enterprise universities has grown from 400 in 1988 to 1,600 in 1998. The phenomenon has attracted the interest of more than 40% of the 500 largest corporations listed in *Fortune* magazine. Estimations are that by 2010 there will be more enterprise universities in the U.S. than traditional universities. For example, Motorola University has 99 locations in 21 countries; Toyota, IBM, Microsoft, Dow Chemical and many others have also joined the club. These universities by and large limit themselves to providing professional training and development for the company employees. But all the signs are that they increasingly want to be considered on a par with their traditional counterparts.

As for private for-profit universities, their numbers in the U.S. have risen by 250% over the last ten years. One of the biggest, the University of Phoenix, founded in 1976, is the property of the Apollo Group, a company listed on the stock exchange. Some of their programs are commercially offered on-line. In 2008, it had 80 campuses (including ones in Vancouver and Calgary), more than 100 training centres and nearly 300,000 students, mainly adults in professional programs.

The University of Phoenix does not stint on the resources it devotes to increasing enrolments and profits. Its dubious recruitment practices have even occasioned lawsuits from the U.S. Ministry of Education. In 2004, without admitting guilt, the university agreed to pay a nine million dollar fine for encouraging its staff to recruit students without pre-requisite qualifications or who were unable to profit from the educational program. The university was pocketing the tuition fees without even having to provide the full service.

Recently, a for-profit company listed on NASDAQ, Laureate Education Inc., has acquired private universities and trade schools in Mexico, Spain, France, Switzerland and India. It is selling courses to more than 60,000 students.

Several Canadian provinces have got on the bandwagon. Until recently, provinces only allowed public universities to develop programs and confer degrees. But some have now relaxed their legislative restrictions. Alberta was the first, in 2001, to authorize a U.S. for-profit company, the DeVry Institute of Technology, to confer degrees. Since 2003, Ontario has also been granting this right to private universities. British Columbia allows such universities to be set up with the sole approval of a quality assessment board, a majority of whose members are from the world of business.

Some public universities have also joined in. The University of Virginia has completely privatized its Graduate School of Business Administration. The school now receives no public funding whatsoever and pays a franchise fee to the university. Dalhousie University in Halifax has done the same thing with its masters program in information technology, in conjunction with the private sector; tuition fees are pegged at $38,000.

As soon as they cross national borders, public universities are usually defined as private in the host country. This has especially been true of Australian universities which, in 2000, provided more than 750 programs abroad to 32,000 students, notably in Newfoundland and Nova Scotia. Their aim is quite simply to generate revenue for the mother house.

But it is overwhelmingly in the field of virtual education that universities are privatizing themselves. On-line instruction quadrupled between 1998 and 2002 to reach two million students. Some see distance education as offering the greatest potential in this new education market. They particularly target students abroad who don't have the means to move away from home. But the dropout rate in these programs is very high and the costs are far from being as economical as expected.

Some public universities are providing on-line instruction with the goal of improving accessibility and equality of opportunity, as they did with distance education. An example is the Open University in Britain, which has more than 200,000 students, of whom 30,000 are pursuing their studies abroad.

According to the OECD, virtual education would have to proliferate for the market to "take off." So huge efforts are put into promotion in order to reach economies of scale. This has pushed the University of California to require all its professors to put their courses on line. In tandem with this, it has collaborated with private businesses to create a private company to make a profit from virtual instruction. The same situation has occurred in Toronto where it triggered one of the longest universities strikes in Canadian history. The York University administration had invited businesses to attach their logos to on-line courses, in exchange for a donation of $10,000. It had also created a private consortium to take care of its commercialization.

These consortia are sprouting everywhere. The most famous one is Universitas 21 (U21), a British law firm, bringing together some fifteen universities in partnership with Thomson Learning, allied with Rupert Murdoch's News Corporation[29]. Its aim is to allow member institutions to make a profit from the global commercialization of higher education. It provides programs in business and technology, but for the time being it is conferring degrees on only a few thousand graduates. In fact, the consortium is the property of Thomson and the participating universities are there to give it credibility; and McGill University has decided to withdraw from the consortium. Major Anglo-Saxon universities, Stanford, Columbia and the London School of Economics are also joining forces to take their products to the commercial market[30].

This all raises the question of accreditation and the quality of education. UNESCO and other bodies have proposed various models of accreditation and a code of ethical conduct. The main fears are of education on the cheap and the risk of a kind of educational neocolonialism. But commercial schools are pushing back; external quality controls would be putting obstacles in the way of market development. They prefer to base themselves on customer satisfaction and self-evaluation.

Students as Paying Guests

The race for foreign students has become a new way to fill the coffers of western educational institutions, including secondary schools. The surfacing of free-market discourse on this subject marks the move from a logic based on educational social values to an economic logic. Global competition for students on a commercial basis conflicts with the values of cooperation, intercultural exchange and aid that prevailed until quite recently.

The percentage of foreign students on the campuses of OECD countries has gone up by 35% on average between 1998 and 2002. It has now reached almost two million. The U.S. is taking the lion's share, with almost 500,000 foreign students, for an estimated revenue of $12 billion in 2003. This makes it the fifth largest sector exporting services. But their overall market share has declined, as other countries have started to compete.

Over the last two decades the number of foreign students has gone up by a factor of four in Britain and by ten in Australia. In the latter case, the unrestricted recruitment of students spending the totality of their tuition costs is part of a move from an aid philosophy to a commercial philosophy. It amounts to more than $900 million a year in a context where public spending on higher education is in decline. Taking revenues as the measure, Canada is now ranked fourth.

Primary and secondary education is also being targeted, the goal for the pupils being to get their first foreign certificate as a stepping-stone for admission to a top class university. Both New Zealand and Australia have been making the recruitment of secondary school students, mainly from Asia, a feature of their trade policy. Education Queensland International is one of the bodies created to promote and export educational services on the international market. One of its goals is to double the number of international students in its public schools.

Several Canadian provinces have leapt on board. In 2001-2002, of the 100,000 or so foreign students in Canada, 38,000 were attending elementary or secondary schools. While Nova Scotia is taking in only a few hundred pupils, there were 10,000 in British Columbia and 18,000 in Ontario. In British Columbia, the Richmond school board takes in more than 5,000 foreign students for a fee of $12,000 per annum each, which allows them to reap a not inconsiderable profit in the tens of millions of dollars. It is mainly the privileged school boards in urban centres that are cashing in on this new goldmine.

With school boards going down the same route as higher education, questions are being raised about equity and social justice. There is the fear that the funding of public services will depend on the sales capacities of school boards. People are asking whether these recruitment practices have anything to do with basic education.

Alongside this growth in the numbers of foreign students, most countries have relaxed their rules about immigration in order to attract highly qualified individuals and students already in the country. This possibility of immigration is an additional attraction for students. The direct consequence of this is that the number of students not returning to their country of origin is going up. This is the case for one student in every five in Australia. In the U.S., almost half the students of Chinese and Indian origin stay on after finishing their thesis.

Canada is part of this new trend. Between 1978 and 1999, only one third of the students from China went back home. Graduates automatically get extra points when their immigration application is assessed. Temporary work permits have been created for graduates, one step on the way to sponsorship by a business and landed immigrant status.

There has been no shortage of protests against the "brain drain" that is being stimulated by developed countries. Universities in the South are becoming suppliers of skills to feed the operating needs of higher education in the countries of the North, without any compensation to the countries of the South for their financial outlay on the earlier levels of education. The poorest countries in the world are the helpless witnesses to this exodus, which is a major obstacle to their development. To be sure, immigrants do send money back to their country, they do facilitate cultural and commercial exchanges between their new country and their mother country, but there can be no question that this is a new "pillage of the Third World", to recall that popular slogan from the 1960s used to condemn the pillage of natural resources back then.

Quebec Rides the Wave

Quebec has also been infected by this current of commercialized education, mainly with the encouragement of the policies of the Canadian Ministry of External Affairs and International Trade. The exporting of Quebec's educational expertise, the opening of private schools abroad, and partnerships of all sorts with the private sector are all examples of alarming trends.

One such example is the memorandum of agreement "concerning the establishment of a combined nursery, elementary and secondary school" in Morocco between the Commission Scolaire des Découvreurs (a school board in the Quebec City region), the Groupe Scolaire Marocain (which already owns one private school) and Éducation Internationale (a services co-operative set up by Quebec's Federation of School Boards). It raises serious questions. This private school, which was about to open its doors in Casablanca, could take in several thousand pupils. Tuition fees ranged from $2,500 to $5,000. Students would graduate with a joint diploma from Morocco and Quebec.

Moroccan parents want to use this opportunity to "help their progeny gain access to North American universities."

It is questionable whether this project would contribute to the "sustainable development of education systems" overseas and to making them "accessible to everyone everywhere in the world" to quote the mission statement of Éducation internationale. It is hard to see how, with a project like this, the service cooperative could say that it was basing its actions on the values of cooperation and solidarity that are claimed to be the foundations of its operation. Fortunately, difficulties at the Moroccan end led to the cancellation of the project and have given rise to second thoughts about this kind of development[31].

The Lester B. Pearson School Board, on the island of Montreal, is apparently getting ready, still with the collaboration of Éducation internationale, to open a school in China that could accommodate up to 3,000 students. According to the senior managers of the school board, this project will be very profitable, since they will be providing the principal, teachers, curriculum, and taking on the management of everything. Tuition fees have not yet been set.

In its strategic plan for the years 2004-2007, the service cooperative proposed increasing "efforts to recruit foreign students" and exporting its members' expertise both nationally and internationally. Some of its export projects are being developed in partnership with private companies. At the same time, the organization declares that it will continue to develop other activities to promote linguistic and cultural exchanges for students and teachers.

In addition, overtures to public-private partnerships are proliferating. Up until recently, several projects have fallen by the wayside, largely thanks to action by unions. Cégeps in the Montreal region planned to hire a private firm of guidance consultants to follow up on high-school dropouts but it came to nothing. Similarly, the Université de Sherbrooke wanted to hand its short MA program in law management over to a private company but that did not materialize either. McGill University's desire to privatize its law faculty also ran into faculty opposition.

Even so, the agreement concluded between the video game multinational corporation Ubisoft and the Matane cégep opened up a deep breach in the traditional role and autonomy of post-secondary institutions. This public-private partnership to create a training centre specializing in electronic games gives the firm a say in the curriculum and the selection of teachers and students, as well as intellectual property rights over any products or innovations that result from the program.

A similar agreement was concluded with the École de design industriel at the Université de Montréal. According to the university's newspaper, the two organizations will work jointly on the concept for a training program at the master's level and in the development of research activities. As for the Université de Sherbrooke, after its agreement with Ubisoft, it will be offering professional training programs at the master's level on video game development leading to a specialized graduate diploma.

Training is generally provided in the firm's own premises, dressed up as the Ubisoft Campus. Not only is professional development made available to staff, but also programs eligible for inclusion in college diploma transcripts and for graduate diplomas jointly conferred by the public institutions and Ubisoft. To start up this new enterprise, the multinational corporation received subsidies from various government sources amounting to several million dollars.

As for the Université de Sherbrooke, after its agreement with Ubisoft, it will be offering professional training programs at the master's level on video game development leading to a specialized graduate diploma.

Some business circles were up in arms to see such a privilege extended to a single company, giving it an undeniable competitive edge. No matter. Several months later the government announced a subsidy of $660,000 to Electronic Arts, the other big player in the video game industry.

Laval University's plan to create a supermarket-school in partnership with the grocery giant Sobeys raised other concerns. This supermarket was set to become a full-scale laboratory for studying consumer behaviour. The corporation was to donate $2 million as well as a percentage of the profits from its university branch to a named research Chair in retail sales and food distribution that would eventually lead to research for its own purposes. The university regretfully had to back off in the face of widespread opposition to such a distortion of its academic mission.

Over at the Université de Québec à Rimouski (UQAR), the green light has been given to a private partnership to develop its Lévis campus. The construction of a new building at a cost of more than $25 million has been awarded to the Groupe Tanguay. The university will become tenant in leases running from 25 to 30 years, a contract that recalls the vicissitudes of other similar projects in both Canada and the United States.

That is precisely what happened at the Université du Québec à Montréal (UQAM) with the development of its Îlot Voyageur, a complex costing $300 million. The Îlot Voyageur P3 project ended in a fiasco. The President had to resign in the fall of 2006, the university was plunged into the worst financial crisis in its history, and a criminal investigation of a misappropriation of funds is now under way. The Liberal minister intends to take advantage of the situation to introduce a new governance model for Quebec universities, one that is more consistent with business models. She has announced that she wants two thirds of the seats on the Board of Governors in each university to be reserved for people outside the university, to the detriment of the traditional internal representation of the university community.

The bill to create the Quebec Public-Private Partnerships Agency enacted in December 2004 is designed to encourage the development of such partnerships. According to the *Notes explicatives* accompanying the Act, the Agency's chief responsibility was to "provide organizations with all the expert services related to feasibility studies of public-private partnership projects, and the negotiation, finalization and management of such contracts". Even though the use of the Agency's services is by and large voluntary, it becomes mandatory when a government body takes the lead in financing the project, directly or indirectly, which will normally be the case. A partnership contract, as stipulated by Article 6, "may have as its object the provision of a public service." Briefly, from now on, the entirety of the public service is now affected.

Finally, the process of "externalizing costs", in the new terminology of globalization, is also having an effect on education. In the fall of 2005, the Montreal Economic Institute published a short piece comparing the average unit cost of school maintenance in school boards that contracted out against that of school boards doing it in-house. For the former, the cost came to $11.39 per square metre as against $17.19 for the latter. It only takes glance at the wage levels to understand the reason for the difference. The public sector workers are paid $17.93 an hour as against $13.55 for the *Class A* employees in the private sector (which is probably more than many of the rest of them are getting). This privatization is going ahead quite simply on the backs of the workers, whose wages in either case must be considered modest.

In short, the education market is now being viewed as a self-evident concept, just like this new education industry that is busily being developed. Like many societies, Quebec is trying to carve out a space in this new market, sometimes forgetting the principles underlying public education. The slide from the internationalization of education towards its commercialization needs to be reversed urgently, if we want Quebec education to go international in a spirit of cooperation, exchange, intercultural understanding and solidarity.

The International Trade Context

The original ideas behind public education led to keeping the space that was available for merchandising within strict limits. But the "education industry" is in full spate. Universities, programs and students are breaking boundaries. Service providers are diversifying, they are scouting new territories, while education exports are continuously rising. But this "industry" is still governed by national laws, even if, in recent years, there has been a shift to laws that favour commercialization. In many countries, national norms have been weakened so as not to interfere with this new commerce, especially where the presence of foreign institutions in domestic territory and their ability to confer diplomas are concerned.

The claim that competition and the market provide the best route to the improvement of the quality and efficiency of education systems is now being extended to include international commerce. Free trade, the expression of free market thinking on the international level, should logically apply equally to education. And that's what some people are trying very hard to get us to believe.

According to the U.S. Department of Commerce, the commercialization of education is one of the major priorities of commercial policy and foreign policy in the country. It would help correct a very deep trade deficit and to "promote the values of freedom and democracy so dear to the United States" (*sic*). In consequence, the hopes are for maximum competitiveness and minimum government regulation.

This is the dynamic that the General Agreement on Trade in Services (GATS) wants to strengthen. Education is in fact one of the 12 service sectors covered by the Agreement. The main goal is to eliminate what educational businesses consider to be "obstacles to trade" in order to turn education into a merchandise like any other, subject to the rules of the international trade agreements. The common good and the public interest would then be reduced to their starkest form. The major exporting countries of "educational services," especially the U.S., Australia and New Zealand, are the ones leading the dance for the most part.

The major trading nations also want to calm potentially troubled waters. And so the Agreement specifies that services supplied in the "exercise of governmental authority" are excluded (Art. 1.3). What are we to understand by this exception? The definition is given just beneath: "any service which is supplied neither on a commercial basis, nor in competition with one or more service suppliers". So it would be jumping the gun to conclude that education is excluded from GATS. Even the WTO admits that the wording is not *"altogether clear"*.

Many analysts have exposed the ambiguity of this exclusion, its inadequate wording and the conflicting interpretations that could arise from it. In fact, in most educational systems there are various service providers who could be considered to be "in competition," particularly in higher education and professional training.

Many questions remain: does the collection of tuition fees constitute a commercial activity? Can public institutions be considered to be in competition with on-line educational businesses? A legal opinion drawn up by the Toronto firm of Gottlieb & Pearson for the Canadian Association of University Teachers does not allay the worst fears and suggests amending Article 1.3 in order to clarify the situation[32].

Article 1.3 would mean that the general provisions of GATS apply equally to educational services within any state, particularly the rule concerning most-favoured-nation treatment. This rule stipulates that all foreign suppliers of education services must be given equal treatment. For example, if an Australian university were allowed to open a university in a Canadian province, all foreign universities would have a right to the same privilege and the same conditions. This does not impinge on the ability of the government to protect national institutions.

For the time being, the consequences of these general provisions have been fairly modest and few countries have made "specific commitments" in the field of education. These commitments need to be made for every service sector and may be of variable geometry; in education, they could force countries to open up their "education market" and confer on foreign businesses the same privileges that national businesses enjoy. In fact, contrary to the general provisions, the specific commitments enforce the application of the so-called rule of most-favoured-nation treatment that requires all businesses to be treated equally.

GATS has divided the "education market" into five categories: elementary, secondary, post-secondary, adult education and other services. It also identifies four different modes of service supply: cross-border supply where a service crosses a frontier without requiring the physical displacement of persons (on-line teaching), overseas consumption (students), commercial presence (a campus) and the physical presence of persons (staff working abroad). A country that makes a specific commitment may do so for one or more categories and for one or more modes of service supply.

When the Agreement was signed in 1994, education was one of the sectors for which there were the fewest commitments. But the Agreement includes an internal virus that provides for progressive liberalization through succeeding negotiations. Education is in its sights.

The WTO has moreover mandated the Global Alliance for Transnational Education, established in 1998 with the support of IBM and other multinationals, to draw up a complete list of restrictive practices impeding trade in education[33]. This is only a beginning, let's keep up the pressure, the educational traders are thundering.

So business organizations on both sides of the Atlantic are demanding a general opening up of the education market. A good example is the National Committee for International Trade in Education, a U.S. coalition of education businesses formed in 1999, and whose board is made up of directors of Motorola University, Educational Testing Services and online education businesses.

Negotiations are currently under way. Four countries have tabled negotiating proposals for the liberalization of trade in education to all members of the WTO: the U.S., Australia, New Zealand and Japan. To stave off the general outcry such demands could trigger, they list the many advantages of a liberalization of trade in education: countries committing to open their markets could benefit from exchanges of knowledge and people, develop a network of profitable alliances and see the growth of their economic prosperity.

There are also reassurances about public education. The U.S. represents the private sector as a supplement to the public sector, Australia insists on the necessity for governments to preserve their sovereign rights in domestic funding and policy, while New Zealand champions a "balance between pursuing domestic education priorities and exploring ways in which trade in education services can be further liberalized".

To keep resistance at bay, there is a clearer definition of the sectors involved, thus opening up "less sensitive" subsectors. New Zealand wants "other services" more clearly defined to cover language training, vocational training, etc., and the addition of a new category for education agency services (advertising, management); the U.S. proposes adding specific categories for training services (particularly on-the-job training) and for educational testing services. Briefly, this is about giving the businesses these countries helped create nationally a level of access consistent with the rules of international trade.

To achieve this, the WTO's members are invited to remove barriers to the desired liberalization. Among the barriers to be removed (the U.S. proposal lists seventeen), are the prohibition on education services offered by foreign entities, the impossibility for them to grant degrees, restricted access to subsidies, national preference for professors, restrictions on imported course materials or on cross-border online teaching.

The removal of these barriers and the opening of markets would allow the businesses in countries exporting educational services to do what they like. The U.S. testing corporations that grew significantly thanks to the requirements of the No Child Left Behind legislation could operate across the planet. Tutoring and school management services would join the rush. Enterprise universities could more easily claim accreditation as universities while online teaching agencies would grant degrees beyond their borders.

If a foreign multinational in education felt that its profits were being threatened by the national regulations of a country having made commitments to "no limitations" in education, the home country could take its case to the Dispute Settlement Body of the WTO. This tribunal's decisions tend to be very favourable to free trade and interpret commercial agreements in this way.

Briefly, then, if countries agreed to buckle under to the demands of the Anglo-Saxon world, which some of them could be forced to do under the pressure of bilateral discussions under way within the GATS framework, this would amount to having to renounce several of their historic responsibilities in education.

Already issues are looming on the horizon. An example is a dispute that pitted Microsoft against the Quebec College of Engineers for several years. The College opposes the multinational's right to award the title of "Microsoft Certified System Engineers" to the technical specialists it is training. Microsoft lost in the Superior Court in June 2005 and again in the Court of Appeal in the fall of that year. The case could go to the Supreme Court. The liberalization of trade to include education would bring joy to Microsoft and those seeking to protect the title of engineer would just have to suck it up.

But the world of education is firmly opposed to such an approach. In a Joint Declaration on Higher Education and the General Agreement on Trade in Services, associations of colleges and universities in Canada and Europe have spoken with one voice. "Given that very little is known about the consequences of including trade in education services in the GATS (...) that it is extremely difficult to clearly define which education services are supplied strictly on a commercial basis (...), our member institutions are committed to reducing obstacles to international trade in higher education using conventions and agreements outside of a trade policy regime (...) Our respective countries should not make commitments in Higher Education Services or in the related categories of Adult Education and Other Education Services in the context of the GATS."

Opposition is even fiercer among teachers' and students' unions. Education International and international student organizations are actively working to ensure that education is excluded from trade agreements. Broad national coalitions are bringing similar pressures to bear on their governments. Even the chairperson of the Council for Trade in Services has admitted that the public campaign has worked and has kept the number of commitments in education small.

Public education is based on non-market principles of equity, justice and solidarity; it is rooted in principles of citizenship and democracy. It is a fundamental right that cannot be subject to the rules of trade. This point of view commands a powerful consensus in the education community throughout the world.

As for Canada, the federal government made no education commitments when GATS was first signed. It even went so far as to specify that it reserved the right to give different treatment to people and service suppliers from foreign countries, particularly where charges were concerned, thereby confirming the policy of charging higher tuition fees for foreign students and the national character of grants to educational institutions.

Since then, it has reiterated its position, but ambiguities remain. In various official declarations, Canada has agreed to make no commitments concerning "public education." But does that leave the door open to commitments on private education? If such were the case, it would risk opening a Pandora's box with unpredictable consequences, given that the boundaries between public and private are far from clear, especially in postsecondary education.

The Canadian position is similar for NAFTA. In an Annex to the Agreement (Annex II-C-9), Canada has reserved "the right to adopt or maintain any measure with respect to the provision of (...) services to the extent that they are established or maintained for a public purpose". Public education and training are listed, along with income security, health and other public services. But the ambiguity about private education services remains.

If trade agreements are not imposing the immediate privatization of education, they continue to push in this direction. The very fact that education is on the table at all is in itself alarming. In the course of such negotiations, countries are discussing the liberalization of a variety of service sectors and it may be feared that some weaker countries will be forced to give up part of their national sovereignty in education.

So this is the rather unreassuring context in which we must assess any legislative measure aiming to liberalize educational trade at the national level, which could later open the door to the greed of the international traders.

A MISSION DERAILED

The growing ascendancy of the neo-liberal educational model in numerous jurisdictions, including Quebec, is deeply worrying in the long run. Competition among schools, the emphasis on individual choices without regard for their social consequences, the obsession with quantifiable results alone, the transformation of knowledge into a commodity that can be bought and sold, the domination of a strictly economic vision, these are all elements that affect education in the deepest core of its mission. That is the conclusion that inexorably flows from the preceding overview.

Almost everywhere, in fact, the reforms are aiming make education more utilitarian, to tie it more closely to the needs of the market. More than ever education is becoming a tool in the service of individual interests alone and is being considered above all as a factor of production. Human resources, human capital, are the new subjects of the educational process. A more pronounced distinction between general education and practical training is being imposed. The competitiveness of national businesses in international markets is claimed to depend on this new turn.

The content of the curriculum and the nature of the degrees and programs are suffering. This is coming about in a variety of ways that are undermining the foundations of an education that seeks to strengthen democracy, promote social justice and secure personal development and well-being, an education based on the intrinsic worth of knowledge, ideas and intellectual discovery.

This explains the protests against the subjugation of all kinds of education to a skills-based approach designed for vocational training that emphasizes skills for use in everyday life to the detriment of the transmission of knowledge. Quebec is not immune from this debate. The new elementary and secondary school programs are still being criticized and with such vehemence that the Minister of Education has been forced to introduce several changes so as to make the learning objectives clearer. The fact that examination results in French in the final year of elementary school have gone down since the reform came in, has only given more ammunition to its opponents.

Rather than building on the democratic reforms of the 1960s and 1970s, the system is moving back to selection at a younger age and every encouragement is being given to greater stratification of schools and students. Schools are now expected to adapt to the need for *practical intelligence.* As the sociologist François Dubet has reminded us, any sociologist can predict the social composition of a set of pupils when they are grouped together by intelligence type (theoretical or practical). "In the common school, there is no differentiation without hierarchization" (2004, p. 69). Despite protestations to the contrary, the objective of a quality education for all has been abandoned. Equality of opportunity is suffering as a result.

In France, Italy, England and Quebec, comprehensive schooling has been questioned and the number of years spent on a common curriculum has been shortened. The prime minister of Italy, Silvio Berlusconi, for example, felt a few years ago that the way to the essentials would come from emphasizing the three "I"s: *Internet, Inglese, Impresa* (Internet, English, Enterprise). In France, the comprehensive middle school (*collège*) is under discussion, with a return to the former streaming system not being ruled out. In Quebec, the plan to implement an applied education stream is going in the same direction. Pupils enrolled in a stream that will in all probability lead to laborious, poorly paid employment could even receive a specialist professional certificate in starting a business.

Entrepreneurship is thus becoming the new skill for the pupils and students to develop, and it enjoys considerable prestige among the teachers. In Quebec, it is now one of the areas of general education in both elementary and secondary schools; pupils are invited to set up businesses, to sell their products. This training, it is insisted, will be useful in the labour market.

In the same vein, a new entrepreneurship-study program at the secondary level is being piloted on the model of existing specialized programs (sports-study, etc.). It is meant to "give an idea of what it means to start up a business and run a company." This program is to be rolled out soon in Quebec. As the Canadian press put it when the government launched this initiative, "as soon as they reach school age, Quebec children are encouraged to develop an entrepreneurial culture in readiness to take over as the corporate leaders of tomorrow" (quoted in Baillargeon, 2006, p.173). The idea is to inculcate in today's youth the values that "are the pride of the business world."

In vocational and technical training, programs are more and more being tailored to meet the immediate requirements of businesses. Short training programs are proliferating to suit the new requirement for "flexibility" in the labour market. Certificate programs, without any general education and not leading to an accredited diploma are now legion; they are no longer limited to adults in training, but open to all pupils. There are fears that the broadening of the authority to issue certificates attesting to a particular skill to a whole range of "service suppliers" will strip the government of its historic prerogatives. The precedent of the Ubisoft campus shows how far business domination of education can go.

On the other hand, "lifelong education" is increasingly coming to be considered as a means of "adaptation" and a market worth exploiting. It would provide a backup for students leaving school early, something that is being encouraged anyhow. In adult education, utilitarian courses now enjoy the stamp of approval; employability is used as the criterion for funding, particularly by *Emploi-Quebec*. In spite of all the fine speeches trotted out along with a succession of policy announcements, universal education, literacy and general education for personal development are being left on the back burner. It's as if, in the long run, a basic quality education is not indispensable for citizenship and professional life.

Universities are being equally affected by the general trend. As one U.S. academic has pointed out, priority is going to the disciplines that make money, study money or attract money. By putting economic development at the top of university's agenda, we are neglecting its traditional mission, and stifling social criticism and basic research, which had been its value.

In vocational and technical training, programs are more and more being tailored to meet the immediate requirements of businesses. Short training programs are proliferating to suit the new requirement for "flexibility" in the labour market.

Fortunately what we can say after this rather gloomy picture is that these are long-term trends. Even if utilitarianism and the market are infiltrating education, they are not dominating all its policies and practices. The resistance being expressed is proof positive of that. But there is a great risk that the neo-liberal educational model will end up being perceived as common sense.

Of course education needs to adapt continuously to the changes going on around it. Globalization carries challenges to which the education system cannot remain indifferent. But the neo-liberal solutions are only making matters worse. We must take them on by coming up with solutions that aim to develop an education system and a society that are more democratic. This is what we shall be discussing in the following chapter.

Notes

1. The *collèges uniques* in France; *écoles polyvalentes* in Quebec.

2. It should be mentioned in passing that one of the authors, John Chubb, was once vice-president of Edison, a profit-making business that promised a fortune to be made in school management.

3. It will come as no surprise to learn that the MEI is still supporting the belief that competition is beneficial. In defiance of the abundant research showing the opposite, especially the studies mentioned below on charter schools, the authors of a research review published in the fall of 2005 claim that its conclusions are taken from "a survey of foreign experiences," actually amounting to nothing more than a few papers on Sweden and the United States.

4. In Canada, only Alberta allows charter schools; no more than 15 can be set up, however, and they must seek authorization from the local school board, subject to an appeal to the Ministry if it is turned down. In 2003-2004, there were 13 of them with an enrolment of 4,500 pupils (fewer than 1%). These schools are not allowed the use of selective admission procedures.

5. This is borne out, with some slight modifications, by a more detailed analysis of the math test scores (Lubienski and Lubienski, 2006).

6. *The New York Times* had to resort to the Freedom of Information Act in order to have the results of this study commissioned by the Clinton administration made public.

7. On this issue, see the model proposed by the MEI (Bernier, 2003) and the critiques of Baby (2003) and the Centrale des syndicats du Québec (CSQ, 2003a).

8. By virtue of Article 15.4 of the Quebec Education Act, a student who "receives home schooling and benefits from an educational experience which, according to an evaluation made by or for the School Board, is equivalent to what is provided at school" may be exempted from the requirement to attend school.

9. This issue gave rise to vigorous debate in Ontario in the Fall of 2005 and again in 2008 after the project of a black-focused school was adopted by the Toronto board. Quebec was not spared its own debate at the end of the 1990s.

10. The Commission was asked to produce a comprehensive report on Quebec education in 1995-1996.

11. According to a similar survey in 1996, these proportions (in constant dollars) were 27% and 37% respectively, which shows that social selection has grown in the private sector in less than a decade.

12. This research study, an initiative of the CSQ, was carried out among the voting members of both French and English school councils (Roy and Deniger, 2001).

13. The law enables each cégep to confer its own graduation diploma, if authorized to do so by the *Commission d'évaluation*. To date, this authority has not been exercised, but it gives rise to fears that local diplomas might come to be considered as "second-class diplomas."

14. Even so, the program won the support of the Democrats, on the condition that the voucher system not be included.

15. A poll conducted by the College of Teachers in Ontario among 1,027 of its members produced the same conclusions. It was also the opinion given by the Civil Rights Project at Harvard.

16. These assessments have become so frequent that experts with the Council of Ministers of Education in Canada attributed a drop in the scores on its own School Achievement Indicators Program, a scheme similar to PISA, to "assessment fatigue."

17. Bills 124 for schools and 123 for cégeps.

18. The doctrine of the new public management is steering government action according to operational criteria derived from customer satisfaction and is playing down its political nature. The citizen is now being replaced by the customer (see L'Italien, 2004).

19. The liberal government came charging back in the spring of 2008. Had the proposed bill been adopted, school boards and schools would have been forced to adopt success targets consistent with Ministry objectives. The bill was postponed until autumn, and then finally shelved with the call for early elections.

20. An article by Christie (2005b) sums up the various measures under way in the USA to improve nutrition and students' well-being.

21. There are many such programs. For example, Pizza Hut gives away pizzas as prizes for its reading contest "Book It!"; the very anti-union Wal-Mart "adopts" schools which it supports financially; Mr. Christie asks pupils to count the number of chocolate chips in its cookies, and so on.

22. Reported in *The Daily News* of New Plymouth, New Zealand, 18 June 1999.

23. Most commonly mentioned are Subway, Dairy Queen, Coca-Cola, Pepsi-Cola, Nike, Reebok, Dell, Apple, IBM and McDonald's. Advertising logos appear mainly on school supplies and the uniforms of sports teams, in corridors, cafeterias and gymnasia. School buses and school internet sites are more rarely cited.

24. These provisions were fought all the way to the Supreme Court. The Irwin Toy Company claimed that they contravened the right to freedom of speech. The Court recognized this to be the case, but that the restrictions were reasonable and justified by the stated goal of protecting children.

25. The contract between Doctor Olivieri, the University of Toronto and Apotex stipulated that any publication of data required the pharmaceutical company's agreement.

26. This is the Foundation that subsidizes 40% of the Canada Research Chairs, while requiring in exchange hat the private sector or other institutional structures make up the difference. The Canadian Association of University Teachers sees this as a threat to university autonomy and an encouragement for the private takeover of research.

27. The relationship between the McGraw family and the Bush family goes back to the 1930s and has continued up to the present day. One of the McGraw heirs was appointed to the George Bush transition team in 2000 and another is linked to the foundation set up by the President's wife.

28. This situation is raising new issues. Anyone teaching the province's programs overseas must hold a B.C. certificate. To get round this, a private agency usually acts as an intermediary between the foreign private school and the service providers, and the staff is not unionized.

29. U21 is registered in Singapore where union rights are restricted. Its head office is registered in the tax haven of Guernsey. Unions have denounced problems with course content and evaluations.

30. Mention could be made of the Western Governors' University, which derives its name from an initiative launched by Governors of Western States in the USA and

brings together universities with businesses such as IBM, CISCO, Microsoft, etc., to provide online instruction.

31. Visit the website www.education-internationale.com. Éducation internationale declares its goal to be the promotion of international exchanges as well as exporting Quebec's *savoir-faire* in education.

32. The suggested wording goes as follows: "except for services supplied in the exercise of governmental authority *as defined by the national laws and regulations of each member*".

33. What is more, the Alliance invited citizens to post any restrictive measures of their government on its website with a guarantee of confidentiality.

CHAPTER THREE

Education and the Common Good

We are at a crossroads: either we keep working at defining and developing a universally accessible public domain; or we turn back. Either we continue on the road to a national education system that puts more emphasis on nation and the people, or we opt for the "survival of the fittest" and "charity begins at home."

Claude Lelièvre, *L'école obligatoire: pour quoi faire?*

Quebec society benefited greatly from the rapid development of public education during the Quiet Revolution. In a few decades, the progress has been remarkable. School attendance and graduation rates in Quebec are now comparable to those of other western societies. Groups once excluded or discriminated against have now found their place within the educational community. Public education has played a major role in the construction of a Quebec identity and in the preservation and teaching of its national language and culture.

Unfortunately, as we have seen, recent years put an end to the linking of public education with the common good. Words like "common" and "public" have even become anathema, associated in some minds with standardization and mediocrity.

The strongly-held belief that we are living in unprecedented times, "the global epoch," has helped in the subjugation of education to narrow economic goals. Globalization has been used and is still being used as an argument in support of the neo-liberal educational agenda. It is true that the changes ushered in by globalization will define the context in which young people grow up, learn, love and work, but the solutions offered by this new educational order are the very opposite of democracy.

Individual educational choices dominate, to the detriment of the interests of society as a whole and of the poor in particular. Competitive learning is encouraged from earliest childhood. Private enterprise is forced on us as the model to imitate. The market is now interfering in some areas for the first time. The common good is being sacrificed.

At the same time, all political stakeholders are crying out for educational improvement. Everyone agrees that education is the key determinant of social and economic development. Massive changes have come with a demand for a high standard of cultural attainment and higher qualifications.

In the face of these changes, we suggest an alternative approach fuelled by a different kind of logic. This approach combines a reaction against the neo-liberal agenda with a response to the issues raised by globalization. It is based on a few important principles: greater equality, better social integration, and educational justice. We shall begin by defining these principles in more detail, and then move on to the things that have to be done to make them work.

We propose a New Deal for education. It begins with a call for policies that will distribute students more fairly across schools and classrooms, notably by limiting school choice. It demands an array of measures designed to ensure success: quality early childhood education, support for the most vulnerable groups, an emphasis on school-community solidarity, and a respect for professional autonomy which provides the only way to guarantee the much-needed diversity of teaching.

A high-quality basic education for all will serve as the foundation for an extended education. The goal of providing young and old alike with a recognized professional qualification must be taken seriously. Higher education and professional development must be made more accessible and democratic. Finally, we must seek inspiration for the internationalization of education in a spirit of cooperation and solidarity.

This approach will not achieve instant unanimity. But it is vital if we want to transform an education system entrenching inequalities of every kind and creating a veritable apartheid in our schools.

Our enterprise is not unrealistic. We shall draw on the experiences of countries that have managed to resist the current trend. We shall look at the results of numerous research studies in Quebec and elsewhere as well as reports about truly innovative and democratic policies and practices, in order to show that our program is not only desirable, but also achievable. The challenge is massive: the creation of a new "virtuous circle" dedicated to the common good (in place of the old vicious circle)[1].

If we are to ground education once again in the common good, we shall need courage to go against the flow. But without such courage, many social changes in the past, now widely accepted, would never have seen the light of day. The public school would still be in limbo, women would still be made to stay at home, and human rights would still be a utopian dream.

EQUALITY, SOCIAL INTEGRATION AND EDUCATIONAL JUSTICE

Public education has been the tool of choice in efforts to achieve the democratic principles of liberty, equality and solidarity. From its inception, we have expected much from it and we still do. It must give everyone an equal opportunity to succeed. It must achieve the lofty goal of emancipation, preparing free people capable of thinking for themselves—enlightened citizens. It must create the soul of an all-embracing nation.

Today, these persistent challenges are becoming more complicated. More than ever before, educational inequalities cast a shadow over the democratic ideal. The increase in social diversity puts heavier demands upon the integrative mission of education. Globalization is increasing the pressure for an enlightened and expanded notion of citizenship. These are the three challenges confronting education in Quebec.

Dramatic Inequalities

Access to the different social levels that characterize democratic societies should not depend on wealth or social status. That principle was at the origin of the notion of equality of opportunity. Since education was universally accessible, merit should be the only criterion for distinguishing "winners" from "losers." But the revelation of glaring inequality among different social groups in the education system has shaken the meritocratic principle to its roots.

In fact, in the 1960s, we began to discover that the dice were loaded. Sociologists spoke with one voice. School, they said, privileges students who are already privileged and contributes to the "construction" of inequalities. Children of poverty do not have access to the same educational resources as children of affluence. Inequalities become apparent right from the first day at school and the gaps widen as time passes. So they wondered whether society or the school system was to blame. They finally concluded that there was shared responsibility, but were far from agreeing where to draw the dividing line.

The concept of equal opportunity was then expanded to include policies that aimed to give more to those who had less, and tried to compensate for what some called "handicaps" and others called "deficits." In the 1970s, Quebec joined the wave of interventions in poor and working-class neighbourhoods, convinced that greater equality of opportunity would come about through the unequal redistribution of resources.

Today, the magnitude of inequalities remaining in Quebec's school system should embarrass even the mildest of democrats. In 2001-2002, the secondary school dropout rate in poor areas was twice as high as in affluent areas[2]; the respective rates for boys and girls who had repeated a grade by the end of elementary school were 2.5 and 3 times higher. As for secondary school graduation rates, the gap between the poorest and the richest had reached 16 percentage points among boys and 13.4 among girls[3].

The failure rate gap between boys and girls "seems less important than the one between children from different socio-economic backgrounds. On the other hand, the gap between girls and boys tends to shorten when the students are from a privileged background, and to widen with disadvantage." (Pelletier and Rheault, 2005, p.23)

The situation is even more critical on the island of Montreal. The rate of those who are a grade or more behind among the most disadvantaged was almost four times higher than the rate among the most privileged (16.6% and 4.9%) while the percentage of students not graduating or graduating late was 2.6 times higher among the former than the latter (62.4% and 24.0%).

In higher education, participation rates also correlated noticeably with parental income. According to 2001 StatsCan data, 35% of 18- to 24-year-olds whose parents' annual income was under $25,000 were enrolled in cégeps and 18% in universities, while these participation rates were 50% and 37% respectively for students with parental incomes over $100,000 (MELS, 2005).

Educational inequalities have very serious lifelong consequences. Education is the major determinant of social class and income in later life. Although these inequalities are a universal phenomenon, their magnitude varies enormously from society to society and schools can do a lot to reduce them, both in their organization and in their practices.

Numerous research studies indicate the path to follow and confirm the urgency of making the struggle against educational inequalities a policy priority. We know, for example, that inequalities are made worse the earlier the process of selection begins. We know that a massive intervention is needed as soon as school attendance begins. We know that the chances of the most disadvantaged are directly affected by streaming children into different schools and different classes.

Policies to combat educational inequality should not be limited to compensatory measures inspired by an "ideology of deficiency." We need a holistic approach to the "war on poverty." The countries that have made most progress towards school democracy are also those that have succeeded in reducing educational inequality and in improving the living conditions of poor families.

Since 1995, the proportion of families living in poverty in Quebec has declined somewhat; but the financial situation of the poorest families has become more precarious and lasts longer. Today, more than 15% of families live below the poverty line. The proportion is higher in the Montreal region and those most affected are children in the 0-5 year age group; almost 40% of them live in poverty[4]. In some city neighbourhoods, this situation leads to a downward spiral accentuating social problems and effectively compromising children's development.

Robert Cadotte[5] has published a description of the physical, social, economic and environmental health of a poor neighbourhood in Montreal (Saint-Henri) and compared it with Westmount, the wealthy neighbourhood next door. In Saint-Henri, life expectancy is ten years lower, diseases are far more frequent and living conditions are desperate. It is no wonder that the suicide rate is 3.5 times greater than in Westmount.

It's worth repeating Gerald W. Bracey's remark that poverty resembles gravity. Gravity affects everything you do on the planet. So does poverty. It gets in the way of the full exercise of your fundamental rights and is fully synonymous with exclusion and discrimination. But, unlike gravity, poverty is not inevitable.

According to the Collective for a Poverty-Free Quebec[6]: "From 1997 to 2002, if the population of Quebec had consciously chosen to exchange the so-called invisible hand of the market and its political glove for a visible, fraternal helping hand, it could have freed itself collectively from neediness and poverty" (Labrie, 2005, p.5). All that was needed was a temporary ceiling on the wealth of the richest fifth of the population, whose income continued to rise, while the income of the poor stagnated, but did not actually fall.

For their part, Léo-Paul Lauzon and his team (2005) exposed the other fiscal imbalance, that of the tax burden, brought about by lowering corporate taxes. In 1964 the share of Quebec's tax revenues borne by individuals stood at 62%. As of 2004 it stood at 88%. The lower corporate share is explained mainly by the fact that more than half of them pay no taxes at all. A modest tax on corporate revenues would allow for a more equitable distribution of wealth and adequate funding for public services.

Education is increasingly being affected by social problems, especially in poor areas. The demands being made of schools continue to grow. Children bring to school their own difficulties and misfortunes, whether exposure to violence, discrimination or poverty. These are societal problems that should be tackled by society as a whole. We must resist, in Antoine Baby's words, "saddling the school with the entire responsibility for saving those whose lives have been shipwrecked and who, by the time they reach schools, are already on a leaky lifeboat" (2005, p.12).

Any policies intended to make education more democratic must be part of a total package of anti-poverty policies: policies on employment, income security, redistribution of wealth, public housing and urban planning.

Growing Diversity and Pluralism

One direct consequence of globalization has been to expose more people to very different cultural experiences. Even in Western societies, pluralism and ethno-cultural diversity have risen constantly, largely as a result of a greater diversity of immigration. People from a wide range of backgrounds are interacting more and more everywhere.

Societies and their educational systems have a double duty: (i) to encourage their citizens to be open to this pluralism, and (ii) to do more to integrate immigrants. There is no ideal integration model, no magic formula. Nations have taken different approaches to pluralism. The French republican model hasn't worked, judging by the suburban "uprisings" of Fall 2005. As for British multiculturalism, it had already hit the skids with the dramatic events of 9/11 and it was badly shaken by the London bombings of July 2005, essentially the work of British citizens.

As for Quebec, it has long seen itself as a society of "French Canadians." The world consisted of "us" and "them." Although we should acknowledge that there has been much progress, changes in cultural identity occur very slowly. It is not unusual to hear experts, politicians, journalists and many others limiting the term "Québécois" to people of francophone stock. At the same time, the passionate reaction against the wearing of Islamic headdress in school, at a time when schools themselves were still denominational, did not show much logical coherence.

In both Quebec and the rest of Canada, demographic projections anticipate a big increase in immigration in the coming years. One Canadian study (Bélanger & Malenfant, 2005) estimates that, between 2001 and 2017, the growth of the immigrant population will be somewhere between 24% and 65% and that almost 85% of this growth will be accounted for by visible minorities. In comparison, the non-immigrant population is expected to rise between four and 12%.

It is estimated that by 2017 the proportion of immigrants in the total Canadian population will be comparable to what it was at the time of the great population movements of the early 20th century. Big cities will be affected most. In Montreal, the proportion of visible minorities is expected to reach 19%, compared to 13% in 2001, while in Toronto it is expected to exceed 50%.

Quebec has already announced that it intends to accept significantly more immigrants than the average levels of the 1990s. It is not hard to imagine the challenge for the Montreal region, which takes in three quarters of all Quebec immigrants and where immigrants already accounted for 28% of the population in 2001. It would be a challenge for all the other regions too, given the intent to spread immigrant settlement out more[7], and for Quebec's population as a whole living in a far more pluralistic society. Judging from how things are now and despite a largely positive record, Quebec society and its schools still have a long way to go in their acceptance of diversity, integration and equality.

Any policies intended to make education more democratic must be part of a total package of anti-poverty policies: policies on employment, income security, redistribution of wealth, public housing and urban planning.

Indeed a certain chill regarding immigration can now be observed in Quebec. A CROP poll for the magazine *L'actualité* (March, 2005) showed that 55% of the population was against the idea that "to counter the effects of the drop in the birth rate on the Quebec economy, the government should accept far more immigrants that it does at present." Only 38% approved of this proposal. Even in the very white, very francophone region of Quebec City, where immigrants account for only 3.3% of the population, one person in five, according to another poll, felt that this was already too much.

As for economic integration, Quebec was, according to the 2001 census, the province where the difference between the unemployment rates for white and black people was highest (7.8% and 17.1% respectively), even though the average level of education among black people was higher. More than one immigrant in four was living below the poverty line (almost twice the average for the whole population), and for visible minorities, the rate reached 40%. Skin colour has a negative impact on how immigrants are viewed and the attitudes that they encounter[8].

Generally speaking, visible minorities are not well-represented. They are almost absent from the National Assembly; they are under-represented (or totally absent) in the media[9], and they are rarely seen in commercial advertising. The civil service, for its part, includes only 2.5% of its staff from "cultural communities."

Being a young immigrant is often synonymous with being poor, bordering on destitute. The usual indicators of school success are quite gloomy. Most of them fail and fewer of them graduate with diplomas either in secondary school or in the cégeps.

The situation is even worse for black youth. After seven years of secondary school, only 51.8% graduated with a diploma as compared to 69% of the total population (McAndrew, 2006). Only 14.7% of black youth entering the first year of secondary school in the mid-1990s went on to graduate with a college diploma, as compared with 29.7% of the total population and 26.2% of students of immigrant backgrounds generally[10]. On the island of Montreal, 55% of schoolchildren from black communities live in disadvantaged neighbourhoods as compared with 30% of the total population. This is a major issue. It calls for a genuine policy on racial equality.

One can imagine the challenges yet to come. Every year, over 30,000 immigrants will settle in Montreal, and one fifth of them will be under 14. Already more than half of the public school population of the island of Montreal is made up of students from immigrant backgrounds[11].

Even so, we should recognize that important steps have already been taken. The French Language Charter has defined one of the determinants of a common civic framework. The secularization of schools and their governing structures in 1997 and the subsequent decision to end the historical privileges of Catholics and Protestants with respect to religious education are measures that will help to improve integration in school.

But more has to be done. Publicly subsidized private schools are left untouched by secularization. The concentration of immigrant schoolchildren in schools located in poor neighbourhoods does not help with an educational policy of inclusion. Finally, the integration of adult immigrants means more than improving their command of French.

Ethno-cultural diversity and pluralism in values and lifestyles can enrich the education of schoolchildren by opening their minds to diverse cultural horizons. But they can also accentuate prejudice and social exclusion. That is why social and educational policies that support integration and interethnic harmony, two factors that contribute to educational success, are so important.

The democratic ideal is based on an equal respect for all citizens, openness to diversity, the protection of fundamental rights and freedoms, and the effort to find effective solutions to the problems encountered by means of debate and cooperation.

There are two pre-conditions for living harmoniously according to this ideal: a shared political culture and the peaceful co-existence of differing lifestyles. The first of these pre-supposes the acceptance of democratically defined norms and rules and the will to be integrated in society as a fully-fledged citizen. The Quebec philosopher Charles Taylor has put it strikingly: just as we shouldn't always be saying "*that's just the way things are here*," nor should we always avoid saying that sometimes things should be "*like that*". The second condition enjoins the host society to respect its own rules, to take into account its own diversity and to integrate this into the totality of its social institutions, while paying special attention to groups suffering from discrimination and exclusion.

These conditions should serve as a guide to educational policies. All education is the education of a given society and that society is the one in which everyone should be invited to integrate. In order to live together, it is all the more important that students learn together, in a setting most closely reflecting the image of the surrounding society.

Research leaves no doubt about this: an ethnic mosaic in the school encourages peaceful coexistence and dialogue while segregation or separation encourages withdrawal into distinct communities. The State should be doing everything possible to avoid such segregation. Secular schooling has a responsibility to show students the basic distinction between universal knowledge and personal belief.

In addition, we cannot overlook the gap between the legally recognized status and the daily reality of native peoples. Aboriginal peoples have special rights as the first occupants of the land. They embody the first historic instance of pluralism in Quebec society. Nevertheless, their living conditions are far too often deplorable. While the challenges they face may be first and foremost their own concern, they do also involve the entire population of Quebec.

Quebec is home to about 70,000 native people belonging to eleven different nations. Apart from the 10,000 Inuit who run their own school boards in line with municipal legislation and under the same tax laws as the rest of Quebec, native affairs come under the Federal government through the Indian Act. Even so, from the 1970s on, these communities have gradually been taking over the management of their schools.

Overall, research has shown that the native population is significantly behind in school, the secondary school graduation rate is often under 10%, and access to higher education is very low. According to the Federal government, improvement is needed in the quality, accessibility and relevance of school programs, in the effectiveness of school systems, and in collaborative efforts. Socio-economic factors, the after-effects of residential schools, the huge diversity of the communities, and their geographical remoteness are all elements that make this mission difficult. They confront the enormous challenge of trying to reconcile tradition and modernity and to ensure the survival of their heritage and culture, while still emphasizing the need to develop fluency in one of the two official languages of Canada and a broader perspective of the world.

But all the youth of Quebec should be made aware of the history, culture, reality and rights of native peoples. It is by no means obvious that the contents of the new Quebec Education Program will succeed in doing this[12].

Greater Demands of Democratic Citizenship

The core function of public education is not to serve families or the business world. From its very beginning, it has been about citizenship, a collective effort in the service of the common good. This function means that all students, indeed all citizens, must be able to acquire the fundamental knowledge and skills necessary to be good citizens. Everyone agrees today that such needs are continually increasing and argue for both a broadening and an improvement of basic education.

In the course of the last few years, the balance between maintaining this citizenship function in the school and the function of selecting and sorting has been lost. Competition is imposed from the beginning of school and actually works against the chances of the majority. We must find a new balance between the objective of individual development and integration for all and the objective of getting students ready for entry into a hierarchical workplace.

More and more educators now think that competition and selection should be put off until the end of compulsory education. This is not to deny differences, but to put off their effect, so that all children learn first to be citizens.

As the U.S. philosopher Michael Walzer has pointed out, there is no royal road to citizenship, no way to get more of it or to get it more quickly, by doing better than others at school. We must not be content with offering all students an equal opportunity to learn to read. They must all succeed. At the same time, you cannot expect everyone to become a literary critic or a doctor. For all to succeed, the principle of corrective justice applies; in the second case, the principle of meritocratic justice.

The determination to teach all students the essentials of democratic citizenship is rooted in the conviction that all students are capable of learning. This affirmation of educability must extend to the way in which schools are organized and resourced. Not that all students are identical, but we must guard against the tendency to attribute to nature differences that are attributable to social factors.

The establishment of this core belief is important both to ensure school justice and to encourage school integration. Rooted in a culture of curiosity and pleasure in learning, this belief could help reverse the tendency to consider education above all as an instrumental good rather than as a good in itself.

François Dubet and Marie Duru-Bellat believe that a common curriculum of at least nine years is needed to cover the requirements of the future life of young people, to take on the evolving uncertainties of the world, to give a whole generation a set of common reference points, and to lay the foundation of social cohesion and a capacity for living together. In their view, this combines an economic necessity, a civic imperative, and an ethical commitment.

We could add that this will raise the academic level too. Studies based on international measures of student achievement support this: countries with undifferentiated school systems, aiming to provide all students with the tools needed to be a good citizen are those which obtain the best academic results and combine these with being the most egalitarian.

For comparative study, school systems were divided into three types. Integrated systems, mainly represented by the Scandinavian countries, have common schools and mixed-ability classrooms for the duration of compulsory education. At the other extreme are differentiated systems that stream students early (sometimes even ten-year-olds) and also segregate schools by ability; this is the case of Germany and Austria. Between these two extremes are systems that have a common structure but stream by program as in France and Quebec.

In a report for the French Ministry of Education, Marie Duru-Bellat and her colleagues have concluded that it "seems fairly clear that the overall organization of school systems correlates with their degree of equity" (2004, p.4). Streaming during compulsory education and the segregation of schools by ability both increase school inequality without any offsetting improvement in the performance of the elite.

Another study aiming to evaluate the specific effects of the structure of school systems, taking into account the relative wealth of each country and the extent of social inequality, comes to the same conclusions. The type of school structure has a direct influence on school performance and the integrated systems come out on top (Dupriez & Dumay, 2005).

International comparisons have made a small country like Finland into an apparent educational paradise. The media have flocked to this new Holy Land of school success where the highest average levels of attainment have been reached along with lowest level of inequality. Germany, on the other hand, is identified as having low average attainment and very pronounced inequalities.

Of course, we need to bear in mind that the admittedly homogeneous Finnish system also has the special distinction of being attended by young Finns who think of reading as their main hobby, and of valuing highly both education and those who dispense it. But this does not take away from the fact that their choice of an integrated school system in the 1970s produced very positive results; and, contrary to the usual refrain, there was no dumbing down to the lowest common denominator.

Unfortunately, Quebec has proposed maintaining a common education only to the end of Year 2 of secondary school (Grade 8 in English Canada) and has allowed selective streams to multiply, thereby abandoning that democratic trend. The introduction of numerous tracks at the end of the Year 2, including a one-year program leading to semi-skilled employment, does not augur well for equalizing opportunity[13].

Aside from the fact that a citizenship-based approach to basic education would lead to greater equality, it could also favour fairer social reproduction by weakening the link between access to the most highly valued programs (leading to the best paid jobs) and any particular social background. Since social reproduction seems inevitable, let us at least make it as obvious and as just as possible, to cite the U.S. philosopher Amy Gutmann.

Only when students have come to the end of the common curriculum should the educational structure adapt to the different abilities and interests of the students and emphasize preparation for the workplace, even while still striving to equalize opportunities. This is a political choice that inevitably entails consequences for teaching and school organization. In the first instance the government has a responsibility to do what is needed to maximize educational opportunity for all future citizens.

A New Deal for Education

As we struggle to achieve greater equality, to accommodate increasing diversity and to meet the ever increasing demands of citizenship, we need an educational structure and an approach to teaching that promotes the mixing of social groupings, ethnic backgrounds and abilities throughout the compulsory years. Obviously such a mix is desirable for integration, since access to full citizenship is quickly lost in a segregated school system, but it is equally effective in achieving academic success.

To be truly democratic, public policies must ensure that the highest number possible attains what our society agrees to be an acceptable educational minimum, i.e. a secondary school diploma, and that youth and adults alike achieve a higher level of schooling. A total package of educational and social reforms is needed to achieve this and they must be a priority.

This means a New Deal for education in Quebec. As with the social policies adopted after the Great Depression of the 1930s, educational policies must place school justice and equality back on the agenda.

ENDING SCHOOL APARTHEID

The notion of school apartheid has surfaced in recent years to expose the ethnic and social segregation affecting the educational systems in many countries. Education in Quebec offers a pretty good illustration of this problem. Ethno-religious schools are financed by public funds. The selective nature of private secondary schools and the proliferation of selective programs in public schools have come about as schools in poor districts are charged with taking in "all the wretched of the earth" and carrying more than their share of the "educational burden."

Practically speaking, basic education is being separated from the democratization we strive to attain. The least favourable school settings are the fate of children of poverty while the wealthier ones benefit from better teaching and learning conditions. As François Dubet has put it, the more a student has a background of privilege, the better the chances of becoming a good student, and the more a student is successful, the more likely is an offer of a high quality education.

Numerous research studies on school mix show that the influence of the SES of others in the school is a determinant of achievement, and that the weakest students are the ones most sensitive to school setting. The Anglo-Saxon world speaks of the effect that school mix and class mix have on achievement. According to researchers in the Harvard Civil Rights Project, the experience of diversity has beneficial long-term and short-term effects on students; attendance at a less segregated school can even succeed in breaking the poverty cycle (Orfield & Lee, 2005).

Other U.S. researchers, using longitudinal studies, have concluded that the average SES level of students in a school has as much influence on performance of individuals as their own SES. In elementary schools, an analysis of NAEP results shows that low-SES students who attend schools where fewer than half of the students are from the same background do better than mid-range SES students who attend a school where 75% of their peers are low-SES. The researchers conclude that the social composition of a school is one of the factors that correlates best with student achievement and that socio-economic integration in the school is the best way to reduce inequality and improve success (Rumberger and Palardy, 2005).

Canadian studies, based on international test results, also conclude that student performance is affected by the dominant SES in the school attended and that this effect is magnified for students of poor backgrounds (Bussière, 2004; McMullen, 2005). The same effect has been observed on the island of Montreal.

To sum up, the higher the proportion of children from privileged backgrounds in a school, the better the results of the whole student body, and the children from poor backgrounds gain most. On the other hand, the higher the proportion of the poor, the lower the results; this situation is explained by the fact that expectations are lowest in schools in poor neighborhoods, the demands of the courses taught are lower, and the level of insecurity is higher.

These are not new findings. This was one of the conclusions of the monumental research study in the Coleman Report, published in the U.S. in 1966 and showing the importance of students' peers on success rates[14]. Being in school with children of wealthier backgrounds and higher academic aspirations was the factor that did most to influence school achievement by black students. These results indicated clearly that school composition was a critical element for equal opportunity; they served as an argument in favour of busing, something we shall return to below.

The common good must reclaim its lost ground in the face of the neo-liberal educational agenda, which extols the virtue of freedom of choice. Education is a public good and it is the State's responsibility to set the benchmarks for educational justice. As we are reminded by the philosopher Michael Walzer, "limits placed on a few are necessary for the freedom of the majority" (1997, p. 154); in this way, we can aim to prevent the most powerful from becoming all-powerful in the name of liberty.

Education is indispensable for the development of society as a whole. It is the responsibility of all citizens and not only of the parents who set their hearts on the education of their own children. While you can opt out of public school education, you cannot opt out of a collective responsibility for public education[15].

The rules will have to be clear if we want everyone to join this common effort. To quote Daniel Weinstock's image, nobody will agree to abandon the weapons of early competition until everyone lays down their arms at the same time. This multilateral disarmament will not be easy. But it is related to social needs and curriculum quality.

We must contest school segregation, which has gathered momentum with increasing private school enrolment, and the concomitant development of streaming initiatives in the public sector. Three things can be done in the short term: a stop to state funding of private schools, greater limits on school choice, and destreaming.

Genuinely Private Education

The choice of private education is a parental right. But this right in no way obliges public authorities to fund it. That is the crux of the debate that has been under way in Quebec ever since the Parent report which stipulated that "the mere fact of opening a private school does not in and of itself confer the right to receive State subsidies, either for the school itself or for the parents who send their children there" (paragraph 357). Neither Ontario nor the U.S. spends a cent of public money on private schools[16].

The reasons for choosing a private school vary. Some maintain that the quality of education is higher[17], some are looking for stricter discipline, some prefer a more homogeneous social mix, etc. Some parents even make huge financial sacrifices, so certain are they that their children's future depends on it.

To defend public funding, it is argued that parents choosing private education are doubly taxed. In opposition to this argument, others insist that people who choose to drink water other than the water provided by municipal services must bear the cost and that public funds should be reserved for public services. It can also be pointed out that people who have no children pay no less of a contribution to the costs of public education.

The choice of private education is a parental right. But this right in no way obliges public authorities to fund it.

In early 2005, two things happened that put this question back on the agenda. First came the decision to increase the funding of Jewish schools from 60% to 100%, which caused such an outcry that the Charest government had to back off. But it raised public awareness of the special situation of ethno-religious schools. Secondly, the Coalition for the Defense and Advocacy of Public Education (*Regroupement pour la defense et la promotion de l'école publique*) put out a statement calling for the phasing out of the public funding of private schools and this too sparked off a great debate.

The *Globe and Mail* newspaper editorialized that "Quebec's approach contrasts sharply with that of Ontario, where a party that announced a tax credit of $3,500 a child toward private-school tuition was defeated by a party that pledged to cancel the credit". The *Globe* concluded that "if Quebec's objective is greater integration, the government should encourage more students to swell the public system and stop subsidizing the private schools, particularly the sectarian ones" (January 21, p. A12).

For the first time in many years, editorials and columnists in Quebec agreed that the current situation could not continue. Some argued for an immediate end to all public funding for private elementary and religious schools. Others wanted to integrate private schools further into the public system, as advocated by the journalist Michel Venne. According to Venne, it would be preferable "to insist on open admission requirements, the retention of students with special needs, French education for immigrants, and closer collaboration with local public school boards. And all this according to one principle: same grants, same rules" (*Le Devoir*, December 13, 2004, p. A7).

Such a recommendation is not inconsistent with the earlier one made by the Coalition above. In fact, an end to the public funding of private schools along with a process for integrating students and teachers into the public sector would have to be phased in. During this transition, private schools would have a tough choice: accept public requirements, such as those proposed by Venne, or lose public funding.

Two experiments are worth mentioning. In the early 1960s, Quebec went from a school system where private schools played an important role—notably in the form of *collèges classiques*—to a genuinely public education system. Volume IV of the Parent report laid out the course to follow. Private schools willing to sign an agreement with the State could receive funding on the same basis as State schools; at the same time, they would be expected to admit all pupils without distinction, they could not charge additional fees, and they would have to guarantee the same employment conditions as the public system. "Behaving otherwise," wrote the commissioners, "would amount to having the State funding its own competition and undermining public education" (paragraph 370). As for private elementary schools, they were receiving no public funds at that time and the Commission recommended that this should continue to be the case.

Changes now under way in Spain are equally enlightening. Educational authorities must now guarantee an equitable distribution of children with special needs among the various schools, public and private, along with equal admission criteria. Publicly funded private schools will also have to retain all admitted pupils until the end of compulsory education; they will not be allowed to discriminate on the basis of religion, ethnic origin, or sex and cannot receive funding from associations or private households. A public school representative must be on every private school council as an advocate for integration and as a monitor of compliance with the new regulations.

Quebec could follow suit, as long as the change would be phased in. A first step could be the cessation of all public funding to ethno-religious schools[18], since they do not conform to government policy either on integration or on the development of democratic citizenship; secular schooling must be the rule in all institutions supported by public grants. As for private elementary schools, there ought to be a rapid return to the situation before the 1960s, when they had no access to public funds.

The integration process in secondary schools could be phased in over several years so that schools could make adjustments and choose the model that works best for them. Even so, the State could immediately require all schools entering into funding agreements to admit all pupils without discrimination or selection and to comply with the rules on compulsory school attendance. This would lay the foundation for comprehensive schooling later within a framework designed to serve the public good.

The private school lobby has already made its position known. The withdrawal of public funding, it says, would lead to the closing of virtually all such existing schools and would cost the State a fortune. This is not the opinion of public school organizations, which estimate that the State would actually save about $75 million. A study by researchers at UQAM, which estimated possible fluctuations in private school enrolments in Quebec based on the experience of provinces across Canada, concluded that the demand for private education would not be affected as severely by tuition increases as the private school advocates are claiming; and the State could save anywhere between $75 million and $200 million.

Of course, there will always be some differences in the way costs and savings are calculated, but what we are talking about here has more to do with principles and democracy than money. Private schools do not serve the public good, and for this reason they cannot justify public funding. So the issue is how to come up with an integration model that will allow the desired changes to occur.

Constraints on Freedom

Residential areas form a patchwork of social and educational inequalities. While urban planning and social housing policies can have some effect on such inequalities, it is still the case that school policies do have a part to play in reducing the consequences of these patterns. A case in point: we know that many Canadian parents consider the local school when choosing where to live.

School policies must aim at reducing the gaps among schools. This means questioning any measure that could exacerbate inequality, as is the case with free school choice. In many other countries, public school choice is limited by statute. This can involve anything from hard-edged school districts to busing, with room for the occasional relaxation of admission limits along the way.

Let's begin with the situation in the U.S., where busing was introduced with a political determination rarely encountered elsewhere. In 1954, the Supreme Court was asked to rule on the case of a black youngster, Linda Brown, who had been refused admission to a white-only school. The Court decided that the separate education of white and black children was unconstitutional; children denied admission could acquire a sense of inferiority from which they would never recover[19]. The famous dictum of "separate but equal," which had always dominated education in the Southern States, was thrown out.

But change came at a snail's pace. The Civil Rights legislation of 1964 demanded a research study on equality of opportunity. The upshot was that James Coleman and his colleagues published a report which, as we have already stated, marked a turning-point in education. *The Equality of Educational Opportunity Report* showed that black students were more successful in schools where they studied alongside white students, and there were no adverse effects on the latter.

These findings weighed heavily in court decisions over the ensuing years. Given the high degree of residential segregation in many large cities, the Supreme Court required integration plans to be put into effect. To ensure the desired racial balance, school boards had to redraw the boundaries of school districts and implement voluntary or compulsory busing of students to other school districts.

In some cases, the Supreme Court actually imposed the integration plan. In the spring of 1974, for example, the Boston Judge Arthur Garrity decided that all schools should reflect the proportion of blacks and whites of the city as a whole, a ratio of 1:2. Race thus became the major factor in the assignment of pupils to schools. Busing created huge tensions. One of the consequences was white flight to the suburbs.

It was not until 1991 that the Court reversed the integration requirement by encouraging admission by school district, on the grounds that such a policy could not be seen as intentionally discriminating. Since that time, an intensification of school segregation in the U.S. has been noted.

This thumbnail history is cited only because, even in as liberal a society as the U.S., the State had been able to impose limits in the choice of school for reasons related to public policy. Thus, the strug-gle against racial segregation and the desire to improve success rates among black youth served as the justification, at one time, for policies which put powerful constraints on individual liberties.

In Europe, a majority of the countries still maintain hard-edged school districts and these regulations are found to keep the extent of inequality down. Where no such controls exist, there is pressure to review free choice policies. As a case in point, the Belgian sociologist Marcel Crahay believes in the necessity of taking back "the right of parents to school choice in order to put the brakes on the spontane-ous gravitation towards sociological consanguinity" (2000, p. 397). His fellow Belgian Nico Hirtt agrees that students should be as-signed to schools.

Others, without going so far as to advocate busing, propose various ways to broaden the social mix: redrawing school district boundaries, huge investments to make schools in disadvantaged areas more at-tractive, and so on. In the latter view, rather than banning flight to the suburbs, a better choice is to give families a reason to stay.

In Quebec, even if, as a result of the Public Education Act, parents can choose their child's school, the choice is limited by language and religion. Until the adoption of the French Language Charter in 1977, one could study in English or French and, until the end of the denom-inational school system in 1997, one could choose between Catholic, Protestant and non-denominational schools. Quebec society would not think of going back to those times, even if the mentioned reforms interfered with the freedom of school choice that is being praised to the skies these days.

But Quebec will have to place even more stringent limits on the freedom to attend the public school of one's choice. The State has a responsibility to ensure that public schools strive for equality and in-tegration. Freedom of choice accentuates the situation where strug-gling students and students from immigrant backgrounds are con-centrated in certain schools.[20] This "segregated schooling" is on the increase. As we have seen, many studies show that free choice encour-ages the avoidance of schools where there are many students strug-gling, from immigrant backgrounds or from visible minorities. This only makes the chances of academic success more remote as well as making compulsory French education tougher.

In this sense, section 240 of the Education Act, which allows for se-lective "schools dedicated to a specific project," should be abrogated or changed to allow only those schools consistent with a national char-acter. The law should stipulate that school districts be drawn to en-sure the greatest social and ethnic diversity possible, so that all public schools can take their share of the responsibility for the education of children with special needs or from immigrant backgrounds.

Reaching this goal will involve locally imposed limits on parental choice, and for this purpose, school boards should be given the power to impose them.

Mixed-ability Classes

A good social mix is not only desirable in the school as a whole, it is also important in the classroom. The make-up of a class has an effect on social and pedagogical interactions, teaching activities, social climate, and even socialization. What sort of class groupings should we consider, when we are taking the interests of the whole student body into account during the years of compulsory school attendance? Marie Duru-Bellat summarizes research on this issue: "Overall, the examination of scholarly achievement across a whole age group shows that the most effective approach involves mixed-ability classes" (2002, p. 140). Such classes maximize progress among the weaker students without adversely affecting the progress of the better ones. On the other hand, segregation broadens the gap. The result is that those who have less get less.

Generally speaking, it was shown that the weaker students gain from being in a mixed class while streamed classes often put them on a downward spiral to failure, since the climate is so non-conducive to learning. A class made up of weak students is subject to more interruptions and more frequent discipline interventions, with the result that learning time is reduced.

Classes streamed by ability accentuate learning disparities, generate inequalities in treatment and status, and extend the gap along socio-economic, cultural and ethnic lines. Labeling students has consequences for their attitude and their self-esteem as well as for teacher expectations. Research in Britain and the U.S. has even shown that the concentration of students with a low predisposition towards schooling in poor classes leads to the emergence of sub-cultures of opposition that pave the road to social exclusion.

On the other hand, research has shown that the better students lose little or nothing at all by attending mixed-ability classes. "The hypothesis that streaming is beneficial for good students has collapsed," concludes Marcel Crahay. "In other words, good students do not suffer from being together with average or weak students" (2000, p. 302). There is no "Robin Hood effect": a mixed-ability class does not take from the rich to give to the poor.

Some countries do encourage mixed classes, while others prefer streaming. In international studies of student performance, mixed classes trump streamed classes. For example, analysis of reading research concludes that the elite does not suffer from mixed ability grouping while weak students benefit from it; on the other hand, in countries that favour streaming by ability, the percentage of poor readers is generally higher than the international average. A culture of integration is particularly helpful for the weaker students.

In Quebec, the situation is, to say the least, paradoxical. On the one hand, the Education Act encourages the integration of students with special needs into regular classes. On the other hand, selective classes for the best students are mushrooming, even in the elementary grades. The devolution to school councils of responsibilities such as the allocation of time spent on different subjects is a contributing factor. Claude Lessard (2006) recalls the usual requirements for participation in such selective projects: students must be performing above average, have demonstrated exemplary behaviour and, in some case, the parents have to bear a financial cost that may be considerable[21].

To illustrate this, here is a very real situation in a medium-sized secondary school. There are nine classes in Year 1 (Grade 7). At the request of the parents, there are two enriched English classes, an arts studies program, a sports studies program, and a program in international studies. These options are open only to students experiencing no difficulty in school. That leaves four so-called regular classes, already made up of weaker students by a process of elimination, and these are the ones that must integrate students with learning difficulties.

So those students who need the most favourable learning conditions are placed in the most difficult school settings. A few randomly collected comments used to describe the students sent to the so-called regular classes now stripped of their good students are a good indication of the injuries inflicted by this practice; they are called classes of "dummies", "slugs", "pukes", "bums". The assignment of teachers to enriched classes is a bone of contention among the staff, since teaching conditions vary enormously from class to class.

However, there are many teachers and parents who do not accept the research results that favour mixed classes. It seems like just plain common sense to group students with similar abilities together to get the benefits of teaching at their level. At the same time, they feel that mixed classes would hold back the good students and that having weak students present would cause major headaches.

A Canada-wide survey has shown that mixed-ability groupings rank third among the problems identified by teachers. This indicates that the vital expedient of de-streaming during the years of compulsory school attendance will have to be accompanied by improvements in teaching conditions and educational support, especially in difficult districts.

The State has a duty to indicate that mixed classes are a priority. That is a political decision motivated by principles of solidarity, consideration for others and the mixing of different students. And so the Public Education Act could specify that until the third year of secondary school, classes must be open to all students, except for students with really special needs that can only be met in a separate class. Themed projects must be open to all without selection based on performance[22].

These mixed classes will need to receive resources in line with their ambitions. The development of enrichment activities on the one hand and booster activities on the other must be a priority. A pedagogy based on cooperative principles, particularly on student collaboration, has long ago proven its worth; you learn best when you are teaching others.

FULL STEAM AHEAD TO SUCCESS

Providing a quality basic education, backed up by a diploma, for the totality of the student population is an aim that should be the foundation on which the entire education system rests. Now it is precisely on this point that the Quebec school system is still failing with respect to a hard core of students — more than one in four. So everything is pointing to the need to take action during early childhood, to take the necessary steps to help the most vulnerable students succeed, to champion schools with strong links to their communities, and to guarantee the professional autonomy so vital to teachers.

In education, there is no technology available to prolong school life expectancy. Nor are there any miracle drugs to cure the suffering that comes from failure. Even so, the problems are no less flagrant; young people who miss out on education will pay for this for the rest of their lives. Education is a profoundly human activity in which only human beings can come to the rescue. And we must be investing in those human beings for the future of our children, all our children.

The State has a duty to indicate that mixed classes are a priority. That is a political decision motivated by principles of solidarity, consideration for others and the mixing of different students.

Coddling the Little Ones

Early intervention and prevention are among the most effective strategies in education. Numerous international studies show the positive outcomes of action during early childhood. Significant improvements in academic achievement and reductions in juvenile delinquency are generally noticeable among children who had the benefit of early interventions, mainly quality childcare, a range of assistance programs and a solid kindergarten education.

While these observations hold true for all children, there is all the more justification for them for children from poor backgrounds. Indeed research has shown that absent such interventions poor children are far less prepared for school than their more affluent peers. This is even more so when these children belong to minority groups who have to learn the language of instruction before learning anything else.

From an international perspective again, here are two models for the provision of early childhood education. One emphasizes childcare until the age of five or six, while the other emphasizes kindergarten education. The former engenders problems of coordination when educational services come under several ministries; the tendency then is to move towards better integration under the aegis of the Ministry of Education. This has been happening mainly in Sweden, Spain, England and Scotland. On the other hand, France, Italy and Belgium have opted for the second model by extending kindergarten and nursery school education down to children as young as three. In some cases, kindergarten is obligatory from the age of five.

In Quebec, childcare legislation sets out the intention to provide all children with a quality setting to advance their cognitive and socio-affective development and prepare them to cope with the later demands of school. The huge rush to take advantage of these services gives ample proof of their relevance. But when they were evaluated some murky areas began to emerge.

Thanks to the Longitudinal Study of Child Development in Quebec, we know that daycare attendance rates increase as children get older[23], but that there are significant differences according to backgrounds. While 89% of the children of affluence attend daycare, this was true of only 54% of the children of poverty.

In addition, compared with the children of the well off, children of the underprivileged were more likely to be receiving a lower quality of daycare. This low-quality daycare is increasingly a feature of private for-profit centres. So the children who need quality daycare the most are the ones least likely to get it.

According to this longitudinal study, the prevailing approach based on universality runs the risk of worsening the gap between rich and poor. We should instead be improving interventions among the most vulnerable children, from poor and immigrant backgrounds, and making every effort to increase their participation rate in quality daycare.[24]

Targeted and varied interventions are also required for these children from littlest infancy. Home visits for children in the 0-4 age range, pre-natal and post-natal support for mothers, educational and recreational activities on public holidays and during vacations would help, judging from the experience in Ontario, to reduce hyperactive behaviour and low-attention span, while at the same time improving children's health and attitude to school.

The recent extension of full-time kindergarten to all five-year-olds has also been a huge success. Today, almost every child in this age group is enrolled. There needs to be an evaluation of the significance of compulsory kindergarten for five-year-olds, with a view to introducing reading there; the situation has changed enormously as daycare attendance has become more and more widespread. The results of an important longitudinal study in the U.S. argue for this, particularly for youngsters from poor backgrounds; the positive effects of learning to read at five could well last for the rest of their time in school.

As for four-year-olds, kindergarten programs have been maintained in disadvantaged areas, but there is much to be said for developing them further. They should be provided on a full-time basis for children of poverty and immigrant backgrounds, rather than on the current half-day basis. This is needed to achieve the long-proclaimed target of equality of opportunity.

Finally, there needs to be much better coordination between child-care services and kindergarten education. It is time to think of following a trend in many other developed countries by giving responsibility for all these services to a Ministry of Education and Childhood.

Increasing Assistance to Groups at Risk

Distributing students more equitably among schools and among classes, coupled with early intervention, will not be enough to bring about the equality, integration and social justice we are looking for. A range of sustained interventions is required to improve the situation for the most vulnerable groups, mainly those of immigrant and poor backgrounds.

Where boys are concerned, there is much to be said for paying more attention to their place in school. For the time being, it's important to remember that all interventions have to occur in a co-educational setting and aim to reduce sexual stereotyping. It is the latter that helps explain not only the achievement gap between girls and boys but also the later persistence of sexual discrimination against women in the workplace. Policies to improve reading are going in the right direction, but not practices that group students by sex.

Where schools in disadvantaged neighbourhoods are concerned, several western countries have adopted policies designed to reduce inequality. The *Title I* program in the U.S. and the designation of educational priority zones in France, Belgium and Britain, all call for a cluster of measures from extra educational resources to smaller class sizes, including free meals programs.

These policies obviously give rise to much debate. Criticism centres on the stigma created by the designation of difficult areas, something that encourages flight to schools in other areas, and on the predominantly charitable nature of some policies that consign the fundamental problem of poverty to the shadows. There are cases where a broader perspective has been advocated so that these policies are integrated into the larger struggle against poverty and exclusion. In other cases, the preference has been to refocus the educational mission of the school.

In Quebec, "inner-city" school policies took off in the mid seventies with Opération Renouveau (school renewal). They have been the object of periodic evaluations that did not always confirm the perceptions of their communities. Gilles Roy and Marc-André Deniger (2003) conducted an excellent overview that is critical of these policies. They conclude by calling for programs not to be scattered across too many schools, for early interventions at both elementary and secondary levels, for better in-service training programs, and for the allocation of adequate funding.

Currently, the Supporting Montreal Schools Program, with an annual budget of $12 million, targets a hundred or so elementary schools. The intervention strategy called *New Approaches, New Solutions (NANS)* has received $125 million for the period 2002-2007 for nearly two hundred secondary schools in Quebec. It has been extended to nearly 600 elementary schools and 70 more secondary schools till 2009 with an annual budget of $44 million.

The two programs have many features in common: interventions tailored to specific communities in order to promote academic achievement, improved relations with parents and the community, professional development and additional teacher positions. It is up to each school to adapt its success plan to include the most appropriate measures and, for Montreal schools, to include a program giving access to cultural resources.

These programs are currently being evaluated, but we should expect difficulties in isolating the variables concerned, given the extent of the changes under way as a result of the present reform. Even so we can conclude from past experience that such measures as the allocation of extra positions to meet special needs will have to be put in place permanently.

As for lowering class sizes, the results of numerous research studies have led to the adoption of such policies in different countries. One example is the U.S., where a federal program costing over $1 billion aims to reduce class size in Grades 1-3 for schools in poor neighbourhoods. Similar policies have been put into effect in the Netherlands, Britain and Ontario.

In support of such measures, the commonly cited references are two major longitudinal studies in the U.S. The STAR project (the Tennessee Student/Teacher Achievement Ratio) was a large-scale experimental K-3 study from 1985 onward that compared the results obtained by students in small classes (13-15 range) with those in larger classes (22-25). Significantly higher results were observed in the smaller classes, especially for students of minority and poor backgrounds. Worthy of note was the observation that STAR students were maintaining their advance five years after the experiment.

The same conclusion was reached by the Wisconsin SAGE project (Student Achievement Guarantee in Education) in the late 1990s, among elementary students (K-3) in disadvantaged areas. An improvement rate of about 25% was observed in these groups, and this improvement was particularly pronounced among young black students.

A report commissioned in 2001 by the Haut conseil de l'évaluation de l'école in France supports the results of these earlier studies and a study under way in Britain is coming to the same conclusions. In France, the economist Thomas Piketty has shown that a reduction in class size has a far greater effect on students from poor backgrounds than on others. His conclusion is that a drop in class size in low-SES areas would lead to a substantial reduction in the inequality of educational opportunities.

A lower class size leads to an increase in the time spent in teaching (an improvement from 80% to 86% in the SAGE project), facilitates instructional strategies better suited to a diverse student population and improves attention levels among struggling students. It is also easier to maintain discipline and an atmosphere conducive to learning. Such a policy seems all the more necessary as classes become more heterogeneous.

In Quebec, sustained intervention from the earliest primary grades is now the consensus. The gradual reduction of the number of students per class to a maximum of 20 for K-3 levels in schools in disadvantaged areas[25] is a step in this direction. If the above research is anything to go by, a reduction in K-3 class size to a maximum of 15 in disadvantaged areas could improve educational opportunity, and for relatively little cost.

On top of this, data from the study conducted by L'Institut de la statistique du Québec among young people reveal the efforts needed outside school in the fight against poverty. Food insecurity is a big problem for 20-30% of youth in poor families; significant numbers of children report that they never eat before going to school in the morning. This raises once more the whole issue of food policies in school.

At this time, compensation is coming from charities and the private sector; in 2004, the Club des petits déjeuners du Québec (Quebec Breakfast Club) served almost two million snacks in 183 elementary schools. In a letter to the editor of *Le Devoir* (April 5, 2006), the Chair of the Montreal School Board (CSDM), Diane de Courcy, was critical of the shortfalls in grants and called upon the government to invest in such programs. Should we not be expanding free lunch programs in poor neighbourhoods, as is done in the U.S. and a handful of schools in Quebec? In Finland, this policy is extended to the whole school population.

The Institut de la statistique study also reports that almost 40% of 16-year-olds who have jobs while still attending school say that they are doing this to help out their parents and to pay for essential school supplies. An improvement of the situation for low-income families could help reduce young people's working hours, which beyond a certain threshold can have negative impacts on achievement.

Moreover, more often than not, schools in disadvantaged areas are also the ones with the highest attendance of students from immigrant backgrounds. This tendency is likely to become more pronounced in the coming years. Along with the attention demanded by the dramatic academic situation affecting some groups and the interventions that they necessitate, there are three special challenges that arise for students of immigrant backgrounds throughout most western school systems: reception and learning the common language, the status of heritage languages, and the acknowledgement of cultural diversity in school programs and practices.

The responses to these challenges vary and are profoundly affected by history and the relationships each society has had with immigration. One of Quebec's specialists in this field, Marie McAndrew (2001), has produced an excellent synthesis using a comparative approach to highlight the many debates looming on the horizon.

Britain favours an approach where students are integrated into regular classes and ESL specialists work in tandem with classroom teachers. In secondary schools, special classes are used only for under-educated students. In English Canada, integration with partial withdrawal in small groups for language support is the preferred model. In some cases, the use of the heritage language is encouraged as a support for the learning of English, as too are buddying with an older student of the same mother tongue and bilingual volunteers as monitors, etc.

In the U.S., given the high concentrations of Spanish speakers and their historic relationship with English speakers, there has been a longstanding preference for bilingual education with gradually increasing emphasis on English, so as not to delay learning in other subject areas. A 1997 study by the U.S. National Research Council concluded that what was actually being done was more important than the choice of model. A structured program aiming to achieve a systematic acquisition of the school language, the recognition and use of the student's home language in the early stages, and maximum integration with English-speaking peers all had things in their favour.

So there is no magic formula. All models are affected by the tension between the need to give special attention to learning the common language and the need to ensure the highest level of integration possible.

In the early 1970s, Quebec stood out by opting for second-language Welcoming Classes with specialist teachers; seen in an international context, this model was the exception to the rule. It was only where immigrant population was small that students were integrated into regular classrooms with French language support.

The success of the Welcoming Class model and the satisfaction that has met it do much to explain opposition to a Ministry pilot program looking to broaden the range of approaches. There is also a fear that the resources now allocated specifically to welcoming programs will disappear, as has been the case in jurisdictions that opted for more rapid integration into regular classes. There need to be successful pilots and an assurance that adequate resources will be maintained if Quebec is to adapt to other FSL models.

This said, it is still necessary to keep providing services better suited to the reality of immigrant students coming into the school system with significant delays in basic education or even illiterate in their home language. Special approaches are called for along with special resources.

Along with this, the Programme d'enseignement des langues d'origine (PELO — "heritage language program") was created in 1977, based on research showing that mastery of the home language was helpful in learning the host language and in creating a sense of belonging to the school community. Despite a relatively broad consensus as to its benefits, its status is marginal, since PELO is thought of as an extra-curricular activity, before or after school hours. And yet, in a context of globalization, this linguistic diversity is an asset that Quebec should be learning to turn to its advantage, and in schools too.

Finally, the treatment of ethno-cultural diversity is still a hot topic. Despite the expressed intent to improve the representation of certain ethnic groups in different employment sectors, progress is occurring at a snail's pace. On the curriculum side, the content of the new curriculum and the textbooks accompanying it will have to be analyzed and improved to take this diversity into account, by including such areas as the history of immigration, the relationship between immigration policies and the exploitation of poor countries, and the mechanisms of discrimination and racism. Even if "citizenship and community life" make up one of the five broad areas of learning, there is nothing to show that the integration of diversity will be the result.

Just as policies for education in low-SES areas should be part of a broader approach to the struggle against poverty, so too an effective integration policy for young immigrants should be accompanied by social policies specifically aimed at improving adult FSL and working against discrimination.

Supports, not Repeats

Educational debates in recent years have exposed the extent to which support for special needs students has been a priority for teachers and parents. This concern is in stark contrast to the controversy over the rethinking of official grade repetition policies. They deserve renewed attention, given that research has conclusively shown the ineffectiveness, to say the least, of grade repetition as a way of helping failing students.

If the evidence suggests that supports and not repeat grades are the way to go, then the necessary supports had better be available.

Internationally speaking, the first point is that the use of grade repetition varies enormously from country to country. In France, 20% of the students entering secondary schools have already repeated a grade, with the proportions varying from 5% for children of executives to 42% for the children of unskilled workers (Duru-Bellat, 2003). Levels in Scandinavian countries, on the other hand, where grade repetition is supposed to be prohibited by law, are lower than 5%.

Next, when we compare, on the basis of student achievement, the countries that still practice grade repetition and those that have dropped it, the results clearly come down on the side of the "abolitionists." Countries with school systems as different as Ireland, the United Kingdom, Denmark and Norway are in the latter category, while Germany, Italy, France and the Netherlands are in the former one[26]. Automatic grade promotion is therefore not synonymous with dumbing down to the lowest common denominator.

Finally, the results of a hundred or so studies spanning several decades all agree, at the very least for elementary grades: comparisons of failing students who repeat and others who move up confirm that grade repetition has hardly any corrective effect while the negative impacts on learning are indisputable (Crahay, 2004).

For many researchers, the evidence against grade repetition is overwhelming. For students, the experience amounts to a painful ordeal as they are brutally cut off from their friends. Some researchers have no hesitation in characterizing the practice as "harmful," in describing a repeated year as a lost year, and in pointing out that cases of "recovery" are in a minority. In the U.S., the National Association of School Psychologists has even issued a position statement denouncing its ineffectiveness.

Despite all this, surveys have revealed that there are educators and parents who remain convinced of its usefulness. Grade repetition, it is believed, will allow students who have fallen behind to master the skills needed to proceed to the next grade or to develop the necessary maturity. At the same time it is believed that this sword of Damocles hanging over students' heads will provide the motivation needed for greater effort.

If the evidence suggests that supports and not repeat grades are the way to go, then the necessary supports had better be available.

In this context, it is hardly surprising that policies aiming to stamp out grade repetition have generally failed. The experience in Belgium and France has been instructive in this respect. In Belgium, the ban on grade repetition between the first and second years of secondary education was reviewed in 2001, following teacher protests. In France, grade repetition, which was supposedly authorized only for key elementary grades (roughly speaking grades 3 and 6), has become possible for every grade, even though this approach is discredited by researchers, educational unions, and parents alike.

In Quebec, the Ministry's policy banning grade repetition has been perceived as a short-sighted expedient mainly inspired by the prospect of quick savings on the backs of the poorest people once more. A Ministry study in the early 90s did actually estimate the annual cost of grade repetition at around $150 million for elementary schools and $350 million for secondary schools. Although the government has been backing off under pressure from communities, the issue is still a hot one.

More than 20% of the students entering secondary school were a grade or more behind in 2003-2004. It was shown that these students were four times more likely to drop out than the rest of the school population. Grade repetition has a stronger effect on children living in straitened circumstances. Children repeating grades have far lower self-esteem and fewer than half of them envisage the possibility of any post-secondary education.

The effectiveness of grade repetition is largely discredited, but simply abolishing it is not the solution. While repetition correlates with difficulties in school, it is not their cause. Those difficulties are just not being remedied by making students repeat a grade. But the difficulties do have to be tackled.

For that to happen, the complexity and weight of teacher's workloads must be taken into account. The proportion of students identified with developmental or learning disabilities has risen continuously in recent years and more and more of them are being integrated into regular classes.[27]

The identification of student disabilities and the guaranteed provision of appropriate services are definitely on the agenda these days. A preliminary study for the Ministère de l'Éducation, du Loisir et du Sport (MELS), carried out by seven research professors at UQAM, concluded that support services were inadequate and that waiting times to get into them were unacceptable[28]. There will need to be an evaluation of the impact of the additional resources that have recently been allocated over a three-year period to increase the numbers of teachers, professionals and support staff, in order to see how effectively they will help meet the needs of students in difficulty.

To sum up, going beyond research results, it is not mainly a question of arguing for or against grade repetition, but of finding the policies most likely to make it unnecessary. There is an urgent need for the development and implementation of effective policies of preventive intervention and support for students with special needs.

School and Community Together

The development of sustained relationships between the school, the parents and the community at large will remain on the list of priorities, especially in schools serving poor communities and those that include a high proportion of children of immigrant backgrounds. The vast majority of parents do attach importance to the success of their child in school. But in the words of Bernard Charlot and his colleagues, there is a gap between "what they know and experience and what they are hoping to achieve" (1992, p.114).

The students who have greatest difficulty are very often those who don't have access to people able to help them with their schoolwork in their immediate surroundings. Where immigrant parents are concerned, a poor command of French is an obvious handicap; their level of integration into Quebec society is part of it. This is why well-structured homework and parenting programs, along with FSL instruction and interpretation services, are still as important as ever.

But we must stop thinking of poor families only as problem cases. The school must adapt to its surroundings and it would have a lot to gain from turning to community resources already in place and from developing relationships of trust and collaboration. A sustained effort to get more representative participation and involvement on school councils, including parents of immigrant backgrounds particularly, could help achieve that.

This is the fundamental meaning of "school and community together." It is not enough for the school to put on a bunch of after-school activities. The school's contributions should also be linked to those of other institutions and of the community at large to reduce the inequalities and injustices affecting poor neighbourhoods.

This approach is quite different from one that favours rationalizing the provision of social services and bringing them together under the school roof. And the government plan for regional and municipal autonomy does have the appearance of sharing the misery around. Of course, neighbourhoods have every interest in pooling their recreational and cultural resources and in making them as accessible as possible. According to a Canadian survey in 1994, 60% of the children aged four to 11 years from very poor family backgrounds had never taken part in organized sports (as opposed to 28% from affluent backgrounds); the high cost of such activities and the lack of recreational facilities in poor neighbourhoods were the main reasons given by way of explanation.

Other studies, from the U.S. this time, showed that having a public library close to home has a direct bearing on how often the library is used and that this is a good way to reduce loss of learning during the summer holidays. There is actually evidence that the gap between students of poverty and students of affluence widens in summer.

A survey by Quebec Ministry of Culture and Communication published in the fall of 2005 revealed that reading is on the wane among young people and that it drops steeply as soon as they leave school. In 1979, 60% of those in the 15-24 age group used to read regularly as opposed to 54% in 2004. The numbers of regular readers and heavy readers have both fallen off significantly. Another survey, this one nationwide, confirms the importance of adequately resourced school libraries (Coish, 2005). It concludes that larger collections, greater funding, and better access to qualified librarians all correlate with better school results. The recent decision of the Quebec government to invest $40 million over three years as part of an action plan to stimulate reading is a step in the right direction, but it will not be enough to provide all schools with adequate collections and services.

As for television, it has the power to dumb down every bit as much as to educate and support success in school. The most recent studies have found a negative correlation between the number of hours spent in front of the TV and school achievement. Public television barely plays an educational role any more. It has massively suffered from being left at the mercy of market forces and cuts in public investment.

The complementary role of other cultural institutions must be emphasized, in particular that of public libraries, museums, recreational organizations and educational TV, in the education of young and old alike. These institutions must be made widely accessible.

A Pedagogy of Liberation

The pedagogy of liberation has two meanings. First of these is the one given to it by the great Brazilian teacher, Paolo Freire: a pedagogy that tries to educate free beings, make them critically aware, and ready and willing to change the world. But it also refers to the liberating the work of teachers, considered as professional pedagogues and not simply drones following ministry orders and passing on the latest academic fashions.

Once again pedagogical freedom is at the centre of a controversy between traditionalists and modernists, a dispute that goes back to the beginning of the twentieth century. There is the basis here for a genuine debate, but there is little room for debate among arguments based on authority, excommunications and a crusading spirit run rampant.

Marie-Claude Blais (in Blais, Gauchet and Ottavi, 2002) describes the situation in France with a reminder of the long controversy pitting republicans against pedagogues, the supporters of the "sanctuary school" dedicated to the transmission of knowledge and the believers in a pedagogical reform based on the needs of the child. She condemns the almost caricature-like exaggeration of the issues, as knowledge and pedagogy, instruction and education are fallaciously opposed.

The same sterile dispute can be observed in Belgium where Nico Hirtt condemns the "extremists" whose almost religious adherence to a sectarian school of pedagogy is curiously matched by their allegiance to the ideal of the "republican school".

These artificial oppositions are denounced with every bit as much verve in the U.S. by the educational historian Larry Cuban. These futile battles, he writes, " between traditional and progressive ideologies (...) have, in their evangelical fervor, like the religious warfare of an earlier century, constricted the search for 'good' schools" (2005, p. 149); indeed, good schools can do very well by seeking nourishment in diversity. He goes on to remind us of the relationship between pedagogy and society. What is commonly called progressive education in the United States arose within a vast movement called the "Age of Reform," while traditionalist movements tended to dominate in conservative periods[29].

Others point out that the idea of failure proof schools recently led to the development of standardized curricula, atomized into multiple objectives followed up by fastidious testing. The proposal to teach the same thing in the same way to everybody was an effort to reproduce the factory-like efficiencies of the division of labour.

In Quebec there has also been a pitched battle. The social constructivism and competency-based pedagogy underlying the new curriculum, along with the recommendation of project method, are roundly condemned by academics insisting on the transmission of knowledge and "good" pedagogy. Some of the criticisms have the virtue of drawing attention to tangents that could threaten the basic instruction al mission of the school and the dangers inherent in top-down pedagogical reform. Others, however, cloak themselves in the virtues of "science" and advocate a conformism that could crush pedagogical spontaneity and freedom.

The analysis offered by Steve Bissonnette, Mario Richard and Clermont Gauthier is imbued with this noisome "scientism." Their goal, a laudable one when all is said and done, is "to identify the teaching methods most likely to improve the school performance of those most at risk of dropping out, namely the children of disadvantaged backgrounds" (2005, p. 1). But their use of the plural of "methods" seems superfluous, since they end up deciding that there is only one that is any good.

Apparently, this "science," invoked so reverently, tells us that the teacher is *the* factor that has the biggest impact on students' learning, an impact that is far greater than that of the family or society. Alongside this first "truth," a disputable one to say the least and indeed widely disputed, comes the corollary claiming that "the most effective measures for students from disadvantaged backgrounds are direct teaching approaches" (p. 55). Let's agree that this kind of "scientific truth" at the very least needs qualification. It places far too heavy a burden on teachers, making them solely responsible for the success or failure of the students. While we must recognize that what happens in the classroom is important for success, many other factors have to be taken into account, as we have already said.

But lo and behold, they seem to have found the magic recipe that will guarantee that all teachers can make all their students successful in all circumstances: that recipe is direct and systematic instruction[30]. This approach is said to constitute an absolute refutation of the constructivist approach, which apparently claims that "the student cannot learn through direct instruction or a teacher-centred method" (p. 78). The results of voluminous research on the question are "all" highly positive and provide proof of the superiority of direct and systematic instruction. The enviable rankings on international tests of certain Asian countries, such as Japan, only serve to confirm these findings.

But educational "science" is not so one-sided. The case of Finland can be cited in opposition, top of the class on the international tests, and where socio-constructivism has found favour[31]. We could equally point out that even in Japan from now on there will be increasing emphasis on project method, drawing topics from the students' own interests.

So qualifications are in order. For example, a recent U.S. study based on the results of the NAEP tests sought to check the relationship between various teaching methods and the scores obtained for mathematics, science and reading (Wenglinsky, 2004). Everything shows that a student-centred project method is more appropriate in math and science, while an eclectic approach seems more fruitful for reading.

Other studies point in the same direction. A longitudinal evaluation of the Direct Instruction (DI) program implemented in disadvantaged schools in Ohio concludes *grosso modo* that there are no significant differences, neither for weak students nor for strong students, between the participating schools and other comparable schools using different approaches (Ross et al., 2004). Another study, in Texas this time, concludes that it is impossible to say that an approach emphasizing basic skills is better than practices based on cognitive development; everything depends on the school's context, on grade level, and on teachers' personal belief system (Muijis et al., 2004).

In addition, it is worth recalling other critiques. In a 1991 landmark paper published in the U.S., Martin Haberman challenged what he called "the pedagogy of poverty" that he described as untouchable, based totally on what was measurable and to which all teachers were expected to submit. Recently, the journalist and essayist Jonathan Kozol condemned "military" pedagogy, forced on the poor schools in New York that had been converted into "sanctuaries" of direct instruction. This "policed" teaching, straitjacketed by a strict program, is imposed only on poor schools, and has contempt for the professional autonomy of the teaching staff.

Pedagogical research in fact does not indicate any particular method as being inherently effective or ineffective. Instead, it implies we should respect professional autonomy in the choice of ways of teach. School is made up of teachers in all their diversity, full of their convictions, and all sharing a love for children. As Claude Lessard (2006a) recalled, in the debate following his colleagues' publication of the analysis mentioned above, in the human professions there is no absolute truth. Research informs, but it cannot dictate.

Going further afield, we can say that approaches focusing on student success and mastery of basic knowledge, which use lots of positive reinforcement, which link learning to students' life experiences, and which set high but realistic expectations seem to be most likely to succeed. On the other hand, teaching that confines itself to a dumbed-down program on the grounds that this is a better fit for the imagined characteristics of children of poverty, or that discards demanding content in favour of physical activity is likely to be depriving students of access to fuller, more complex understanding. If "respecting students" means "*anything goes*", you are not respecting students, you are condemning them, as Nico Hirtt has observed.

These remarks are not meant to trash all criticism of current reforms nor to let reformers off the hook for any of the errors of their ways. For one thing, we may justifiably be worried that aberrations arising from a competency-based curriculum will simply replace the aberrations of an objectives-based curriculum, and that what we want our children to know and understand will become secondary. And project method does sometimes take on the appearance of a new dogma and some programs do impose rather than proposing.

In several countries, current curriculum reform is just part of a much broader transformation of education that is shaking up teachers' work. The Belgian Christian Maroy reviewed the literature on how teachers' work has been evolving in Europe. He found that the notion of the ideal teacher as one who teaches from constructivist principles, who accommodates student differences, who works with other teachers, and who gets involved in student life generally is running into stiff resistance.

In most places, teachers' workloads have been increased to include longer hours in school, more time in committee meetings, as well as numerous administrative chores in the name of accountability, with no accompanying increase in salary and no offsetting reduction in the teaching load. The profession is becoming more complex and more varied, the workload is becoming heavier, mainly through greater social and emotional demands. Sociologists have observed a deep sense of pain and suffering occasioned by the impossibility of carrying out the school's mission fully, something that leads to teacher burnout. This distress is described as the symptom of a certain de-skilling of the profession. This explains why many teachers are thinking of quitting altogether.

Professional autonomy is also a way to guarantee teaching that raises consciousness. This is not indoctrination, but a way of teaching consistent with the values and principles that undergird democracy.

Some of these observations apply to Quebec. Such were the findings of a study by the Fédération des syndicats de l'enseignement (FSE-CSQ) that tracked the implementation of the Ministry reform. While teachers generally seemed well-disposed and willing and, in elementary schools especially, did see the advantages of a more dynamic approach to teaching and a curriculum that they found more stimulating, they also said they lacked the time, the training and the means to engage in it. They felt that their expertise was not always recognized and that what they did was being dictated to them, with the result that they ended up expressing doubts about the kind of ideal school that seems to have inspired the reforms.

This distress and these new requirements are the key to why many teachers are thinking of leaving the profession and why so many are suffering from burnout. This analysis could be extended to the other school professionals among whom there has also been an alarming rise in psychological stress and exhaustion[32].

Moreover, the learning of liberty calls for rooting curriculum content in an ideal, in a democratic project. Education passes on a sense of tradition and prepares for the future. It serves the goals of emancipation, community development and social change. We agree with Nico Hirtt that its job is not to reproduce a world of inequalities, ecological threats to our planet, or starving peoples.

On the contrary, basic education should provide the weapons of knowledge to everyone, enabling them to understand the world in all its complexity, equipping them with the competencies to help them work to change it, making citizens for a more just and genuinely democratic world. The goal is to educate for a future everyone wants, for a shared vision of humanity.

Professional autonomy is also a way to guarantee teaching that raises consciousness. This is not indoctrination, but a way of teaching consistent with the values and principles that undergird democracy. On this subject, the CSQ's curriculum materials designed primarily for the Green Brundtland Schools (GBS)[33] are really valuable.

Education is liberation. The practice of teaching and the content of the curriculum must be thought through, discussed, and clarified, but they cannot be imposed without making nonsense of the professional autonomy so critical to their success.

STAYING IN SCHOOL LONGER

The numerous changes accompanying the current round of global-ization argue for keeping more students in school for more time, so as to prepare them for the demands of a more developed citizenship and a labour market experiencing radical changes.

In this context, several States have set themselves ambitious goals for school completion rates. This is true in France with its goal of an 80% success rate for the "Bac" (secondary school graduation exams). For Europe overall, the goal is that by 2010 at least 80% of the popula-tion between 25 and 59 would have completed senior grades in second-ary school and that the drop-out rate would have fallen below 9%.

In Quebec, the goals set in 1997 are just as ambitious. By 2010, the aim was for 85% of all students to graduate with a secondary school diploma before the age of twenty, 60% with a cégep diploma and 30% with a university degree. As this deadline approaches, the situation does not look very hopeful. The secondary graduation rate by the age of twenty was down 1.4 percentage points in 2006-2007 (to 71.9%) compared with 1995-1996 while admission to cégeps had dropped slightly, even though cégep graduation rates were holding steady at around 40%.

There is also room for improvement in higher education. In 2002, the graduation rate for university degrees stood at 27.7%, which was 4.8 points lower than the average for OECD countries. However, it should be noted that female students have already surpassed the goal.

But improving school completion should not lead us to neglect es-sential professional qualifications. The goal is not to get a complete generation of youth into university. "Diploma inflation," to translate the term used by Marie Dubu-Bellat, does not necessarily pave the road to social justice.

Whatever the case, while it is true that a diploma does not neces-sarily guarantee a job, it is becoming more and more vital in order to avoid being shut out. In particular, it can still provide good protec-tion against unemployment. Thus, as educational attainment rises, unemployment falls. In 2004, unemployment was over 15% for work-ers with no secondary school diploma but under 6% for those with a university degree.

L'Institut de la statistique du Québec has published studies con-firming the fact that jobs for people with low qualifications are be-coming rarer while the opposite tendency can be observed for highly skilled jobs. Thus, between 1990 and 2004, people without a secondary school diploma were affected most by a 36% drop in jobs; on the other hand, jobs requiring higher educational qualifications were showing a healthy growth rate, reaching 82.3% for university graduates.

Over at StatsCan, a study reports that from 1981 to 2001 employment had skyrocketed in high knowledge sectors (84%), more than twice the rate for low knowledge sectors (32%). This is easily explained by the massive relocation of industrial jobs and the increase in service sector jobs.

There is then no doubt that, if we are going to maintain our commitment to the goal of emancipation and the development of Quebec society, an improvement in school participation is vital. We must work to raise the status of vocational and technical training, improve access to post-secondary education, and provide a wide range of continuing education programs.

Occupational and Technical Training

Models of pre-service career training vary a great deal from society to society. They can be summed up as belonging to three distinct types: those where general education plays the dominant role, those that accentuate occupational training, and those that emphasize on-the-job apprenticeships. The third model is usually the one with the highest youth intake, often following a highly inegalitarian form of streaming. By way of contrast, models focusing on initial vocational training, without close links between education and work, as was historically the case in Quebec, attract few students into career training programs later.

In fact, each system is rooted in specific historical, institutional, economic and social conditions. There is no ready-made model to be found by seeking out experiences elsewhere, only general trends worth considering inasmuch as they affect Quebec society.

These days, most reforms are trying to cut down on overlapping among training programs and to clarify qualification standards. At the same time, there has been an observable increase, at least for OECD countries, in partnerships with the private sector, closer ties between education and the workplace, and approaches focusing more sharply on the demands of the labour market. Moreover, the clear division that once existed between preliminary education in a school setting and continuing education in the workplace is now breaking down.

There is no shortage of critics emphasizing the dangers of company-sponsored training schemes that prepare narrowly specialized individuals who have difficulty coping with the inevitable job transfers that come later. On the contrary, more stress should be put on the importance of training multiple, transferable skills, and lifelong learning, chiefly in a world where work seems to be organized less and less along Taylorist lines.

In Quebec, policy-making in recent years has been marked by the desire to improve the relationships between schools and workplaces, to streamline transitions between education levels, and to provide a general education that paves the way to lifelong learning. Even so, despite numerous campaigns to improve the status of vocational and technical training, the results never measure up to expectations. More than one third of the students are leaving school without any kind of professional qualification; 35% receive a Diploma of Vocational Studies or a Diploma of College Studies (technical program), compared with 45% on average in OECD countries.

A 2004 MELS survey of more than 7,000 senior high school students revealed that nothing much had changed over the previous ten years. Young people perceive those of their peers who choose a secondary school vocational program as hating school and wanting to get out of it and into the workforce. The jobs in question are thought of as low-status, dirty and physically demanding, even if they offer good employment possibilities. So it is not surprising if only a few young people think of taking a vocational program. Mostly, the ones who do are students way behind in their schooling or getting poor grades and whose parents have a low educational background. The better a student is doing in school, the more likely he or she will be expected to go to university.

The conclusions in Christian Payeur's study of this question in the early 1990s are just as valid today. "Vocational training," he wrote, "is a dead-end stream entered more as a result of poor grades than of any enlightened career choice" (1991, p.57). Secondary school vocational training is still just as unattractive to young people.

Even so, some improvements are noticeable. For one thing, efforts to improve perceptions have apparently worked with parents and employers. Also, the number of young people under twenty enrolled in vocational training programs has gone up as a proportion of the total secondary school cohort, from 12.8% in 1994-1995 to 16.6% in 2002-2003.

In its annual report for 2003-2004, the Conseil supérieur de l'éducation (CSE) has brought out an excellent analysis titled *CareerTtraining: Promoting the value of all paths*. In practice, according to the CSE, high school career training does not match the needs of young people; concurrent training programs (general education and vocational studies taken simultaneously) after grade 9 and workplace apprenticeship programs under the supervision of an experienced worker have no appeal for them. Programs alternating in-school and on-the-job training, are more popular, but they suffer from a lack of stable funding and there are problems finding enough work placements.

In fact, vocational education mainly caters to adults and high school graduates now. Indeed, many students in the 20-24 age bracket go back to school after a spell of varying length in the workforce, either to learn a trade or to change careers. Two thirds of the youth in such programs have a secondary school diploma and 14% of them have attended a cégep. The fact that there is no longer any general education after entrance to the program and the existence of a separate diploma only reinforces the idea, according to the CSE, that it is a dead end; only 2% of those with a Diploma of Vocational Studies ever get into a cégep.

Among CSE's proposals for improving the situation, we can endorse the one to restore a general education component in vocational training, so as to keep up necessary communication skills and improve the prospects of long-term career development. Next, there needs to be an improvement in pedagogical support and supervision — guidance services in particular — as well as a consolidation of career exploration in grades 10 and 11 (secondary 4 and 5). As for articulation between secondary school and cégeps, the CSE recommends the coordination of the sequence of competencies in preparation for lifelong learning.

But we must also face up to facts. The talk of improving the image of vocational training is condemned to remain purely symbolic as long as the jobs these programs lead to are unattractive. Improving the image of vocational training means also improving the jobs that follow.

Youth perceptions of technical training are much more favourable. According to the Ministry study mentioned earlier, young people believe that such training does lead to a paying job and gives a variety of job options, and that you have to be good in mathematics and technology to get into them.

This is also borne out by the CSE analysis. Polytechnic education has been maintained in technical education programs, and this smoothes the way to lifelong learning. Almost one quarter of technical programs graduates are admitted to university, and in some programs the proportion climbs to 50%. Reservations expressed concern mainly the insufficient length of some programs: only 35% of young people graduate within the expected period of three years, a percentage that climbs to about 60% after five years. The report also finds that enrolments reached a plateau after 1993-94 and that there was even a slight decline after 1997-98, even though the demand for technical staff kept rising.

Among the proposals for improvement, the CSE proposed to ratchet up the length of some programs and to review the general education content in order to bring it into line with youth needs in this area. Given the regional importance of cégeps and the threats looming over several technical programs, the regional merging of programs to avoid overlapping, the development of local specializations and a better articulation between educational levels are all viewed as desirable.

In addition, especially in union circles, there is concern over the proliferation of new cégep certificates (Attestations of College Studies or AECs) and the possibility they will be open to younger students. The number of AECs has gone up from 260 in 1987 to more than 1,300 in 2003. The growth is alarming, when the cégeps who have sole responsibility for their content are embroiled in a fierce competition for students. The programs vary in length, their content being sometimes equivalent to that of technical programs, but without any general education. They are designed for adults and young people who dropped out of school a year or more earlier. Among the recommendations, there is an emphasis on improving the coordination of content, rationalizing the range of programs on offer, and including a general education component.

For both vocational and technical education, the CSE insists on the importance of career guidance, "an essential factor in students' success" (p. 9). The education system should be organized so as to help develop students' skills in making choices, testing their abilities, and eventually changing career directions.

Some countries have opted for grant schemes to support school retention and regular attendance, in order to maximize the number of students who stay in school and complete the desired job qualifications. One example is in the United Kingdom where the government brought in Education Maintenance Allowances (EMAs) of up to thirty pounds ($60) a week for young people in the 16-19 age group from low-income families, reinforced by periodic incentive bonuses of one hundred pounds ($200) for keeping on track. The student signs an EMA contract with a school or college after which the assigned sum is paid into his or her bank account. This arrangement has apparently increased school retention by 10% in poor communities.

But the preferred approach in many countries is raising the school-leaving age. For this to work, it is usually bolstered by arrangements to accommodate the needs of a diverse school population. In the U.S., 11 states have raised the age to 18 and nine others to 17. In Europe, the Netherlands, Germany and Belgium have followed suit, in some cases on a part-time basis, and Britain is looking at a similar policy. This is not universally welcomed; in Belgium, specifically, questions have arisen as to whether such a constraint has contributed to an increase in school violence.

In Canada, New Brunswick took the lead in 1999, followed by Alberta in 2001. Ontario joined in as of December 2005; young people are required to continue their education to the age of 18, either in school or in an approved apprenticeship program. Failure to observe the new Ontario law is subject to penalties running from fines to the loss of a driver's license.

Two Canadian studies have demonstrated the worth of this policy. The first, based on data from OECD countries, concluded that it could have positive outcomes, as long as secondary school programs made room for more career-related options. The second told the history of the situation in Canada from the 19th century on and showed that each change of the school leaving age led to a significant improvement in grade attainment and incomes and in the well-being of citizens throughout their lives. This confirmed findings in the U.S. and the UK.

Quebec has always lagged behind in this matter, often simply framing laws for situations that already existed. Thus it was only in 1988 that the school leaving age was raised to 16. According to the official figures, 97% of the students stay in school until that age, but the participation rate declines rapidly afterwards[34].

The Ministère de l'Éducation, du Loisir et du Sport (MELS) estimates that it would cost about $133 million a year to raise school leaving age from 16 to 18. The requirement would be waived, as it is now, for any student graduating earlier. Such a policy, according to MELS, would effectively increase enrolments in cégeps and, indirectly, improve productivity since more young people would be graduating with a secondary school diploma.

A serious evaluation of the pros and cons of such a step is needed. Historically, raising the school leaving age has been a victory for equality. But it is just as important that it not turn the school into a kind of prison for young people.

It is equally important to assess the value of awarding grants in support of extended schooling for those least able to afford it. The Comité consultatif sur l'accessibilité financière aux études (CCAFE, advisory committee on financial accessibility to education) has proposed a credit for postsecondary students of up to $3,000. It would be awarded annually for each secondary school grade passed and would be available for later use. The expansion of such a policy, along the lines adopted in Britain, would also be worth studying.

Higher Education

Besides the commercialization of research and the reconsideration of the traditional role of universities discussed in the previous chapter, along with internationalization, a subject taken up further below, the relatively low charge for higher education and its public character have given rise to debates in many parts of the world.

While there is a trend to reduce the public financing of universities and to raise tuition fees, this is far from being as widespread as some would have us believe. Despite the assault on free tuition in Britain and in some German Länder (provinces), the majority of European countries have stayed the course on almost free access to postsecondary education. This is particularly true in France, Spain, Italy, the Scandinavian countries and Ireland.

On the other hand, there are cases such as Australia, where cutbacks in public expenditures and increases in tuition fees were clearly designed to force the universities to bow to market forces and to respond to the demands of students viewed as "clients." This kind of policy could lead to the privatization of higher education and its commodification, as tuition fees come closer to covering actual costs.

In Canada, the cuts in federal transfers for education that began in the mid-1990s exerted powerful upward pressure on tuition fees. In fact, federal transfers for postsecondary education were cut by almost $5 billion in constant dollars from 1994 to 2005; in Quebec this amounted to a loss of $1.2 billion.

Between 1992 and 2002, tuition fees increase on average by 100% in constant dollars and far more for students in some programs. In Ontario, for example, tuition increases were vertiginous. In 1998, that province deregulated tuition for certain professional faculties, principally medicine, dentistry and law. The consequences were not long in coming.

A study by StatsCan, based on the National Graduates Survey and comparing the periods preceding and following the Ontario deregulation, showed a significant increase in inequality. The authors concluded that the "findings suggest that the advantages enjoyed by students of higher SES backgrounds increased during the period of deregulation" (Frenette, 2005, p. 9)[35]. The middle class bore the brunt of this impact, since those with the lowest incomes were generally able to benefit from corresponding increases in financial aid.

At the same time, StatsCan's Postsecondary Education Participation Survey showed that a third of the students who dropped out of postsecondary institutions in 2002 did so for financial reasons. From 1986 to 1998, according to the Canadian Association of University Teachers (CAUT), the gap in access to higher education widened in favour of higher-income families.

Quebec chose to improve access to higher education thanks to a tuition-free policy at the cégeps and low tuition fees at the university level and, by doing so, they have done much to support democratization. In 1961-1962, only 16% of young people got into college and only a handful of poor children could escape their fate in life. Today, 58% of the graduating age group get in and, while inequalities do still persist, they are not as glaring.

Free tuition, the journalist reminds us, loudly proclaims the truth that knowledge and culture are as vital to us as air and water, that the university is not a market commodity and that making it free expresses the desire to make it a common good, a gift of society to future generations.

From time to time, the cégep model comes under renewed fire, even though it has proved its worth, mainly for sustaining educational, cultural and economic growth in the regions. We should be working on their success and adequate funding rather than dwelling on arguments about their structure. Cégeps had to absorb cuts amounting to a quarter of their budgets between 1994 and 1998, about $260 million. The funding is just not there to help them succeed. For instance, the Explorations programs (Sessions d'Accueil et d'Intégration or SAI), in which one out of every eight students were enrolled in 2002-2003, does not have enough places. Mentorship programs, learning centres and practicum courses are all having a tough time surviving.

University tuition fees have been frozen at a little over $1,600 a year (for Quebec students) since 1994, whereas the Canadian average was reaching $4,000 in 2004. To keep its promise to maintain the freeze while increasing university revenues, the Liberal government decided to take a scythe to student grants. This decision, in the winter of 2005, triggered the longest student strike in Quebec history. In the face of massive public support for the student cause[36], the government was forced to back down. The government finally decided to lift the freeze and introduced an increase of $100 a year for the next five years (2007-2011) with an indexing policy thereafter. Only minor adjustments were made to the Student Financial Assistance program.

In *L'Annuaire du Québec 2006*, the journalist Christian Rioux gives a very nice summary of the principles involved. He specifically lashes out at the market vocabulary and the arguments of the "bean-counters" for whom free tuition is nothing more than a subsidy to the rich and high tuition fees the price individuals ought to pay for the opportunity to get rich afterwards. These are arguments advanced most particularly by the Montreal Economic Institute even if we do get pleasure from seeing this group climbing the barricades ostensibly to defend the interests of the poorest members of society[37].

Free tuition, the journalist reminds us, loudly proclaims the truth that knowledge and culture are as vital to us as air and water, that the university is not a market commodity and that making it free expresses the desire to make it a common good, a gift of society to future generations. Since the whole of society benefits from higher education, it is up to the entire citizenry to pay for it through income taxes.

Moreover, the former president of the AUCC, Robert Giroux, insists on the importance of higher education's return on investment for society. University graduates account for 15% of the Canadian population over 18, but they contribute almost 35% to the fiscal purse. In contrast, they receive only 8% of the transfer payments to individuals, that is, only half of their proportion in the population as a whole.

The finding that the children of the wealthiest families are the ones who benefit the most from inexpensive higher education serves only to underline two imperatives. The first is the need to reduce social disparities and the second is the need to improve financial assistance for students in order to sustain the participation of those of disadvantaged backgrounds. A significant rise in tuition fees would tend to appear as an insurmountable obstacle for poor youth.

The committee charged with advising the government on the issue of financial assistance recommended a series of improvements to the current arrangement. These were to raise the base amount for living expenses (indexed to only 50% of inflation over the last ten years), to reduce the mandatory parental contribution by adjusting it to the levels in effect in other provinces, to increase the amounts of first-year grants, and to bring in a postsecondary education credit scheme for those from the lowest income families. The committee equally pointed out the inequity for Quebec of federal tax measures that gave refunds to individuals on the basis of actual tuition payments. Taking all these tax measures into account, including the subsidy provided since 1998 to parents who had been investing in a registered educa-

tion savings program[38], governments were paying out as much mon
ey for education to the most affluent as they were providing through
financial assistance programs for the least affluent. The adjustments
made by the government to the Student Financial Assistance program, after the tuition fees increase, were far from an adequate response to these recommendations.

Generally speaking, the whole of the financing of higher education
needs to be rethought within the context of a rebalancing of federal
transfer payments to provinces. The current under-funding is bla-
tantly stifling postsecondary institutions and forcing them to engage
in practices that endanger the critical function of higher education.
Public authorities have a duty to provide sufficient funding to guarantee essential independence of cégeps and universities along with
their public service function.

The policies of government research-funding agencies must also be
reconsidered from this perspective, in a spirit of respect for the constitutional responsibilities of provinces. There has also been a call
for universities to adopt a code of ethics guaranteeing that private
funding will not undermine the fundamental goals of university research, i.e. the pursuit of truth and the advancement of knowledge.
The university also has an important social function, the necessity
to re-affirm its contribution to the common good and to stop giving
in into instrumental motivations.

Continuing Education

Lifelong education has become one of the slogans of what some call
the new economy. The evolution of disciplines and their role in production and innovation is encouraging governments, educational institutions and businesses to put the stress on continuing education.
Moreover, anybody lacking the required educational minimum, and
unable to adapt to the changes under way, is either excluded from the
job market or threatened with exclusion.

But the emphasis on the flexibility of labour sweeps aside much of
the broader mission of adult education. Such are the major trends visible in Europe where, to use the title of an article by Céline Mahieu
and Frédéric Moens, we are moving "from the liberation of mankind
to the liberalization of education." Now there is a shift away from offering adults a critical distance with which to understand society and
towards equipping them to respond narrowly to current changes in
our economy. Government support is now essentially directed towards
people facing the threat of exclusion. According to the two authors,

"there is no longer any question of education for personal growth, but of training or apprenticeship in order to serve" (2003, p. 53).

While that is the dominant tendency, supported notably by the OECD, it doesn't get the backing of numerous educational organizations, including UNESCO. The Hamburg Declaration, adopted at the International Conference on Adult Education in 1997, is testimony to that. Adult education is viewed there as a fundamental right that must be recognized concretely by creating the conditions to facilitate its task. It is "both a consequence of active citizenship and a condition for full participation in society" (Article 2). It should allow "people, whatever their age, [to] have an opportunity, individually and collectively, to realize their potential" (Article 9).

The same tensions between two divergent views of adult education are found in Quebec. The development of "human potential" is being progressively reduced to the development of "human capital" [39]. Customized training has become the "cash cow" of lots of institutions. School boards and cégeps are competing with one another to attract a "clientele". At the same time, less and less general education is available.

To be sure, the policy on adult education and continuing studies that the government made public in the spring of 2002 acknowledges the importance for everyone to acquire a basic education. A secondary school diploma is to be the "social benchmark." But overall, according to the Institut de Coopération pour l'Éducation des Adultes (ICEA), we are witnessing a fundamental shrinking of the idea of adult education, a "quiet regression" (Baril, 2006).

Government policy is limited in its application; it notably excludes adult education in cégeps and the universities, as well as general, cultural and scientific education. The government's responsibilities are equally limited where funding is concerned and individual learners are expected to shoulder the burden themselves for any programs outside the common curriculum of Secondary Three (Grade 9).

There is also a stated intent to confine the educational objectives to the maintenance and upgrading of manpower competencies, to the detriment of the individual right of adults to an education that fits their needs. Success would thus become synonymous with employability.

Despite this concern, the Liberal government has waived the obligation to devote 1% of the wage bill to training for almost two thirds of all businesses. In 2002, only one third of the workers in the 25-64 age bracket were involved in any training; the proportion is lower still if only the least educated are considered. So there is still not a genuine training culture in Quebec businesses.

A consensus has nevertheless emerged over the importance of recognizing prior learning and competencies at the different levels of education. On this subject, Quebec is way behind what is happening in several European countries. The costs of not recognizing prior learning and competencies are high, both for the individuals involved and society at large. According to the CSE, this is the "cornerstone" of a new economy in the education system, a "major undertaking."

This recognition takes on special significance in the context of the increasing mobility of populations, particularly of immigrants who are often the victims of a major downgrading of their educational qualifications. It is also noted that almost two thirds of all newcomers do not have mastery of the national language even though this is an essential requirement in most trades and occupations.

The proposal is to harmonize the approaches adopted by different authorities responsible for vetting credentials and issuing an official document attesting to prior competencies. The current provision of reception, orientation and job coaching services should be expanded.

In addition, we must come back to the priorities set by the Estates General on Education: literacy and basic education. These are in fact the essential pre-conditions to lifelong learning. Literacy must be understood in its broadest sense, as defined by UNESCO, i.e. education intended to fulfill the desire for social, cultural and economic advancement and which helps bring about equality.

In Quebec, according to the International Adult Literacy and Skills Survey, more than one in four adults are considered to be functionally illiterate. There is a clear relationship between literacy and employment. While almost two thirds of the employed people between 16 and 65 have reached the minimal level of functional literacy, this is true of only half of those who are unemployed.

More efforts are needed to support the wide range of organizations working in this field. In fact, beyond the more traditional programs provided by school boards, there are more than one hundred local literacy organizations who prefer an approach based on active participation, emancipation and working for social change.

Today, more than a million people in Quebec have not attained the "social benchmark" of a secondary school diploma and, of these, 600,000 have not even made it to Secondary Three (Grade 9). There will have to be financial assistance for adults who choose to pursue their studies, if we want this social benchmark to be reached by the maximum number. Today, adults enrolled in general education courses are excluded from the MELS financial assistance program; only those receiving employment insurance and employment assistance benefits qualify for support from Emploi Québec and that is for a maximum of three years.

A recent longitudinal study from StatsCan, based in part on the Survey of Labour and Income Dynamics, showed the value of a policy for the development of adult education. It begins with the observation that younger workers and better educated workers as well as women generally are the most likely to continue with their studies in adulthood and that Quebec is lagging behind Ontario, with continuing education figures lower by three to five percentage points depending on which variable is considered. However, people returning to school have seen their wages go up more than those who did not, particularly when their studies led to graduation. The annual gains for the returners went up almost 24% between 1994 and 2001, compared with only 15% of the others. The situation improves further for students who go on to obtain a postsecondary diploma.

There is every reason then for school boards, cégeps and universities to develop their adult education programs in order to promote the acquisition of the highest level of education possible. Free access to part-time cégep studies and general education courses in both secondary schools and cégeps, along with increases in tax incentives or financial assistance should also be part of a move to democratize adult education.

INTERNATIONALIZATION, COOPERATION AND SOLIDARITY

The major directions marking the internationalization of education evolved throughout the 20th century. Originally, they were strongly influenced by the movement for peace and understanding among peoples. Later the program was subjected to the imperatives of the cold war. International aid and cooperation policies nevertheless gained the upper hand in the years between 1960 and 1980, before being put on the back burner again.

Today, two main internationalization approaches may be contrasted: one is commercial, the other is based on cooperation and solidarity. The former is the preferred practice in Anglo-Saxon countries that give priority to economic considerations in the recruitment of foreign students and qualified immigrants. From the point of view of the developing countries, these commercial approaches are often part and parcel of the "brain drain."

The latter approach is dominant in Europe whose member states subscribe to objectives of mutual understanding, cultural exchanges and aid for development. They advocate a policy of openness aiming mainly at imbuing their young people with a feeling for European citizenship and respect for diversity. This reality is wonderfully illustrated in Cédric Kapisch's 2002 film *The Spanish Apartment* (*L'auberge espagnole*).

A majority of European countries (with the notable exception of England) have also adopted a policy of cooperation in their dealings with countries that are not members of the Union. And so, for the most part, foreign students benefit from free education or low tuition fees at the same rates as domestic students. Development aid is rising regularly there (except in Germany). The five countries that have reached the target 0.7% of GDP set by the United Nations for development aid are all in Europe.

This is the approach preferred by UNESCO for whom internationalization "should lead to the mutual enrichment of peoples throughout the world through the promotion of sustainable development, democratic progress, respect for fundamental human rights, stronger social cohesion and a culture of peace" (quoted by CSE, 2005, p. 79).

At an international colloquium called *Universities and Globalization* (Fall 2002), Gilles Breton, the then-director of the international office at l'Université Laval, argued for establishing the worldwide regulation of higher education based on more equitable access and new kinds of relationships. In particular he recommended building a common global space in the academic world founded on the notion of the common good and as part of a project for sustainable human development.

This is the perspective adopted by Canada's institutions of higher learning, at least on paper. In this spirit, the *AUCC Statement on Internationalization and Canadian Universities* (1995) recommends to universities and colleges that they share "their expertise and resources with other people who require them to realize their own legitimate aspirations ...[and that they] contribute to these countries' efforts to find their own paths to development."

There is a need to link internationalization closely with cooperation, rather than with competition and neo-liberal globalization. This means favouring approaches based on learning exchange rather than on a kind of neocolonialism.

Unfortunately, since 1988, the record shows that the foreign students attending Canadian universities increasingly come from the more affluent families. In 2004, 33% of them indicated that they came from an affluent family, as opposed to 27% in 1999 and 24% in 1988. Despite the higher SES intake, half of the international students still indicated, in 2004, that they had encountered financial difficulties during their education. The majority said that they had to depend in large measure on their own resources or those of their families.

Generally speaking, studies and declarations about the internationalization of education refer only to higher education. But the ideas about both curriculum content and student mobility in this field would profitably be extended to cover the whole of the education system and the general educational objectives adopted by the international community. International cooperation and solidarity should be the focal points of discussion.

This is, in part, the vision underlying the Quebec strategy on the internationalization of education adopted in 2002. It took its inspiration from the two dominant currents: mutual understanding and commerce. The parts on education and training as well as on the free movement of ideas and people come under the first rubric, while the part on exporting expertise comes under the second. The existence of Éducation internationale, the school board services cooperative, and of Cégep international attests to the seriousness paid to these questions at all levels of education.

The education system as a whole is mainly concerned with the internationalization of content, with the effort to modify the curriculum at the different levels to include, in addition to the learning of modern languages, knowledge, skills and attitudes that improve our understanding of the world and the state of the planet, that respect cultural diversity and that prepare the younger generation to become full participants in the changing world.

This is the mission accepted by Quebec's ninety or so international education schools in the public sector both at the elementary and secondary level. Not the least of the paradoxes in all this is the fact that these programs are reserved for high performing students alone, thus running counter to the declared efforts to foster respect for the other and the acceptance of difference amongst all students. Such programs would only really make a significant contribution if they were open to all students.

Where universities are concerned, the creation of joint programs and international networking are a big plus. In a recent opinion sent to the minister, the CSE recalled the advantages of recruiting foreign students; this will soften the effects of declining enrolment, increase the recruitment of top students, internationalize education and improve the image of Quebec abroad. But the issues of higher tuition fees, exemptions and links with immigration policy are central to the debates.

Today, Quebec universities charge higher tuition fees to foreign students, about $9,000 a year, but these fees are still lower than the average cost per student. At the same time, exemption agreements with a number of countries mean that only 40% of foreign students pay these higher fees. Should Quebec ask foreign students to pay the same tuition fees that it charges to its domestic students? We are far from reaching consensus on this. There is agreement, even so, that merit should be the basis for admitting candidates and that financial assistance should be improved so that young foreigners of modest circumstances can come to Quebec universities.

Finally, in order to avoid "brain drain," a clear code of conduct should be put in place with the goal of encouraging students to return to their country of origin. Granting joint degrees with foreign university partners and travel grants in aid of upgrading for graduates educated overseas are ways to encourage this movement back and forth.

The international mobility of Quebec students is hard to evaluate. All the same, everything suggests that the proportion of Quebec students studying abroad is far lower than it is for students in other countries. The bursary programs for short-term study (under four months) are considered insufficient and the fear of excessive debt puts a brake on mobility. Assistance levels must be sufficient to ensure that such experiences are not the exclusive right of wealthy students.

From another point of view, there is a need to link international-ization closely with cooperation, rather than with competition and neo-liberal globalization. This means favouring approaches based on learning exchange rather than on a kind of neocolonialism. The goal should be to contribute to the development of institutions so-cially relevant to the South and to objectives based on respect for the right to education.

The affirmation of this right is not new. It appears in the Univer-sal Declaration of Human Rights and in various international agree-ments. The recognition of this fundamental social right was the ba-sis for the program called Education For All (EFA) whose objectives were re-affirmed at the World Forum on Education held in Dakar in the year 2000. It also explains why education is included in the Mil-lennium Development Goals adopted by the United Nations.

These various commitments notably include ensuring that "all boys and girls complete a full course of primary schooling", the elimination of "gender disparity … at all levels [of education] by 2015"[40], as well as cutting in half the illiteracy rate of 1990. The World Forum affirmed that "no countries seriously committed to education for all will be thwarted in their achievement of this goal by a lack of resources."

As we passed the halfway point towards the target dates, it is now estimated that, unless there is a significant change in direction, these will not be reached. The resources and facilities have just not been forthcoming. Teachers are not adequately trained and classes are too large. To reach the objectives set for 2015, according to Oxfam Inter-national, aid for basic education would have to rise from $1.5 billion a year to $5.6 billion.

The situation is similar for the commitments made by heads of state at the Summits of the Americas. We are still long way from the targets set for 2010 of a 100% completion rate for primary schooling, of a 75% rate of entry into secondary education and the elimination of illiteracy.

Development aid is not up to the level of the needs. The wealthy countries today are contributing only half the amount for develop-ment aid (as a percentage of GDP) that they were contributing in the 1960s. Canada was only contributing 0.34% of its GDP for aid pur-poses in 2005, and 35% of that was in the form of linked aid, tied to the purchase of Canadian goods and services. If the trend of re-cent years continues, the 0.7% goal will not have been reached before 2025. There is also the pressing question of debt forgiveness. Poor countries have, since 2003, disbursed $39 billion in debt repayments while receiving only $27 billion in aid. Over that period, staggering sums have been spent on military expenditures.

Internationalization based on cooperation and solidarity supposes that the wealthy countries will be devoting sufficient efforts and resources to guarantee education for all, an urgent democratic need. It also invites us to ensure that knowledge becomes a common good dedicated to the equitable development of humanity, to put that knowledge to work for the right of every human being to live in dignity, and to avoid any deepening of the gap in higher education participation and in the production of knowledge between the countries of the North and those of the South.

Notes

1. On the question of the common good in French, see the Spring 2004 issue of *Éthique publique* on the theme "What's left of the common good?"

2. Dropping out in this context means interrupting studies during the year in question. This is not the same as non-graduation. The rate was 36.6% for schools in the bottom 20% of the disadvantage index and 19.6% for schools in the top 20%. The average across Quebec stood at 27.2%

3. The repeat-grade gap between the rate in the most disadvantaged schools and that in the most advantaged was between 34.2% and 14.5% for boys, and between 26.8% and 8.4% for girls. As for graduation rates, they stood respectively at 58.3% and 74.4% for the boys, and at 72.1% and 85.5% for the girls. This indicator refers to the number of students graduating with a secondary school diploma as a percentage of the total enrolments in Year Five of Secondary School in a given year.

4. The situation is even more dramatic in the Montreal School Board where 53% of the children live in poverty as opposed to 35% on average for the island as a whole.

5. Was, till 2007, Director of the Centre de formation sur l'enseignement en milieux défavorisés, Université du Québec à Montréal (A training centre for teaching in disadvantaged areas).

6. Collectif pour un Québec sans pauvreté.

7. For the regions, many schools will depend on such a demographic trend for their survival.

8. According to an IPSOS-Reid poll conducted on the International Day for the Elimination of Racial Discrimination, one out of every six adults in Canada had personally been the victims of racism and 15% of Quebecers were hostile to the idea of welcoming people of another "race" as neighbours.

9. We should acknowledge as an exception the show *Pure laine*, broadcast on Télé-Québec in 2006.

10. By students of immigrant backgrounds, we mean students born abroad or with one or both parents born abroad.

11. 17% of the total were foreign-born, and 33% were born in Quebec with either or both parents born abroad.

12. A 2002 cross-Canada study by the Coalition for the Advancement of Aboriginal Studies revealed that very few young Canadians had access to an adequate curriculum and that they knew very little about First Nations.

13. In doing this, the Quebec government has rejected a proposal of the Estates General of Education, even though the Working Group on Curriculum Reform had also picked up on it. The proposal was for a common curriculum extending over nine years and a maximization of secondary school graduation for young and adults alike.

14. The scope of this research study means that it is still one of the most important pieces of social science research in the history of the USA. It covered almost 600,000 students, 60,000 teachers in more than 3,000 schools.

15. David Labaree uses the catchy slogan "fight rather than flight."

16. There are, however, some tax credits for private schools tuitions in the U.S.

17. When you compare the results of students in the public and private systems in France, you find that "the raw differences in success rates disappear once you control for the totality of social and familial characteristics of the students(...)" (Tavan, 2004, p. 41). The same is found in Canada based on a comparison of students' scores on the PISA tests: the results are similar, once the social differences between the two populations is taken into account.

18. There are currently thirty or so such schools in Montreal enrolling 10,000 pupils from the Jewish, Greek, Armenian and Moslem communities.

19. This decision is known as *Brown vs. Board of Education*.

20. Currently, more than 60% of the students from immigrant backgrounds attend schools that have an enrolment of minority students in excess of 50%.

21. On this matter, the TV show *La Facture*, broadcast on Radio-Canada on January 17, 2006, instanced special programs in elementary schools with parental contributions varying between $1,500 and $2,500.

22. In a memorandum entitled *Les projets pédagogiques particuliers au secondaire : diversifier en toute équité*, the CSE recommended opening these projects to all students and abandoning selection procedures so as to meet the needs of all students. It also underlined the negative impact that the proliferation of selective projects had on the weakest students. Neither MELS nor the school boards have followed these recommendations.

23. From 42% at age 1.5, it rises to roughly 75% for 3.5 and 4-year-olds, and reaches 81% at kindergarten age (see Japel, Tremblay and Côté, 2005). In the fall of 2003, 67% of the children ranging in age from 6 months to 5 years were in daycare programs.

24. The Harper government's decision to provide grants directly to parents is not going to make a difference here, any more than the steps taken by the Charest government that aim to encourage the use of private daycares and the privatization of daycare generally.

25. Compared to maximum hovering between 22 and 24 by level in other schools.

26. For the whole picture, see the special feature in *Le Monde de l'Éducation* (October 2005), pp. 25-43.

27. The proportion of these students rose from 13.2% in 2002-2003 to 14.7% in 2004-2005. Integration has been proceeding rapidly since the early 1990s: in 2004-2005 the integration rate had reached 80% in elementary schools and 44% in secondary schools.

28. See Marie Allard, "Un système coûteux et très peu efficace," in *La Presse* (19 March 2006) pp. A3-A4.

29. As was the case with the National Defense Education Act in 1958 and the publication of *A Nation at Risk* under the Reagan administration.

30. This teacher-centred pedagogy includes three steps: the teacher presents something to be learnt, the learner practices under supervision and then the learner practices alone. It relies on the fragmentation of programmed learning into short sequences. The model called Direct Instruction is one of its more developed forms.

31. On this subject, see *La Presse* of March 2, 2005 and the journal *Cahiers pédagogiques* (issue 432, April 2005) which allowed teachers to speak for themselves, along with French and Finnish students.

32. This is revealed in survey conducted by Angelo Soares at UQAM with more than 1,800 education professionals at school boards. According to the title of this study, they have *Le travail dans la peau, mais l'âme maganée*, i.e. they are, roughly speaking, "crazy about their work, but worked to death."

33. Particular mention should be made of *S'investir dans nos communautés... en citoyens du monde* (a French variant of "Think globally, act locally") which proposes opening a window on the world in a spirit of solidarity and engagement, *Tirer le diable par la queue*, which deals with poverty in Quebec and elsewhere, and *La Terre dans votre assiette* which raises young people's awareness of North-South relations and tackles the whole issue of responsible consumption.

34. The participation rate stood at 86% for 17-year-olds and at 77.2% for 18-year-olds. The normal age for graduation with a DES (secondary school diploma) is 17.

35. This is our own translation of the French version. Interestingly, the English version tones this finding down: "The findings suggest that enrolment patterns by socioeconomic background changed substantially in Ontario, where tuition fee increases were largest." The inference is the same, but the sense of injustice is less evident.

36. According to a Léger marketing survey in January 2004, 57% of the people in Quebec were in favour freezing tuition fees, while 35% favoured their indexation.

37. The same arguments were voiced by the World Bank in its questioning of public funding for higher education within the framework of structural adjustment policies.

38. According to the Survey of Approaches to Educational Planning (SAEP), two thirds of the families in the higher income bracket make contributions to this program as opposed to 30% of those in the lower income bracket and the contributions of the former were on average twice as large.

39. This was the view of Paul Inchauspé, commissioned by the Ministry of Education to provide advice on the question.

40. For primary and secondary education, the target date was 2005. The target was not reached.

Conclusion

Education does not evolve in isolation. It is constantly being compelled to adapt to social change. From time to time it has to review the programs it is charged with providing to young and adults alike. It is also profoundly influenced by the great ideological and political currents that permeate societies at important moments in their history. Those are the times when efforts are made to subordinate it to aims that are way beyond its scope.

The current phase of globalization is indisputably one of those important moments. A new global model for education is taking over just about everywhere. The great international economic institutions are imposing it and coordinating its implementation. This is a radical change, a major break with the national character of the preceding model. This is the central thesis of this book.

A short summary of the history of globalization and an analysis of the great issues that today's societies are confronting have allowed us to describe the context in which educational systems are evolving. We have laid out the major characteristics of the "new global educational order," which is keeping in tune with neo liberal globalization. The market is playing a central role.

In many countries, the education system is being reformed in favour of competition fed by school choice, greater autonomy for local schools, and a system of rewards and penalties, allowing the new "consumers" of education to make choices, with complete liberty for individuals and complete indifference to the collective good. These tendencies, as we have seen, are bearing down heavily on Quebec education.

Quite typically, again, this model presents business as the panacea. Educational institutions are invited to adopt business values and to copy its practices. But wait, there's more. Education itself is becoming an industry and its profiteers are predicting a rosy future for it. There are even efforts afoot to give preference to trade agreements over national education policies.

The examples we have been citing sometimes send shivers down the spine, so fundamental is the damage being done to the ideas that inspired education for more than a century before. And, as we have recalled, the results of many research studies agree: the new educational model does not live up to its promises. Resistance is widespread, both nationally and internationally. It would be presumptuous to announce the defeat of the democratic model but it would be equally presumptuous not to admit that it is under threat.

Criticism is certainly enlightening. It is the first step in raising awareness of the ups and downs of Quebec education and the forces that are energizing it. But it would have been a mistake to stop there. Opposition is not enough. *Pro*position is becoming a necessity if we want education to continue making progress on the road to equality, social integration, school justice and democracy.

The proposals in this book did not arise by spontaneous generation. They are inspired by the results of a great deal of research. There may well be disagreement about the appropriateness of this or that policy. Indeed, in some cases, there is more room for debate than for hard proposals. We are not claiming the authority to lay out the most desirable solutions. The aim is to stimulate discussion on the basis of foundational democratic principles.

The proposals made here do not need the investment of astronomic sums of money. In the first place, political choices are needed to allow us to define priorities. For example, a moratorium on school choice wouldn't cost a cent; but it could reap rich rewards in school justice and in success for the greatest number.

We could draw a host of conclusions from the proposals being advanced, particularly in pre-service and in-service teacher training. The social aspects of education have largely run out of steam in faculties of education these days. And yet, there is a need for critical distance if we want to grasp the paradoxes of the situation in Quebec education and move forward with renewed cogency. At the same time, research results are not as widely known as they deserve to be.

The directions we are advocating include imperatives that go far beyond the usual boundaries of education. Educating is a job for all of society, its social, cultural, and scientific institutions, its media, its communities and its families. Education and society are closely linked; the democratization of one goes along with the democratization of the other. The considerable progress made over the last half century is indeed the proof that we do not hope in vain and that the commitments made in support of democratization are bearing fruit. The future is under construction and, as in the past, it belongs to all humanity.

Now that this lengthy task is over, all that remains is the hope that this rethinking reaches its objectives: shedding light on the great issues permeating Quebec education today, and helping to make it more just, more egalitarian and more democratic.

References

CHAPTER ONE

Changing Times

On globalization in general
Berger (2003), Brunelle (2003), Clayton (2004), George (2004), Golub (2005), Latouche (2001), Robertson and al. (2002), Rocher (2001), Saul (2004), Scholte (1997), Sklair (1999), Sousa Santos (2001), Torres (2002a) and Wallerstein (2002a).

Globalization, a Long History
Arrighi (1994), Berger (2003), Berthelot (1991), Brunelle (2003), Burbules and Torres (2000), Cavanagh and Mander (2003), Clarke (1997), Coastworth (2004), Delâge (2001), Foner (1998), Friedman and Friedman (1980), Gélinas (2000), George (2004), Golub (2004 and 2005), Halimi (2004), Hobsbawm (1994), Latouche (2001), Manzagol (2003), Piotte (2003), Polanyi (1944), Rouillard (1989) and Wallerstein (2002b), Stiglitz (2002 and 2003).

Putting the Market in its Place
Berger (2003), Dostaler (2001), Foner (1998), Friedman (1982), Friedman and Friedman (1980), Gélinas (2000), George (1999), Giddens (2000), Halimi (2004), Latouche (2001), Laval (2003), Mander (1997), McQuaig (2002), Petrella (2004), Polanyi (1944), Robertson (2000), Rocher (2001), Sader (2006), Stiglitz (2002) and Torres (2002a).

Civilizing Free Trade
Brunelle (2003), Cassen (2005), Chang (2002 and 2003), Clarke (1997), Dale and Robertson (2002), Deblock (2005b), Gélinas (2000), George (2004), Halimi (2004), Manzagol (2003), Morris (1997), Polanyi (1944), Sader (2006), Sinclair and Traynor (2004), Stiglitz (2003) and Wallach (2001).

Reinforcing Democratic Institutions
Astiz and al. (2002), Berger (2003), Castonguay (2005), Dale and Robertson (2002), Deblock (2005a), Gélinas (2000), Giddens (2000), Graz (2005), Hardt and Negri (2000), Mander (1997), Parizeau (1998), Priestley (2002), Scholte (1997), Sklair (1999), Smith (2001) and Torres (2002b).

Controlling Economic Restructuring
Burbules and Torres (2000), Dubet (2001), George (2000), Halimi (2004), Labrosse (2005), Lapierre (2005), Morrow and Torres (2000), Robertson (2000), Scholte (1997), Stiglitz (2002), Tison (2005) and Torres (2002a).

Protecting our Planet
Ariès (2005), Francoeur (2005), Gélinas (2000), Latouche (2001), Lemieux (2005), Le Prestre (2005), Petrella (2004), Reeves and Lenoir (2003) and Wallach (2001).

Globalizing Solidarity
Berger (2001), Fairbrother and Hammer (2005), Foner (1998), George (2004a), Kriegel (1978), Launey (1990), Polanyi (1944), Rouillard (1989) and Wallach (2001).

CHAPTER TWO

Business Goes to School

For the Introduction
Apple (2000), Ball (2004), Ball and Van Zanten (1998), Blackmore (2000), Burbules and Torres (2000), Crahay (2000), Daun (2002), Isambert-Jamati (1981), Johsua (2003), Laval (2003), Laval and Weber (2002), Lelièvre (2004), Léon and Roche (2003), Popkewitz (2000), Priestley (2002), Robertson (2000), Saint-Pierre (2001), Tyack (2003), Tyack and Cuban (1995), Walford (2003) and Weber (2005).

The Market as Solution
Apple (2000), Ball and Van Zanten (1998), Barroso (2000), Bélisle and al. (2005), Chubb and Moe (1990), Daun (2003), Duru-Bellat and Meuret (2001), Friedman (1982), Hughes and al. (1999), Ladd (2003), Lessard and al. (2002), Meirieu (2005a), Migué and Marceau (1989), Walford (2003) and Whitty, Power and Halpin (1998).

School Choice: Failure to Remain at the Scene
Apple (2001), Ascher and Wamba (2005), Baby (2003), Ball and Van Zanten (1998), Bernier (2003), Berthelot (1986 and 1988), Bracey (2005), Careil (2002), Commission (1996), CSQ (2003b), Daun (2002 and 2003), Davies and Guppy (1997), Duru-Bellat and Meuret (2001), Felouzis, Liot and Perroton (2005), Fiske and Ladd (2003), Glass

and Matthews (2000), Hatcher (2005), Hughes and al. (1999), Ladd (2003), Lankford and Wyckoff (2005), Laval (2003), Lewis (2003), Lubienski and Lubienski (2006), Marceau and Migué (1998), Massé (2005), Meirieu (2005a), Migué and Marceau (1989), Molnar (2005a), Nelson and al. (2004), Plank and Sikes (2003), Priestley (2002), Princiotta and Chapman (2006), Proulx (1987), Reich (2002), Robertson (2000), Tondreau (2003), Tyack (2003), Van Zanten (2001), Wells and al. (1999 and 2002) and Whitty, Power and Halpin (1998).

The Paradox of School Autonomy
Angus (2003), Barroso (2000), Barroux (2002), Berthelot and Brouillette (2002), Brunet and al. (2004), Curie and Newson (1998), Duru-Bellat and Meuret (2001), Johsua (2003), Kuehn (2004a), Laval (2003), Laval and Weber (2002), MEQ (1997), Migué and Marceau (1989), Pelletier (2004), Plank and Sykes (2003), Poupeau (2003), Roy and Deniger (2001), Saint-Pierre (2004), Whitty, Power and Halpin (1998) and Williams (2003).

Punishments and Rewards
Ball (2004), Bracey (2004a and 2004b), Broadfoot (2000), Carnoy and al. (2003), Crespo (2001), CSQ (2002 and 2003a), Demailly (2004), Deniger and al. (2004), CTF (2004), Goldberg (2005), Gouvernement du Québec (2000), Gratz (2005), Karp (2006), Kohn (2005), Kuehn (2004a and 2005), Lessard (2004a and 2004b), Lessard and al. (2002), L'Italien (2004), McNeil (2000), MEQ (2003), Mintrop (2004), Moll (2004), Neill (2003), Normand (2003), Pedulla (2003), Polster and Newson (1998), Popham (2005), Robertson (2000), Russell and al. (2004), Sunderman and al. (2004), Tyack (2003), Tyack and Cuban (1995) and Walford (2003).

He who Pays the Piper...
Allard (2000), Anderson and Hatcher (2005), Ball (2004), Berthelot and Brouillette (2002), Breton (2003), Crespo (2001), Currie (2003), Currie and Newson (1998), Deglise (2005), Doherty-Delorme (1999), CCPA (2006), Fisher and Rubenson (1998), Froese-Germain (2004), Hébert (2001), Hess (2005), Klein (2000), Kohn (2002), MEQ (1999), Molnar (2005a and 2005b), Robertson (1999), Shaker (1999), Washburn (2005) and Weiner (2003).

The Education Industry
Alexiadou and Lawn (2000), Ball (2004), Bracey (2002 and 2004b), Brouillette and Fortin (2004), Bruno-Jofré and Henley (2002), Deglise (2006), Dennison and Schuetze (2004), Froese-Germain (2004), Hatcher (2005), Jones (2004), Klein (2000), Kuehn (2004b), Laval (2003), L'Homme (2001), Matthews (2002), Molnar (2005a and 2005b), Muller (2005), Nelles (2001), OECD (2001 and 2004), Porfilio and Hall (2005), Robertson (2000), Robertson (2002), Robinson (2004), Savage (2005), Shaker (2004), Tremblay (2005), Weiner (2003), Welch (2002) and Whittle (2005).

The International Trade Context
AUCC and al. (2001), Brouillette and Fortin (2004), Gottlieb and Pearson (2001), Education International (2006), Knight (2003), Laval and Weber (2002), WTO (2000, 2001a, 2001b), Petrella (2000) and Robertson and al. (2002).

A Mission Derailed
Baillargeon (2006), Dubet (2004), Hirtt (2004), Kohn (2002), Laval (2003), Mahieu and Moens (2003), Petrella (2000), Shipps (2000) and Washburn (2005).

CHAPTER THREE

Education and the Common Good

Equality, Social Integration and Educational Justice
INAC (2005), Baby (2005), Baillargeon (2006), Bélanger and Malenfant (2005), Blais, Gauchet and Ottavi (2002), Bracey (2004a), Broucker (2005), Cadotte (2006), Charlot (1997), Conférence régionale des élus (2004), Connell (2006), Crahay (2000), CSDM (2004), Cuban (2003), David (2004), Dubet (2003), Dubet and Duru-Bellat (2000), Dupriez and Dumay (2005), Duru-Bellat (2002), Duru-Bellat, Mons and Suchaut (2004), Gutmann (1987), Hirtt (2004), Johsua (2003), Labaree (2005), Lauzon and al. (2005), McAndrew (2006), McAndrew, Ledent and Aït Saïd (2005), MELS (2005a), MEQ (2004), Pelletier and Rheault (2005), Pena Ruiz (2005), Roy and Deniger (2003), Sarjala (2005), Sévigny (2003), St-Jacques and Sévigny (2003), Taylor (1992), Walzer (1984) and Wong and Nicotera (2004).

Ending School Apartheid
Bourgeault (2006), Bussière (2004), Crahay (2000), CSE (2007), Dubet (2004), Duru-Bellat (2002), Duru-Bellat and Mingat (1999), Federación de Enseñanza CC. OO. (2006), Felouzis, Liot and Perroton (2005), Ferguson and Mehta (2004), Garon (2006), Hirtt (2004), Hughes and al. (1999), Kozol (2005), Labaree (2005), Lessard (2006b), Massé (2005), McAndrew (2001), McMullen (2005), Orfield and Lee (2005), Rumberger and Palardy (2005), Sévigny (2003), Tavan (2004), Walzer (1997), Weinstock (2004), Willms (2004) and Wong and Nicotera (2004).

Full Steam Ahead to Success
Allard (2006), Baillargeon (2006), Bissonnette, Richard and Gauthier (2005), Bjork and Tsuneyoshi (2005), Blais, Gauchet and Ottavi (2002), Bracey (2004b), Caille (2004), Charlot, Bautier and Rochex (1992), Coish (2005), Crahay (2003 and 2004), Cuban (2003 and 2005), Dubet (2003), Dupriez and Draelants (2004), Duru-Bellat (2003), Ferguson and Mehta (2004), FSE (2006), Goldberg (2005), Haberman (1991), Herry (2005), Hirtt (2004), Japel, Tremblay and Côté (2005), Kamerman (2005), Kozol (2005), Lessard (2006a), McAndrew (2001), MELS (2005b, 2005c), Meuret (2001), Ministère de la Culture et des Communications (2005), Muijis and al. (2004), Piketty (2004), Ross and al. (2004), Roy (2003), Roy and Deniger (2003), St-Jacques and Sévigny (2003), Terrail (2002 and 2004), Van Haecht (2001), Warren (2005) and Wenglinsky (2004).

Staying in School Longer
Baril (2006), Broucker (2005), Caron (2004), Caron and Lanthier (2003), Comité (2004), CSE (2003b and 2004), CSQ (2004 and 2008), Doray and Maroy (2005), Duru-Bellat (2006), Kozhaya (2004), Lefebvre (2004), Lefresne (2005), Mahieu and Moens (2003), Martin (2005), Meirieu (2005b), MELS (2005b and 2005d), Oreopoulos (2005), Payeur (1991), Saysset (2005), Talbot (2005) and Zhang and Palameta (2006).

Internationalization, Cooperation and Solidarity
Breton (2003), Brouillette and Fortin (2004), Cégep international (2004), CSE (2005), Feldfeber and Saforcada (2005), Knight (2005), Lessard (2006b), MEQ (2002), OECD (2004), Oxfam International (2005), Salmi (2003) and Teather (2004).

Bibliography

Abrams, Lisa M. and Madaus, George F. (2003). The Lessons of High-Stakes Testing, *Educational Leadership*, November, p. 31-35.

Indian and Northern Affairs Canada (2005). *Action Plan for Education*, Ottawa, Government of Canada, INAC.

Alexander, Nancy (2002). Réforme de l'éducation: le rôle de la Banque mondiale, *Problèmes économiques*, no 2782, p. 14-18.

Alexiadou, Nafsika and Lawn, Martin (2000). Le nouveau discours éducatif sur l'influence entrepreneuriale: les secteurs public et privé dans les zones d'action éducative, *Revue française de pédagogie*, no 133, p. 25-36.

Allard, André (2000). Les enfants ont-ils besoin d'être protégés contre la publicité?, *Options*, no 20, Centrale des syndicats du Québec, p. 27-36.

Allard, Marie (2006). Un système coûteux et très peu efficace, *La Presse*, March 19, p. A3.

Anderson, Bill and Hatcher, Richard (2005). The Blairite Vision: School in England Under New Labour, *Our Schools/Our Selves*, vol. 14, no 3, p. 89-102.

Angus, Max (2003). School Choice Policies and Their Impact on Public Education in Australia, in David N. Plank and Gary Sykes (dir.), *Choosing Choice. School Choice in International Perspective*, New York, Teachers College Press, p. 112-142.

Apple, Michael (2001). *Educating the «Right» Way*, New York, RoutledgeFalmer.

Apple, Michael (2000). Between Neoliberalism and Neoconservatism: Education and Conservatism in a Global Context, in Nicholas C. Burbules and Carlos Alberto

Torres, *Globalization and Education: Critical Perspectives*, New York and London, Routledge, p. 57-77.

Ariès, Paul (2005). La décroissance en débat, *Relations*, March, p. 15-18.

Arrighi, Giovanni (2000). Globalization and Historical Macrosociology, in J. Abu-Lughod (dir.), *Sociology for the Twenty-First Century. Continuities and Cutting Edges*, Chicago, Chicago University Press, p. 117-133.

Arrighi, Giovanni (1994). *The Long Twentieth Century. Money, Power and the Origins of Our Times*, London and New York, Verso.

Ascher, Carol and Wamba, Nathalis (2005). An Examination of Charter School Equity, in Janelle T. Scott (dir.), *School Choice and Diversity. What the Evidence Says*, New York, Teachers College Press, p. 77-92.

Association of Universities and Colleges of Canada (1995). *AUCC Statement on Internationalization and Canadian Universities*, Ottawa, AUCC.

Association of Universities and Colleges of Canada, American Council of Education, European University Association and Council for Higher Education Accreditation (2001). *Joint Declaration on Higher Education and the General Agreement on Trade in Services*, authors.

Astiz, Fernanda M., Wiseman, Alexander W. and Baker, David P. (2002). Slouching towards Decentralization: Consequences of Globalization for Curricular Control in National Education Systems, *Comparative Education Review*, vol. 46, no 1, p. 66-88.

Baby, Antoine (2005). *Pédagogie des poqués*, Québec City, Presses de l'Université du Québec.

Baby, Antoine (2003). Des bons? À quoi bon? Une analyse de la question des bons d'études, *Notes de recherche*, no 50, Québec City, Centrale des syndicats du Québec.

Baillargeon, Normand (2006). La réforme québécoise de l'éducation: une faillite philosophique, *Possibles*, vol. 30, nos 1-2, p. 139-184.

Ball, Stephen J. (2004). *Education for Sale! The Commodification of Everything?*, King's Annual Education Lecture 2004, University of London.

Ball, Stephen J. and Van Zanten, Agnès (1998). Logiques de marché et éthiques contextualisées dans les systèmes français et britannique, *Éducation et Sociétés*, no 1, p. 47-71.

Baril, Daniel (2006). L'éducation des adultes: entre employabilité et citoyenneté, *Options*, CSQ, spring-summer, p. 247-261.

Barroso, Jorge (2000). Autonomie et modes de régulation locale dans le système éducatif, *Revue française de pédagogie*, no 130, p. 57-71.

Barroux, Rémi (2002). La décentralisation se fera de bas en haut, *Le Monde de l'éducation*, November, p. 46-48.

Bélair, Louise M. (2001). Les dérives de l'obligation de résultats: l'exemple de l'Ontario, *L'Éducateur*, no 15, p. 24-26.

Bélanger, Alain and Malenfant, Éric C. (2005). Ethnocultural Diversity in Canada : Prospects for 2017, *Canadian Social Trends*, no 79, p. 18-21.

Délisle, Jean-François, Belzile, Germain and Gagné, Robert (2005). *La concurrence entre les écoles: un bilan des expériences étrangères*, Montreal, Montreal Economic Institute.

Berger, Suzanne (2003).*The First Globalization : Lessons from the French*, available on line.

Bernier, Sylvain (2003). *Le choix de l'école pour tous. Un projet de bons d'étude adapté au Québec*, in French with an English executive summary, Montreal, Montreal Economic Institute.

Berthelot, Jocelyn (1991). *Apprendre à vivre ensemble. Immigration, société et éducation*, Montreal, Éditions Saint-Martin and CEQ, Second Edition.

Berthelot, Jocelyn (1988). *L'école privée est-elle d'intérêt public?*, Québec City, Centrale de l'enseignement du Québec, D9080.

Berthelot, Jocelyn (1986). *L'école de son rang*, Montreal, Éditions Saint-Martin and CEQ.

Berthelot, Jocelyn and Brouillette, Véronique (2002). *Convictions démocratiques et menaces marchandes. Analyse de l'opinion des membres votants des conseils d'établissement des écoles francophones*, Québec City, Centrale des syndicats du Québec, D11100.

Bissonnette, Steve, Richard, Mario and Gauthier, Clermont (2005). *Échec scolaire et réforme éducative. Quand les solutions proposées deviennent la source du problème*, Québec City, Presses de l'Université Laval.

Bjork, Christopher and Tsuneyoshi, Ryoko (2005). Education Reform in Japan: Competing Visions for the Future, *Phi Delta Kappan*, April, p. 619-626.

Blackmore, Jill (2000). Globalization: A Useful Concept for Feminists Rethinking Theory and Strategies in Education?, in Nicholas C. Burbules and Carlos Alberto Torres, *Globalization and Education: Critical Perspectives*, New York and London, Routledge, p. 1-26.

Blais, Jean-Guy (2004). L'obligation de résultats à la lumière de l'interaction entre le quantitatif et le social, in Claude Lessard and Philippe Meirieu (dir.), *L'obligation de résultats en éducation*, Québec, Presses de l'Université Laval, p. 123-144.

Blais, Marie-Claude, Gauchet, Marcel and Ottavi, Dominique (2002). *Pour une philosophie politique de l'éducation*, Paris, Éditions Bayard.

Bourgeault, Guy (2006). Plaidoyer pour une école publique, *Possibles*, vol. 30, nos 1-2, p. 48-65.

Bracey, Gerald W. (2005). Checking Up on Charters, *Phi Delta Kappan*, March, p. 554-555.

Bracey, Gerald W. (2004b). *Setting the Record Straight. Responses to Misconceptions About Public Education in the U. S.: Second Edition*, Portsmouth (N.H.), Heinemann.

Bracey, Gerald W. (2004a). The 14th Report on The Condition of Public Education, *Phi Delta Kappan*, October, p. 149-167.

Bracey, Gerald W. (2002). *The Market in Theory Meets the Market in Practice: The Case of Edison Schools*, Arizona State University, Education Policy Research Unit, EPSL-0202-107-EPRU.

Breton, Gilles (2003). Higher Education : From Internationalization to Globalization, in Gilles Breton and Michel Lambert (dir.), *Universities and Globalisation : Private Linkages, Public Trust*, Paris, Unesco/Économica/Presses de l'Université Laval, p. 21-34.

Broadfoot, Patricia (2000). Un nouveau mode de régulation dans un système décentralisé: l'État évaluateur, *Revue française de pédagogie*, no 130, p. 43-55.

Broucker, Patrice de (2005). *Without a Paddle: What to do About Canada's Young Dropouts*, Ottawa, Canadian Policy Research Network.

Brouillette, Véronique and Fortin, Nicole (2004). La mondialisation néolibérale et l'enseignement supérieur, *Notes de recherche*, no 51, Centrale des syndicats du Québec.

Brunelle, Dorval (2003). *Dérive globale*, Montreal, Éditions du Boréal.

Brunet, Luc, Brassard, André and De Saedeleer, Sylvie (2004). La décentralisation dans le système d'enseignement au Québec: la Loi sur l'instruction publique (loi 180) et ses effets perçus, in Marjolaine Saint-Pierre and Luc Brunet, *De la décentralisation au partenariat. Administration en milieu scolaire*, Sainte-Foy, Presses de l'Université du Québec, p. 95-120.

Bruno-Jofré, Rosa and Henley, Dick (2002). The Canadian Education Industry: An Historical Critique of Education as Merchandise, *Canadian and International Education*, vol. 31, no 1, p. 1-17.

Burbules, Nicholas C. and Torres, Carlos Alberto (2000). Globalization and Education: An Introduction, in Nicholas C. Burbules and Carlos Alberto Torres (dir.), *Globalization and Education: Critical Perspectives*, New York and London, Routledge, p. 1-26.

Burris, Carol and Welner, Kevin G. (2005). Closing the Achievement Gap by Detracking, *Phi Delta Kappan*, April, p. 594-598.

Bussière, Patrick (2004). *Measuring up :Canadian Results of the OECD PISA Study*, Ottawa, Statistics Canada.

Cadotte, Robert (2006). La réussite éducative dans les écoles de milieux défavorisés, *Options*, CSQ, spring-summer, p. 219-235.

Caille, Jean-Paul (2004). Le redoublement à l'école élémentaire et dans l'enseignement secondaire: évolution des redoublements et parcours scolaires des redoublants au cours des années 1990-2000, *Éducation & formations*, no 69, p. 79-88.

Canadian Centre for Policy Alternatives and al. (2006). *Commercialism in Canadian Schools: Who's Calling the Shots?*, Ottawa, CCPA and CTF. Quebec City, FSE.

Canadian Teachers Federation (2004). *Responsabilisation à visage humain en éducation*, Ottawa, CTF.

Careil, Yves (2002). *École libérale, école inégale*, Paris, Éditions Nouveaux regards and Éditions Sylepse.

Carnoy, Martin, Loeb, Susanna and Smith, Tiffany (2003). The Impact of Accountability Policies in Texas High Schools, in Martin Carnoy, Richard Elmore and Leslie S. Siskin, *The New Accountability. High Schools and High-Stakes Testing*, New York, RoutledgeFarmer.

Caron, Laurier (2004). La formation professionnelle des jeunes: des modèles et des résultats différents, *Possibles*, vol. 28, nos 3-4, p. 54-65.

Caron, Laurier and Lanthier, Pierre (2003). Éducation des adultes et formation professionnelle. Une nouvelle norme sociale déjà en péril, *Options*, no 22, CSQ, p. 107-122.

Cassen, Bernard (2005). Marchandages sur la marchandisation, *Le Monde diplomatique*, December, p. 5.

Castonguay, Alec (2005). Diversité culturelle: c'est oui à Paris, *Le Devoir*, october 18, p. A1 and A8.

Cavanagh, John and Mander, Jerry (2003). World Bank, IMF Turned Poor Third World Nations into Loan Addicts, *The CCPA Monitor*, July-August, p. 19-22.

Cégep international (2004). *L'internationalisation des établissements d'enseignement. Un guide pratique*, Montreal, Cégep international.

Centrale des syndicats du Québec (2008). *Portrait des enjeux éducatifs du Québec*, Québec City, CSQ.

Centrale des syndicats du Québec (2004). *Et si on parlait d'éducation... Mémoire présenté dans le cadre du Forum sur l'avenir de l'enseignement collégial des 9 et 10 juin 2004*, Québec City, CSQ, D11422.

Centrale des syndicats du Québec (2003b). *Choix de l'école et bons d'études*, Québec City, CSQ, D11278.

Centrale des syndicats du Québec (2003a). *Une mobilisation qui a porté fruit. Analyse des modifications apportées à la Loi sur l'instruction publique par la loi 124 adoptée en décembre 2002*, Québec City, CSQ, D11253-1.

Centrale des syndicats du Québec (2002). *La réussite ne se décrète pas. Mémoire présenté à la Commission parlementaire portant sur le projet de loi no 124 proposant des modifications à la Loi sur l'instruction publique*, Québec City, CSQ, D11241.

Centrale des syndicats du Québec (1996). *Une éducation différente pour une société différente. Manifeste pour l'éducation publique*, Québec City, CSQ, D10348.

Centrale des syndicats du Québec and other organizations (2003). *Le projet éducatif et le plan de réussite*, Québec City, CSQ, D11289, D11295.

Chang, Ha-Joon (2003). Kicking Away the Ladder: The «Real» History of Free Trade, *Foreign Policy In Focus*, December, ‹www.globalpolicy. org/socecon/ trade/2003/12historyoftrade. pdf›.

Chang, Ha-Joon (2002). History Debunks the Free Trade Myth, *The Guardian*, June 24.

Charlot, Bernard (1997). *Du rapport au savoir: Éléments pour une théorie*, Paris, Anthropos.

Charlot, Bernard, Bautier, Élizabeth and Rochex, Jean-Yves (1992). *École et savoir dans les banlieues... et ailleurs*, Paris, Armand Colin.

Christie, Kathy (2005b). Setting Food and Exercise Standards for Kids, *Phi Delta Kappan*, September, p. 5-7.

Christie, Kathy (2005a). Critical Mass, *Phi Delta Kappan*, March, p. 485-486.

Chubb, John E. (2003). Ignoring the Market, *Education Next*, spring, ‹www.education-next. org/20032/80.html›.

Chubb, John E. and Moe, Terry M. (1990). *Politics, Markets and America's Schools*, Washington (D.C.), The Brookings Institution.

Clarke, Tony (1997). Mechanisms of Corporate Rule, in Edward Goldsmith and Jerry Mander (dir.), *The Case Against the Global Economy : And for a Turn Toward the Local*, San Francisco, Sierra Club Books, p. 297-308.

Clayton, Thomas (2004). «Competing Conceptions of Globalization» Revisited: Relocating the Tension between World-systems Analysis and Globalization Analysis, *Comparative Education Review*, vol. 48, no 3, p. 274-294.

Coastworth, John H. (2004). Globalization, Growth, and Welfare in History, in Marcelo Suarez-Orozco and Desirée B. Qin-Hilliard (dir.), *Globalization, Culture and Education in the New Millennium*, Los Angeles and London, University of California Press, p. 38-55.

Coish, David (2005). *Canadian Schools Libraries and Teachers-librarian : Results from the 2003-2004 Information and Communication Technologies in Schools Survey*, Ottawa, Statistics Canada.

Comité consultatif sur l'accessibilité financière aux études (2004). *L'accessibilité financière à la réussite du projet d'études. Avis au ministre de l'Éducation*, Québec City, CSE.

Commission for the Estates General on Education (1996). *Renewing our Education System. Ten Priority Actions. Final Report*, Québec City, Ministère de l'Éducation du Québec.

Commission scolaire de Montréal (2004). *Au-delà des apparences, des chiffres et des questions. Diagnostic organisationnel*, Montreal, CSDM.

Conférence régionale des élus de Montréal (2004). *Rapport sur la pauvreté à Montréal. Document de recherche et de réflexion*, Montreal, Forum régional sur le développement social de l'île de Montréal.

Connell, Raewyn (2006). The New Right Triumphant: The Privatization Agenda and Public Education in Australia, *Our Schools/Our Selves*, spring, p. 143-162.

Conseil supérieur de l'éducation (2007). *Les projets pédagogiques particuliers au secondaire : diversifier en toute équité. Avis au ministre de l'Éducation*, Québec City, CSE

Conseil supérieur de l'éducation (2005). *L'internationalisation: nourrir le dynamisme des universités québécoises. Avis au ministre de l'Éducation, du Loisir et du Sport*, Québec City, CSE.

Conseil supérieur de l'éducation (2004). *Career Training : Promoting the Value of all Paths. Report on the State and Needs of Education (2003-2004). Abridged Version*, Québec City, CSE.

Conseil supérieur de l'éducation (2003b). *L'éducation des adultes: partenaire du développement local et régional. Avis au ministre de l'Éducation*, Québec City, CSE.

Conseil supérieur de l'éducation (2003a). *L'appropriation locale de la réforme: un défi à la mesure de l'école secondaire. Avis au ministre de l'Éducation*, Québec City, CSE.

Cowell, Robert (1981). L'évolution des idées et des pratiques pédagogiques en Europe occidentale, in Gaston Mialaret and Jean Vial (dir.), *Histoire mondiale de l'éducation. Tome IV: De 1945 à nos jours*, Paris, PUF, p. 11-20.

Crahay, Marcel (2004). Peut-on conclure à propos des effets du redoublement?, *Revue française de pédagogie*, no 148, p. 11-23.

Crahay, Marcel (2003). *Peut-on lutter contre l'échec scolaire?*, Paris, Brussels, De Boeck Université, Second Edition.

Crahay, Marcel (2000). *L'école peut-elle être juste et efficace? De l'égalité des chances à l'égalité des acquis*, Brussels, De Boeck Université.

Crahay, Marcel and Delhaxhe, Arlette (2004). *L'enseignement secondaire inférieur: entre culture de l'intégration et culture de la différenciation*, ‹www.recherche.gouv.fr/recherche/fns/crahay.pdf›.

Crespo, Manuel (2001). Tendances actuelles des politiques publiques à l'égard de l'enseignement supérieur: une analyse comparative, *Canadian Public Policy/Analyse de politiques*, vol. XXVII, no 3, p. 279-295.

Cuban, Larry (2005). Why Is It So Hard to Get Good Schools?, in Larry Cuban and Dorothy Shipps (dir.), *Reconstructing the Common Good in Education. Coping with Intractable American Dilemmas*, Stanford, Stanford University Press, p. 148-169.

Cuban, Larry (2003). *Why Is It So Hard to Get Good Schools?*, New York, Teachers College Press.

Cuban, Larry and Shipps, Dorothy (dir.) (2005). *Reconstructing the Common Good in Education. Coping with Intractable American Dilemmas*, Stanford, Stanford University Press.

Currie, Jane (2003). Universités entrepreneuriales: de nouveaux acteurs sur la scène mondiale (le cas australien), in Gilles Breton and Michel Lambert (dir.), *Universities and Globalisation : Private Linkages, Public Trust*, Paris, Unesco/Économica/Presses de l'Université Laval, p. 179-194.

Currie, Janice and Newson, Janice (1998). Globalizing Pratices: Corporate Managerialism, Accountability, and Privatization, in Janice Currie and Janice Newson (dir.), *Universities and Globalization. Critical Perspectives*, London, Sage Publications, p. 141-151.

Dale, Roger (1999). Specifying Globalization Effects on National Policy: A Focus on the Mechanisms, *Journal of Education Policy*, vol. 14, no 1, p. 1-17.

Dale, Roger and Robertson, Susan L. (2002). The Varying Effects of Regional Organizations as Subjects of Globalization of Education, *Comparative Education Review*, vol. 46, no 1, p. 10-36.

Danis, Gabriel (2004). Les partenariats public-privé (PPP): mythes, réalités et enjeux. *Notes de recherche*, no 54, Québec City, Centrale des syndicats du Québec.

Daun, Holger (2003). Market Forces and Decentralization in Sweden: Impetus for School Development or Threat to Comprehensiveness and Equity?, in David N. Plank and Gary Sykes (dir.), *Choosing Choice. School Choice in International Perspective*, New York, Teachers College Press, p. 92-111.

Daun, Holger (dir.) (2002). *Educational Restructuring in the Context of Globalization and National Policy*, New York and London, RoutledgeFalmer.

David, Françoise (2004). *Bien commun recherché. Une option citoyenne*, Montreal, Écosociété.

Davies, Scott and Guppy, Neil (1997). Globalization and Educational Reforms in Anglo-American Democracies, *Comparative Education Review*, vol. 41, no 4, p. 435-459.

Deblock, Christian (2005b). Lorsque l'accès au marché des États-Unis devient un privilège..., *Asymétries*, no 1, p. 48-50.

Deblock, Christian (2005a). Repenser la gouvernance globale, *Asymétries*, no 1, p. 38-39.

Deglise, Fabien (2006). L'Université Laval s'associe à Sobeys, *Le Devoir*, February 16, p. A1 and A8.

Deglise, Fabien (2005). Pepsi fait son entrée au primaire, *Le Devoir*, June 6, p. A5.

Delâge, Denys (2001). Identités autochtones à travers l'histoire, in Daniel Mercure (dir.), *Une société-monde? Les dynamiques sociales de la mondialisation*, Québec City, Presses de l'Université Laval, p. 133-147.

Demailly, Lise (2004). Enjeux et limites de l'obligation de résultats: quelques réflexions à partir de la politique d'éducation prioritaire en France, in Claude Lessard and Philippe Meirieu (dir.), *L'obligation de résultats en éducation*, Québec City, Presses de l'Université Laval, p. 105-122.

Deniger, Marc-André, Brouillette, Véronique and Kananzi, Canisius (2004). Réorientation, refinancement et obligations de résultats: réforme ou dérive politique des universités québécoises?, in Claude Lessard and Philippe Meirieu, *L'obligation de résultats en éducation*, Québec City, Presses de l'Université Laval, p. 145-166.

Dennison, John D. and Schuetze, Hans G. (2004). Extending Access, Choice and the Reign of the Market: Higher Education Reforms in British Columbia, 1989-2004 *The Canadian Journal of Higher Education*, vol. XXXIV, no 3, p. 13-38.

Doherty-Delorme, D. (1999). The Corporate Takeover of our Universities and Colleges *Education Limited*, vol. 1, no 4, p. xi-xx.

Doray, Pierre and Maroy, Christian (2005). L'analyse du rapprochement école-entreprise: les pratiques d'alternance dans l'enseignement technique, *Cahiers de recherche sociologique*, no 40, p. 199-225.

Dostaler, Gilles (2001). *Le libéralisme de Hayek*, Paris, Éditions La Découverte and Syros.

Dubet, François (2004). *L'école des chances. Qu'est-ce qu'une école juste?*, Paris, Éditions du Seuil and La République des Idées.

Dubet, François (2003). Éducation: pour sortir de l'idée de crise, *Éducation et Sociétés*, no 11, p. 47-65.

Dubet, François (2001). Les inégalités multipliées ou les épreuves de l'égalité, in Daniel Mercure (dir.), *Une société-monde? Les dynamiques sociales de la mondialisation*, Québec City, Presses de l'Université Laval, p. 93-114.

Dubet, François (2000). L'égalité et le mérite dans l'école démocratique de masse *L'année sociologique*, vol. 50, no 2, p. 383-408.

Dubet, François and Duru-Bellat, Marie (2000). *L'hypocrisie scolaire. Pour un collège enfin démocratique*, Paris, Éditions du Seuil.

Dubuc, Pierre (2005). L'Éducation a trois vitesses, *L'Apostrophe*, no 8, p. 13-22.

Dupriez, Vincent and Draelants, Hugues (2004). Classes homogènes versus classes hétérogènes: les apports de la recherche à l'analyse de la problématique, *Revue française de pédagogie*, no 148, p. 145-165.

Dupriez, Vincent and Dumay, Xavier (2005). L'égalité des chances à l'école: analyse d'un effet spécifique de la structure scolaire, *Revue française de pédagogie*, no 150, p. 5-17.

Duru-Bellat, Marie (2006). *L'inflation scolaire. Les désillusions de la méritocratie*, Paris, Éditions du Seuil.

Duru-Bellat, Marie (2003). Social Inequality at School and Educational Policies, *Fundamentals of Education Planing Series*, No 78, Paris, Unesco.

Duru-Bellat, Marie (2002). *Les inégalités sociales à l'école. Genèse et mythes*, Paris, Presses Universitaires de France.

Duru-Bellat, Marie and Meuret, Denis (2001). Nouvelles formes de régulation dans les systèmes éducatifs étrangers: autonomie et choix des établissements scolaires. Note de synthèse, *Revue française de pédagogie*, no 135, p. 173-221.

Duru-Bellat, Marie and Mingat, Alain (1999). Implications en termes de justice des modes de groupement d'élèves, in Denis Meuret (dir.), *La justice du système éducatif*, Brussels, De Boeck and Larcier, p. 99-112.

Duru-Bellat, Marie, Mons, Nathalie and Suchaut, Bruno (2004). Inégalités sociales entre élèves et organisation des systèmes éducatifs: quelques enseignements de l'enquête PISA, *Les Notes de l'IREDU*, ‹www.u-bourgogne. fr/IREDU›.

Education International (2006). *The General Agreement on Trade in Services. What is it and what Does it Mean for Education ?*, Brussels, EI, available online http://www. ei-ie.org/gats/file/(2006)%20EI%20GATS%20Information%20Kit%20en.pdf.

Fairbrother, Peter and Hammer, Nikolaus (2005). Global Unions. Past Efforts and Future Prospects, *Relations industrielles/Industrial Relations*, vol. 60, no 3, p. 405-431.

Federación de Enseñanza CC. OO. (2006). La LOE: una ley positiva, *T.E. Revista mensual*, Madrid, no 269, January.

Fédération des syndicats de l'enseignement (2006). *Opération Groupes témoins. Rapport phase 3*, Québec City, FSE, A0506-CF-035.

Feldfeber, Myriam and Saforcada, Fernanda (2005). *La educación en las Cumbres de las Américas. Un análisis crítico de las políticas de la última década*, Buenos Aires, Miño and Dávila. Available online, http://www.lpp-buenosaires.net/LPP_BA/Publicaciones/documentos/EI1_Cumbres-Informe.pdf.

Felouzis, Georges, Liot, Françoise and Perroton, Joëlle (2005). *L'apartheid scolaire. Enquête sur la ségrégation ethnique dans les collèges*, Paris, Éditions du Seuil.

Ferguson, Ronald F. and Mehta, Jal (2004). An Unfinished Journey: The Legacy of Brown and the Narrowing of the Achievement Gap, *Phi Delta Kappan*, May, p. 656-669.

Finnie, Ross, Lascelles, Eric and Sweetman, Arthur (2005). *Who Goes? The Direct and Indirect Effects of Family Background on Access to Post-secondary Education*, Ottawa, Statistics Canada.

Fisher, Donald and Rubenson, Kjell (1998). The Changing Political Economy: The Private and Public Lives of Canadian Universities, in J. Currie and J. Newson (dir.), *Universities and Globalization. Critical Perspectives*, London, Sage Publications, p. 77-98.

Fiske, Edward B. and Ladd, Helen F. (2003). School Choice in New Zealand: A Cautionary Tale, in David N. Plank and Gary Sykes (dir.), *Choosing Choice. School Choice in International Perspective*, New York, Teachers College Press, p. 45-67.

Foner, Eric (1998). *The Story of American Freedom*, New York, W. W. Norton & Company.

Francoeur, Louis-Gilles (2005). Un bar ouvert plutôt qu'un plan de match serré, *Le Devoir*, April 16, p. B3.

Frenette, Marc (2005). *The Impact of Tuition Fees on University Access : Evidence from a Large-scale Price Deregulation in Professional Programs*, Ottawa, Statistics Canada, 11F0019MIE2005263.

Friedman, Milton (1982). *Capitalism and Freedom*, Chicago, The University of Chicago Press.

Friedman, Milton and Friedman, Rose (1980). *Free to Choose : A Personal Statement*, New-York : Harcourt Brace Javanovich.

Froese-Germain, Bernie (2004). Getting a Read on Privatization, *Perspectives*, vol. 4, no 1, Ottawa, CTF, p. 1-6.

Fulton, Kathleen, Burns, Mary and Goldenberg, Lauren (2005). Teachers Learning in Networked Communities: The TLINC Strategy, *Phi Delta Kappan*, December, p. 298-301 and 305.

Garon, Jean-François (2006). Retrait des subventions aux écoles primaires et secondaires privées: évaluation de l'argument financier, *Notes de recherche*, no 57, Québec City, CSQ, D11657.

Gélinas, Jacques B. (2000). *La globalisation du monde. Laisser faire ou faire?*, Montreal, Les Éditions Écosociété.

George, Susan (2004). *Un autre monde est possible si...*, Paris, Fayard.

George, Susan (2000). *Corporate-led Globalization*, Colloque de la Fundación Marcelino Botín, Madrid, January 2000, ‹www.tni.org/archives/george/botin. htm›.

George, Susan (1999). *A Short History of Neoliberalism. Conference on Economic Sovereignty in a Globalizing World*, ‹www.globalpolicy. org/globaliz/econ/histneol. htm›.

Giddens, Anthony (2000). *Runaway World*, New York, Routledge.

Giroux, Robert J. (2004). Enrolment Demand versus Accessibility at Canada's Universities, *The Canadian Journal of Higher Education*, vol. XXXXIV, no 1, p. 83-96.

Glass, Gene V. and Matthews, Dewayne A. (2000). *Are Data Enough? Review of Chubb and Moe's Politics, Markets and America's Schools*, in ‹www.glass.ed.asu.edu/gene/papers/chubbrev. html›. Initialy published in Educational Researcher, 1990.

Goldberg, Mark (2005). Test Mess 2: Are We Doing Better a Year Later?, *Phi Delta Kappan*, January, p. 389-395.

Golub, Philip S. (2005). Le grand tournant de Washington, *Le Monde diplomatique*, July, p. 1, 20-21.

Golub, Philip. S. (2004). Retour de l'Asie sur la scène mondiale, *Le Monde diplomatique*, October, p. 18-19.

Gottlieb and Pearson (2001). *GATS Impact on Education in Canada. Legal Opinion*, Ottawa, CAUT.

Gouvernement du Québec (2000). *Déclaration commune faisant état des consensus dégagés par les participantes et participants associés au Sommet du Québec et de la Jeunesse*, Québec City.

Granier, Karine (dir.) (2005). *Collège: peut mieux faire!*, Paris, Éditions Syllepse.

Gratz, Donald B. (2005). Lessons from Denver: The Pay for Performance Pilot, *Phi Delta Kappan*, April, p. 569-581.

Graz, Jean-Christophe (2005). La gouvernance mondiale, *Asymétries*, no 1, p. 8-10.

Guppy, Neil (2005). *Parent and Teacher Views on Education*, Kelowna, Society for the Advancement of Excellence in Education.

Gutmann, Amy (1987). *Democratic Education*, Princeton, Princeton University Press.

Haberman, Martin (1991). The Pedagogy of Poverty Versus Good Teaching, *Phi Delta Kappan*, December, p. 290-294.

Halimi, Serge (2004). *Le grand bond en arrière. Comment l'ordre libéral s'est imposé au monde*, Paris, Fayard.

Hardt, Michael and Negri, Antonio (2000). *Empire*, Cambridge and London, Harvard University Press.

Harvey, James (2003). The Matrix Reloaded, *Educational Leadership*, November, p. 18-21.

Hatcher, Richard (2005). L'école britannique livrée au patronat, *Le Monde diplomatique*, April, p. 3.

Hébert, Pierre (2001). *La nouvelle université guerrière*, Québec City, Les Éditions Nota bene.

Herry, Yves (2005). Un programme de prévention destiné à la petite enfance: ses effets sur les enfants, les familles et la communauté, *Éducation et francophonie*, vol. XXXIII, no 2, p. 67-84.

Hess, Frédérick M. (2005). Inside the Gift Horse's Mouth: Philanthropy and School Reform, *Phi Delta Kappan*, October, p. 131-137.

Hirtt, Nico (2004). *L'école de l'inégalité. Les discours et les faits*, Brussels, Éditions Labor.

Hivon, René and Martin, Yves (1981). *Conceptions nord-américaines en éducation, in Gaston Mialaret and Jean Vial, Histoire mondiale de l'éducation. Tome IV: De 1945 à nos jours*, Paris, Presses Universitaires de France, p. 57-68.

Hobsbawm, Eric J. (1994). *The Age of Extremes : A History of the world, 1994-1991*, London, Michael Joseph.

Hughes, David and al. (1999). *Trading in Futures. Why Markets in Education Don't Work*, Philadelphia, Open University Press.

Isambert-Jamati, Viviane (1981). À quoi attribuer les changements?, in *Gaston Mialaret and Jean Vial (dir.), Histoire mondiale de l'éducation. Tome III: De 1815 à 1945*, Paris, Presses Universitaires de France, p. 99-114.

Japel, Christa, Tremblay, Richard E. and Côté, Sylvana (2005). La qualité des services de garde à la petite enfance: résultats de l'Étude longitudinale du développement des enfants du Québec (ELDEQ), *Éducation et francophonie*, vol. XXXIII, no 2, p. 7-27.

Johsua, Samuel (2003). *Une autre école est possible! Manifeste pour une éducation émancipatrice*, Paris, Les Éditions Textuel.

Jones, Glen A. (2004). Ontario Higher Education Reform, 1995-2003: From Modes Modifications to Policy Reform, *The Canadian Journal of Higher Education*, vol. XXXIV, no 3, p. 39-54.

Kamerman, Sheila B. (2005). Early Childhood Education and Care in Advanced Industrialized Countries: Current Policy and Program Trends, *Phi Delta Kappan*, november, p. 193-195.

Karp, Stan (2006). Leaving Public Schools Behind: The Bush Agenda in American Education, *Our Schools/Our selves*, spring, p. 181-196.

Klein, Naomi (2000). *No Logo. Taking Aim at the Brand Bullies*, Toronto, Vintage Canada.

Knight, Jane (2005). *Crossborder Education: Programs and Providers on the Move*, Ottawa, Canadian Bureau for International Education.

Knight, Jane (2003). Les accords commerciaux (AGCS): implications pour l'enseignement supérieur, in G. Breton and M. Lambert (dir.), *Universities and Globalisation : Private Linkages, Public Trust*, Paris, Unesco/Économica/Presses de l'Université Laval, p. 81-106.

Kohn, Alfi (2005). Test Today, Privatize Tomorrow:Using Accountability to 'Reform'Public Schools to Death, *Perspectives*, vol. 5, no 2, CTF.

Kohn, Alfi (2002). The 500-Pound Gorilla, *Phi Delta Kappan*, October, p. 113-119.

Kozhaya, Norma (2004). *La hausse des droits de scolarité réduirait-elle l'accessibilité aux études universitaires? Les Notes économiques*, Montreal, Montreal Economic Institute, February.

Kozol, Jonathan (2005). The Shame of the Nation. Confections of Apartheid: A Stick-and-Carrot Pedagogy for the Children of our Inner-City Poor, *Phi Delta Kappan*, December, p. 265-275.

Kriegel, Annie (1975). *Les Internationales ouvrières*, Paris, Presses Universitaires de France, coll. «Que sais-je?», no 1129.

Kuehn, Larry (2005). Education Roundup, *Our Schools/Our Selves*, vol. 14, no 3, p. 9-19.

Kuehn, Larry (2004b). School District Business Companies, *Perspectives*, vol. 4, no 1, p. 11-16.

Kuehn, Larry (2004a). Leaning between conspiracy and hegemony: OECD, Unesco and the tower of PISA, in Monica Moll (dir.), *Passing the Test: The False Promise of Standardized Testing*, Ottawa, Canadian Centre for Policy Alternatives, p. 57-66.

Labaree, David V. (2005). No Exit: Public Education as an Inescapably Public Good, in Larry Cuban and Dorothy Shipps (dir.), *Reconstructing the Common Good. Coping with Intractable American Dilemmas*, Stanford, Stanford University Press, p. 110-129.

Labrie, Vivian (2005). Écarts grandissants entre riches et pauvres, *Relations*, no 705, p. 4-6.

Labrosse, Alexis (2005). *La présence syndicale au Québec en 2004*, Québec, Ministère du Travail, Direction de la recherche et de l'évaluation.

Ladd, Helen F. (2003). Introduction, in David N. Plank and Gary Sykes (dir.), *Choosing Choice. School Choice in International Perspective*, New York, Teachers College Press, p. 1-23.

Lankford, Hamilton and Wyckoff, James (2005). Why are Schools Racially Segregated? Implications for School Choice Policies, in J. T. Scott (dir.), *School Choice and Diversity. What the Evidence Says*, New York, Teachers College Press, p. 9-26.

Lapierre, Jean-Marcel (2005). La détérioration des droits collectifs du travail sous le gouvernement Charest, *Options*, no 23, CSQ, p. 77-95.

Latouche, Serge (2001). La mondialisation démystifiée, in E. Goldsmith and J. Mander (dir.), *Le procès de la mondialisation*, Paris, Fayard, p. 7-27.

Launay, Michel (1990). *Le syndicalisme en Europe*, Paris, Imprimerie nationale.

Lauzon, Léo-Paul and al. (2005). *Le déplacement du fardeau fiscal des compagnies vers les particuliers au cours des dernières décennies*, Montreal, Chaire d'études socio-économiques de l'UQAM.

Laval, Christian (2003). *L'école n'est pas une entreprise. Le néo-libéralisme à l'assaut de l'enseignement public*, Paris, Éditions La Découverte.

Laval, Christian and Weber, Louis (2003). Comme si l'école était une entreprise..., *Le Monde diplomatique*, no 591, June, p. 6-7.

Laval, Christian and Weber, Louis (dir.) (2002). *Le nouvel ordre éducatif mondial. OMC, Banque mondiale, OCDE, Commission européenne*, Paris, Éditions Nouveaux regards.

Lefebvre, Sophie (2004). *Saving for postsecondary education,*, Perspective, autumn, p. 26-35, Ottawa, Statistics Canada, no 75-001-XIE.

Lefresne, Florence (2005). Une comparaison européenne des dispositifs d'insertion, *Problèmes politiques et sociaux*, no 915, p. 101-105.

Lelièvre, Claude (2004). *L'école obligatoire: pour quoi faire?*, Paris, Éditions Retz.

Lemieux, Raymond (2005). Mémoire de glace, *Québec Science*, March, p. 23-25.

Léon, Antoine and Roche, Pierre (2003). *Histoire de l'enseignement en France*, Paris, Presses Universitaires de France, coll. «Que sais-je?», no 393.

Le Prestre, Philippe (2005). Quel avenir pour le Protocole de Kyoto?, *Asymétries*, no 1, p. 29-31.

Lessard, Claude (2006b). Différenciation des formations et pratiques sélectives à l'école publique: le système éducatif est-il en train d'imploser?, *Options*, CSQ, spring-summer, p. 169-184.

Lessard, Claude (2006a). Déficit de recherche? Pas certain. Plutôt question de rapport à la recherche, *Formation et Profession*, vol. 12, no 1, p. 37-42.

Lessard, Claude (2004b). Conclusion synthèse, in C. Lessard and P. Meirieu (dir.), *L'obligation de résultats en éducation*, Québec City, Les Presses de l'Université Laval, p. 295-309.

Lessard, Claude (2004a). L'obligation de résultats en éducation: de quoi s'agit-il? Le contexte québécois d'une demande sociale, une rhétorique du changement et une extension de la recherche, in Claude Lessard and Philippe Meirieu (dir.), *L'obligation de résultats en éducation*, Québec City, Les Presses de l'Université Laval, p. 23-48.

Lessard, Claude, Brassard, André and Lusignan, Jacques (2002). *Les tendances évolutives des politiques éducatives en matière de structures et de régulation, d'imputabilité et de reddition de comptes. Les cas du Canada (Ontario et Colombie-Britannique), des États-Unis (Californie), de la France et du Royaume-Uni*, LABRIPROF-CRIF-PE, Faculté des sciences de l'éducation, Université de Montréal.

Lewis, Anne C. (2003). Students as Commodities, *Phi Delta Kappan*, April, p. 563-564.

L'Homme, Christina (2001). Quand la mondialisation accélère la fuite des «cerveaux», *Problèmes économiques*, no 2731, p. 14-16.

L'Italien, François (2004). La «mondialisation» des politiques managériales et les transformations du mode de régulation interne des États occidentaux contemporains. Le Québec en perspective, in Raphaël Canet and Julie Duchastel (dir.), *La régulation néolibérale. Crise ou ajustement?*, Montreal, Athéna Éditions, p. 349-362.

Lubienski, Christopher and Lubienski, Sarah T. (2006). *Charter, Private, Public Schools and Academic Achievement: New Evidence from NAEP Mathematics Data*, National Center for the Study of Privatization in Education, Columbia University, New York.

Maclure, Jocelyn (2000). *Récits identitaires. Le Québec à l'épreuve du pluralisme*, Montreal, Québec Amérique.

Mahieu, Céline and Moens, Frédéric (2003). De la libération de l'homme à la libéralisation de l'éducation. L'éducation et la formation tout au long de la vie dans le discours et les pratiques européennes, *Éducation et Sociétés*, no 12, p. 35-55.

Mander, Jerry (1997). Facing the Rising Tide, in E. Goldsmith and J. Mander (dir.), *The Case Against the Global Economy : And for a Turn Toward the Local*, San Francisco, Sierra Club Books, p. 3-19.

Manzagol, Claude (2003). *La mondialisation. Données, mécanismes et enjeux*, Paris, Armand Colin.

Marceau, Richard and Migué, Jean-Luc (1998). La question scolaire au Canada, *Options politiques*, vol. 19, no 6, p. 58-62.

Maroy, Christian (2005). Les évolutions du travail enseignant en Europe. Facteurs de changement, incidences et résistances, *Les Cahiers de recherche en éducation et formation*, no 42, Louvain, Groupe interfacultaire de recherche sur les systèmes d'éducation et de formation (GIRSEF).

Martin, Marie-France (2005). Évolution de l'emploi et du taux de chômage selon les niveaux de scolarité, *Flash-info*, Québec City, Institut de la statistique du Québec, June.

Massé, Denis (2005). *La situation socioéconomique des clientèles du réseau de l'enseignement privé*, Montreal, Fédération des établissements d'enseignement privés.

Matthews, Julie (2002). International Education and Internationalization are not the Same as Globalization: Emerging Issues for Secondary Schools, *Journal of Studies in International Education*, vol. 6, no 4, p. 369-390.

McAndrew, Marie (2006). La réussite éducative des élèves issus de l'immigration: enfin au cœur du débat sur l'intégration?, *Options*, CSQ, spring-summer, p. 109-128.

McAndrew, Marie (2001). *Immigration et diversité à l'école. Le débat québécois dans une perspective comparative*, Montreal, Les Presses de l'Université de Montréal.

McAndrew, Marie, Ledent, Jacques and Aït-Saïd, Rachid (2005). *La réussite scolaire des jeunes des communautés noires au secondaire*, Montreal, Immigration et Métropoles, Publication no 26.

McMullen, Kathryn (2005). Student Achievement in Mathematics. The roles of attitudes, perceptions and family background, *Education Matters*, vol. 2, no 1, Ottawa, Statistics Canada, 81-004-XIE.

McNeil, Linda M. (2000). *Contradictions of Reform. Educational Costs of Standardized Testing*, New York, Routledge.

McQuaig, Linda (2002). *All you Can Eat : Greed, Lust and the New Capitalism*, Totonto, Penguin Books.

Meirieu, Philippe (2005b). *Lettre à un jeune professeur*, Paris, ESF Éditeur.

Meirieu, Philippe (2005a). *Nous mettrons nos enfants à l'école publique...*, Paris, Mille et une nuits.

Meirieu, Philippe (2004). L'école entre la pression consumériste et l'irresponsabilité sociale, in Claude Lessard and Philippe Meirieu (dir.), *L'obligation de résultats en éducation*, Québec City, Presses de l'Université Laval, p. 5-21.

Mercure, Daniel (dir.) (2001). *Une société-monde? Les dynamiques sociales de la mondialisation*, Québec City, Presses de l'Université Laval.

Meuret, Denis (2001). *Les recherches sur la réduction de la taille des classes*, IREDU, Université de Bourgogne, ‹cisad. adc. education. fr/hcee/documents/rapportmeuret rtc. rtf›.

Mialaret, Gaston and Vial, Jean (1981). *Histoire mondiale de l'éducation. Tome III: De 1815 à 1945. Tome IV: De 1945 à nos jours*, Paris, Presses Universitaires de France.

Migué, Jean-Luc and Marceau, Richard (1989). *Le monopole public de l'éducation: l'économie politique de la médiocrité*, Sainte-Foy, Presses de l'Université du Québec.

Ministère de la Culture et des Communications (2005). *La pratique culturelle en 2004—recueil statistique*, Québec City, MCC.

Ministère de l'Éducation, du Loisir et du Sport (2005d). *Indicateurs de l'éducation. Édition 2005*, Québec City, MELS.

Ministère de l'Éducation, du Loisir et du Sport (2005c). *L'école communautaire. Un carrefour pour la réussite des jeunes et le développement de la communauté. Rap-*

port de l'équipe de travail sur le développement de l'école communautaire, Québec City, MELS.

Ministère de l'Éducation, du Loisir et du Sport (2005b). *La veille ministérielle*, cédérom.

Ministère de l'Éducation, du Loisir et du Sport (2005a). *L'éducation: l'avenir du Québec. Rapport sur l'accès à l'éducation*, Québec City, MELS.

Ministère de l'Éducation du Québec (2004). L'éducation des populations scolaires dans les communautés autochtones du Québec, *Bulletin statistique de l'éducation*, no 30, May.

Ministère de l'Éducation du Québec (2003). *Les nouvelles dispositions de la Loi sur l'instruction publique*, Québec City, MEQ.

Ministère de l'Éducation du Québec (2002). *Pour réussir l'internationalisation de l'éducation... Une stratégie mutuellement avantageuse*, Québec City, MEQ.

Ministère de l'Éducation du Québec (1999). *Publicité et contributions financières à l'école*, Québec City, MEQ.

Ministère de l'Éducation du Québec (1997). *A New Direction for Success: Ministerial Plan of Action for the Reform of the Education System*, Québec City, MEQ.

Mintrop, Heinrich (2004). High-Stakes Accountability, State Oversight, and Educational Equity, *Teachers College Record*, vol. 106, no 11, p. 2128-2145.

Moberg, David (2004). How Edison Survived: Discredited and Broke, the School Privatizer Found an Unlikely White Knight, *The Nation*, March 15, p. 22.

Moll, Marita (2004). *Passing the Test. The False Promise of Standardized Testing*, Ottawa, Canadian Center for Policy Alternatives.

Molnar, Alex (2005b). Ivy-Covered Malls and Creeping Commercialism, *Educational Leadership*, February, p. 74-79.

Molnar, Alex (2005a). *School Commercialism. From Democratic Ideal to Market Commodity*, New York, Routledge.

Monkman, Karen and Baird, Mark (2002). Educational Change in the Context of Globalization, *Comparative Education Review*, vol. 46, no 4, p. 497-508.

Morin, Edgar (2001). Le monde comme notion sociologique, in Daniel Mercure (dir.), *Une société-monde? Les dynamiques sociales de la mondialisation*, Québec City, Presses de l'Université Laval, p. 191-197.

Morris, David (1997). Free Trade : The Great Destroyer, in Edward Goldsmith and Jerry Mander (dir.), *The Case Against the Global Economy : And for a Turn Toward the Local*, San Francisco, Sierra Club Books, p. 218-228.

Morrow, Raymond A. and Torres, Carlos Alberto (2000). The State, Globalization, and Educational Policy, in Nicholas C. Burbules and Carlos Alberto Torres (dir.), *Globalization and Education: Critical Perspectives*, New York and London, Routledge, p. 27-56.

Muijis, Daniel and al. (2004). Improving Schools in Socioeconomically Disadvantaged Areas—A Review of Research Evidence, *School Effectiveness and School Improvement*, vol. 15, no 2, p. 149-175.

Muller, Paul D. (2005). *Entretien ménager dans les écoles. les avantages de la sous-traitance*, Montreal, Montreal Economic Institute, august 25.

Neill, Monty (2003). Leaving Children Behind: How No Child Left Behind Will Fail Our Children, *Phi Delta Kappan*, November, p. 225-228.

Nelles, Wayne (2001). The World Education Market Comes to Canada, *Our Schools/ Our Selves*, January, p. 93-100.

Nelson, Howard F., Rosenberg, Bella and Van Metre, Nancy (2004). *Charter School Achievement on the 2003 National Assessment of Educational Progress*, Washington (D.C.), American Federation of Teachers.

Normand, Romuald (2003). Les comparaisons internationales: problèmes épisté-mologiques et questions de justice, *Éducation et Sociétés*, no 12, p. 73-89.

Oreopoulos, Philip (2005). *Canadian Compulsory School Laws and their Impact on Educational Attainment and future Earnings*, Ottawa, Statistics Canada, Research Paper no 251.

Orfield, Gary and Lee, Chungmei (2005). *Why Segregation Matters: Poverty and Educational Inequality*, The Civil Rights Project, Harvard University, Cambridge.

Organisation for Economic Co-operation and Development (2004). *Internationalisation and Trade in HigherEducation. Opportunities and Challenges*, Paris, OECD

Organisation for Economic Co-operation and Development (2001). *Cyberformation. Les enjeux du partenariat*, Paris, OECD.

Oxfam International (2005). *Paying the Price. Why rich countries must invest now in a war on Poverty*, Oxford, Oxfam Publishing.

Pagani, Linda and al. (2005). Une approche longitudinale-expérimentale sur l'impact des mesures d'éducation au préscolaire sur le rendement scolaire des enfants défa-vorisés de Montréal, *Éducation et francophonie*, vol. XXXIII, no 2, p. 224-246.

Parent Commission (1963-1966). *Report of the Royal Commission on Education in the Province of Quebec*, Québec City, Editour Officiel.

Parizeau, Jacques (1998). *Le Québec et la mondialisation. Une bouteille à la mer?*, Montreal, VLB Éditeur.

Payeur, Christian (1991). *Formation professionnelle. Éducation et monde du travail au Québec*, Montreal, CEQ and Les Éditions Saint-Martin.

Pêcheur, Julie (2002). Au secours, Nike et McDo envahissent les écoles!, *Le Nouvel Ob-servateur*, November 21-27, p. 20-21.

Pedulla, Joseph J. (2003). State-mandated Testing. What do Teachers Think?, *Educational Leadership*, November, p. 42-46.

Pelletier, Guy (2004). La décentralisation du système scolaire québécois: une variation sur un thème majeur, in Marjolaine Saint-Pierre and Luc Brunet (dir.), *De la décen-tralisation au partenariat. Administration en milieu scolaire*, Sainte-Foy, Presses de l'Université du Québec, p. 151-171.

Pelletier, Michelle and Rheault, Sylvie (2005). *La réussite scolaire des garçons et des filles. L'influence du milieu socioéconomique*, Québec City, MELS.

Pena-Ruiz, Henri (2005). *Qu'est-ce que l'école?*, Paris, Gallimard.

Perlstein, David (2005). «There Is No Escape... from the Ogre of Indoctrination»: George Counts and the Civic Dilemmas of Democratic Educators, in Larry Cuban and Dorothy Shipps (dir.), *Reconstructing the Common Good. Coping with intractable American Dilemmas*, Stanford, Stanford University Press, p. 51-67.

Petrella, Riccardo (2004). *Désir d'humanité. Le droit de rêver*, Montreal, Écosociété.

Petrella, Riccardo (2000). *L'éducation, victime de cinq pièges. À propos de la société de la connaissance*, Montreal, Fides.

Piketty, Thomas (2004). *L'impact de la taille des classes et de la ségrégation sociale sur la réussite scolaire dans les écoles françaises: une estimation à partir du panel primaire 1997*, Paris-Jourdan, École des hautes études en sciences sociales, ‹83.snuipp.fr/chiffres/piketty 2004.pdf›.

Pineault, Éric (2005). Vers un nouveau consensus de Washington?, *Asymétries*, no 1, p. 17-19.

Piotte, Jean-Marc (2003). Syndicalisme: démocratie et solidarité, in Marie Gagnon (dir.), *De mémoire vive. La CSQ depuis la Révolution tranquille*, Montreal, Lanctôt Éditeur, p. 295-303.

Plank, David N. and Sykes, Gary (2003). Why School Choice?, in David N. Plank and Gary Sykes (dir.), *Choosing Choice. School Choice in International Perspective*, New York, Teachers College Press, p. vii-xxi.

Polanyi, Karl (1944). *The Great Transformation : The Political and Economic Origins of our Time*, New-York, Farrar and Rinehart.

Polster, Claire and Newson, Janice (1998). Don't Count your Blessings: The Social Accomplishments of Performance Indicators, in J. Currie and J. Newson (dir.), *Universities and Globalization. Critical Perspectives*, London, Sage Publications, p. 173-191.

Popham, W. James (2005). How to Use PAP to Make AYP under NCLB, *Phi Delta Kappan*, June, p. 787-791.

Popkewitz, Thomas J. (2000). Reform as the Social Administration of the Child: Globalization of Knowledge and Power, in Nicholas C. Burbules and Carlos Alberto Torres (dir.), *Globalization and Education: Critical Perspectives*, New York and London, Routledge.

Porfilio, Brad and Hall, Julia (2005). «Power City» Politics & the Building of a Corporate School, *Journal for Critical Education Policy Studies*, vol. 3, no 1.

Poupeau, Frank (2003). La révolte des enseignants français. Décentraliser l'éducation pour mieux la privatiser, *Le Monde diplomatique*, June, p. 6.

Priestley, Mark (2002). Global discourses and National Reconstruction: The Impact of Globalization on Curriculum Policy, *The Curriculum Journal*, vol. 13, no 1, p. 121-138.

Princiotta, Daniel and Chapman, Christopher (2006). *Homeschooling in the United States: 2003*, Washington (D.C.), U. S. Department of Education, National Center for Education Statistics.

Proulx, Jean-Pierre (1987). Devant la concurrence de l'école privée, l'école publique se lance en campagne de marketing, *Le Devoir*, August 31, p. 1.

Ramonet, Ignacio (2001). Enseigner à l'heure de la mondialisation, in *Enseigner, c'est s'engager de A à Z. Actes du Colloque de la Fédération des syndicats de l'enseignement*, Québec City, FSE, D11227.

Reeves, Hubert and Lenoir, Frédéric (2003). *Mal de terre*, Paris, Éditions du Seuil.

Reich, Rob (2002). The Civic Perils of Homeschooling, *Educational Leadership*, April, p. 56-59.

Rioux, Christian (2005). *Éloge de la gratuité, L'annuaire du Québec 2006*, Montreal, Fides.

Robertson, Heather-Jane (2003). «Incent» This!, *Phi Delta Kappan*, May, p. 713-714.

Robertson, Heather-Jane (2002). *Why P3 Schools are D4 Schools or How Private-Public Partnerships Lead to Disillusionment, Dirty Dealings and Debt*, British Columbia, CCPA, ‹www.bctf.ca/Education/NotForSale/privatization/WhyP3SchoolsAreD4 Schools. html›.

Robertson, Heather-jane (1999). In Canada: Son of One, *Phi Delta Kappan*, September, p. 91-92.

Robertson, Susan L. (2000). *A Class Act. Changing Teachers' Work, the State, and Globalization*, New York, Falmer Press.

Robertson, Susan L., Bonal, Xavier and Dale, Roger (2002). GATS and the Education Service Industry: The Politics of Scale and Global Reterritorialization, *Comparative Education Review*, vol. 46, no 4, p. 472-496.

Robinson, Chris (2004). Universitas 21: A Network for International Higher Education, in David Teather (dir.), *Consortia. International Networking Alliances of Universities*, Victoria, Melbourne University Press, p. 178-190.

Rocher, Guy (2001). La mondialisation: un phénomène pluriel, in Daniel Mercure (dir.), *Une société-monde? Les dynamiques sociales de la mondialisation*, Québec City, Presses de l'Université Laval, p. 17- 31.

Roman, Joël (2005). Identités et laïcité. Les dynamiques de l'engagement social en question, *La Revue de la CFDT*, numéro hors-série, November-December.

Ross, Steven M. and al. (2004). Using School Reform Models to Improve Reading Achievement: A Longitudinal Study of Direct Instruction and Success For All in an Urban District, *Journal of Education for Students Placed at Risk*, vol. 9, no 4, p. 357-388.

Rouillard, Jacques (1989). *Histoire du syndicalisme québécois*, Montreal, Boréal.

Roy, Gilles and Deniger, Marc-André (2003). Des mesures compensatoires à l'obligation de résultat—Bilan critique des politiques scolaires d'intervention auprès des milieux défavorisés québécois, *Notes de recherche*, no 49, Québec City, CSQ.

Roy, Gilles and Deniger, Marc-André (2001). *Enquête auprès des membres votants des conseils d'établissement des écoles du Québec, Rapport final*, Québec City, CRIRES.

Roy, Sylvie (2003). *Pour améliorer les pratiques éducatives: des données d'enquête sur les jeunes*, Québec City, MEQ.

Rumberger, Russell W. and Palardy, Gregory J. (2005). Does Segregation Still Matter? The Impact of Student Composition on Academic Achievement in High School, *Teachers College Record*, vol. 107, no 9, p. 1999-2045.

Russell, Michael, Higgins, Jennifer and Raczek, Anastasia (2004). Accountability, California Style: Counting or Accounting?, *Teachers College Record*, vol. 106, no 11, p. 2102-2127.

Sader, Emir (2006). Alternatives latino-américaines, *Le Monde diplomatique*, February, p. 1 and 16-17.

St-Jacques, Marcel and Sévigny, Dominique (2003). *Défavorisation des familles avec enfants en milieu montréalais*, Montreal, Comité de gestion de la taxe scolaire de l'île de Montréal.

Saint-Pierre, Céline (2001). Éduquer autrement pour un monde complexe et pluraliste, in Daniel Mercure (dir.), *Une société-monde? Les dynamiques sociales de la mondialisation*, Québec City, Presses de l'Université Laval, p. 275- 284.

Saint-Pierre, Marjolaine (2004). La décentralisation scolaire en action: le processus de prise de décision en partenariat, in Marjolaine Saint-Pierre and Luc Brunet (dir.), *De la décentralisation au partenariat. Administration en milieu scolaire*, Sainte-Foy, Presses de l'Université du Québec, p. 121-149.

Salmi, Jamil (2003). Construction des sociétés du savoir: nouveaux défis pour l'enseignement supérieur, in G. Breton and M. Lambert (dir.), *Universities and Globalisation : Private Linkages, Public Trust*, Paris, Unesco/Économica/Presses de l'Université Laval, p. 51-68.

Sarjala, Jukka (2005). Why Finland Ranks High in Public Education, *Our Schools/ Our Selves*, vol. 14, no 4, p. 95-107.

Saul, Raston John (2005). *The Collapse of Globalism and the Reinvention of the World*, Toronto, Penguin Canada.

Savage, Christine (2005). *The National Report on International Students in Canada 2002*, Ottawa, Canadian Bureau for International Education.

Saysset, Valérie (2005). *Regard sur la formation professionnelle. Une enquête auprès d'élèves du 2e cycle du secondaire*, Québec City, MELS.

Scholte, Jan Aart (1997). Global Capitalism and the State, *International Affairs*, vol. 73, no 3, p. 427-452.

Scott, Peter (1998). Massification, Internationalization and Globalization, in Peter Scott (dir.), *The Globalization of Higher Education*, Buckingham, Open University Press, p. 108-129.

Seidman, Karen (2005). Pearson Board Might Run New School in China, *The Gazette*, February 8, p. A4.

Sévigny, Dominique (2003). *Impact de la défavorisation socioéconomique sur la diplomation des élèves inscrits dans les écoles secondaires publiques de l'île de Montréal*, Montreal, Comité de gestion de la taxe scolaire de l'île de Montréal.

Shaker, Erika (2004). The Devil in the Details: The P3 Experience in Nova Scotia Schools, *Perspectives*, Ottawa, CTF, p. 7-10.

Shaker, Erika (1999). Higher Education Limited: Private Money, Private Agendas, *Education Limited*, vol. 1, no 4, Ottawa, CCPA, p. ii-ix.

Shipps, Dorothy (2000). L'école des managers, *Le Courrier de l'Unesco*, november, p. 19-20.

Sinclair, Scott and Traynor, Ken (2004). *Divide and Conquer. The FTAA, U.S. trade strategy and public services in the Americas*, Brussels, Public Services International.

Sklair, Leslie (1999). Competing Conceptions of Globalization, *Journal of World-Systems Research*, vol. 5, no 2, p. 143-162.

Smith, Michael (2001). La mondialisation a-t-elle un effet important sur les marchés du travail des pays riches?, in Daniel Mercure (dir.), *Une société-monde? Les dynamiques sociales de la mondialisation*, Québec City, Presses de l'Université Laval, p. 201-214.

Sousa Santos, Boaventura de (2001). La globalisation contre-hégémonique et la réinvention de l'émancipation sociale, in Daniel Mercure (dir.), *Une société-monde? Les dynamiques sociales de la mondialisation*, Québec City, Presses de l'Université Laval, p. 45-63.

Stevenson, Kathryn (1999). Family characteristicsof Problem Kids, *Canadian Social Trends*, winter, p. 2-7.

Stiglitz, Joseph E. (2003). *The roaring nineties : a new History of the World's Most Prosperous Decade*, New-York : W.W. Norton.

Stiglitz, Joseph E. (2002). *Globalization and its Discontents*, New-York, W.W. Norton.

Suarez-Orozco, Carola (2004). Formulating Identity in a Globalized World, in Marcelo Suarez-Orozco and Desirée B. Qin-Hilliard (dir.), *Globalization, Culture and Education in the New Millennium*, Los Angeles and London, University of California Press, p. 173-202.

Sunderman, Gail L. and al. (2004). *Listening to Teachers: Classroom Realities and No Child Left Behind*, The Civil Rights Project, Harvard University, Cambridge (Mass.).

Talbot, Geneviève (2005). La reconnaissance des acquis et des compétences au Québec: à l'aube d'une relance, *Notes de recherche*, no 55, Québec City, CSQ.

Tavan, Chloé (2004). Public, privé. Trajectoires scolaires et inégalités sociales, *Éducation & formations*, no 69, p. 37-48.

Taylor, Charles (1992). *Multiculturalism and « the Politics of Recognition »*, Princeton, Princeton University Press.

Teather, David (2004). The Changing Context of Higher Education: Massification, Globalization and Internationalization, in D. Teather (dir.), *Consortia. International Networking Alliances of Universities*, Victoria, Melbourne University Press, p. 8-27.

Terrail, Jean-Pierre (2004). *École, l'enjeu démocratique*, Paris, La Dispute.

Terrail, Jean-Pierre (2002). *De l'inégalité scolaire*, Paris, La Dispute.

Tison, Marie (2005). L'assemblage final des avions, un gros jeu de construction international, *La Presse*, April 16, p. A7.

Tondreau, Jacques (2003). Diversifier sans sélectionner: le défi de l'école publique, *Options*, no 22, CSQ p. 41-64.

Torres, Carlos Alberto (2002b). Globalization, Education, and Citizenship: Solidarity versus Markets?, *American Educational Research Journal*, vol. 39, no 2, p. 363-378.

Torres, Carlos Alberto (2002a). The State, Privatization and Educational Policy: A Critique of Neoliberalism in Latin America and Some Ethical and Political Implications, *Comparative Education*, vol. 38, no 4, p. 365-385.

Tremblay, Karine (2005). Academic Mobility and Immigration, *Journal of Studies in International Education*, vol. 9, no 3, p. 196-228.

Tyack, David (2003). *Seeking Common Ground. Public Schools in a Diverse Society*, Cambridge and London, Harvard University Press.

Tyack, David and Cuban, Larry (1995). *Tinkering Toward Utopia. A Century of Public School Reform*, Cambridge (Mass.), Harvard University Press.

United State Department of Education (2004). *A Guide to Education and No Child Left Behind*, Washington, U. S. Department of Education.

Van Haecht, Anne (2001). *L'école des inégalités*, Mons, Éditions Talus d'approche.

Van Zanten, Agnès (2001). *L'école de la périphérie. Scolarité et ségrégation en banlieue*, Paris, Presses Universitaires de France.

Venne, Michel (2004). L'école privée… publique, *Le Devoir*, décembre 13, p. A7.

Walford, Geoffrey (2003). School Choice and Educational Change in England and Wales, in David N. Plank and Gary Sykes (dir.), *Choosing Choice. School Choice in International Perspective*, New York, Teachers College Press, p. 68-91.

Wallach, Lori (2001). Cinq ans d'OMC: le bilan. Seattle dans son contexte, in Edward Goldsmith and Jerry Mander (dir.), *Le procès de la mondialisation*, Paris, Fayard, p. 289-311.

Wallerstein, Immanuel (2003). The Ambiguities of Free Trade, *Commentaries*, no 127, décembre 15, ‹fbc.binghamton. edu/127en. htm›.

Wallerstein, Immanuel (2002b). The U.S.-Iraqi War, Seen from the longue durée, *Commentaries*, no 99, October 15, ‹fbc.binghamton. edu/99en. htm›.

Wallerstein, Immanuel (2002a). *La mondialisation n'est pas nouvelle. Postface à la deuxième édition de Le capitalisme historique*, Paris, Éditions La Découverte.

Walzer, Michael (2004). *Morale maximale, morale minimale*, Paris, Bayard.

Walzer, Michael (1984). *Spheres of Justice. A Defense of Pluralism and Equality*, New-York, Basic Books.

Walzer, Michael (1997). *Pluralisme et démocratie*, Paris, Éditions Esprit.

Warren, Mark R. (2005). Communities and Schools: A New View of Urban Education Reform, *Harvard Educational Review*, vol. 75, no 2, p. 133-173.

Washburn, Jennifer (2005). *University Inc.: The Corporate Corruption of American Higher Education*, New York, Basic Books.

Watson, James L. (2004). Globalization in Asia: Anthropological Perspectives, in Marcelo Suarez-Orozco and Desirée B. Qin-Hilliard (dir.), *Globalization, Culture and Education in the New Millennium*, Los Angeles and London, University of California Press, p. 141-172.

Weber, Louis (2005). L'école républicaine mise en bière, *Le Monde diplomatique*, March, p. 8.

Weiner, Harvey (2003). Le financement de l'éducation publique au Canada: l'AGCS est-il un facteur clé?, CTF, see ‹www.ctf-fce/F/NOTRE/mondial/mondial. htm›.

Weiner, Lois (2005). Neoliberalism, Teacher Unionism, and the Future of Public Education, *New Politics*, vol. X, no 2, ‹www.wpunj.edu/~newpol/issue38/Weiner38.htm›.

Weinstock, Daniel M. (2004). L'actualité du bien commun, *Éthique publique*, vol. 6, no 1, p. 117-123.

Welch, Anthony (2002). Going Global? Internationalizing Australian Universities in a Time of Global Crisis, *Comparative Education Review*, vol. 46, no 4, p. 433-471.

Wells, Amy-Stuart, Lopez, Alejandra, Scott, Janelle et Holme, Jennifer J. (1999). Charter Schools as Postmodern Paradox: Rethinking Social Stratification in an Age of Deregulated School Choice, *Harvard Educational Review*, vol. 69, no 2, p. 172-204.

Wells, Amy-Stuart, Slayton, J. and Scott, Janelle (2002). Defining Democracy in the Neoliberal Age: Charter School Reform and Educational Consumption, *American Educational Research Journal*, vol. 39, no 2, p. 337-261.

Wenglinsky, Harold (2004). Facts or Critical Thinking Skills? What NAEP Results Say, *Educational Leadership*, september, p. 32-35.

Whittle, Chris (2005). The Promise of Public/Private Partnerships, *Educational Leadership*, February, p. 34-36.

Whitty, Geoff, Power, Sally and Halpin, David (1998). *Devolution and Choice in Education. The School, the State and the Market*, Buckingham, Open University Press.

Williams, Nancy (2003). Voices. Thinking Outside the Bubble, *Educational Leadership*, November, p. 82-83.

Willms, Douglas J. (2004). Provincial Variation in Reading Scores of 15-year-olds, *Canadian Social Trends*, winter, p. 31-36.

Wong, Kenneth K. and Nicotera, Anna C. (2004). Brown v. Board of Education and the Coleman Report: Social Science Research and the Debate on Educational Equality, *Peabody Journal of Education*, vol. 79, no 2, p. 122-135.

World Trade Organization (2001b). *Communication from New Zealand. Negociating Proposal for Education Services*, Geneva, WTO, doc. S/CSS/W/93.

World Trade Organization (2001a). *Communication from Australia. Proposal for Education Services*, Geneva, WTO, doc. S/CSS/W/110.

World Trade Organization (2000). *Communication from the United States. Higher (Tertiary) Education, Adult Education and Training*, Geneva, WTO, doc. S/CSS/W/23.

Zhang, Xuelin and Palameta, Boris (2006). *Participation in Adult Schooling and its Earnings Impact in Canada*, Ottawa, Statistics Canada, no 11F0019MIE.

List of Acronyms

ADQ   Action démocratique du Québec

AEC   Attestation d'études collégiales

AFT   American Federation of Teachers

ALBA   Alternativa Bolivariana para la América

ATTAC   Association pour la taxation des transactions financières pour l'aide aux citoyens (Association for the Taxation of Financial Transactions for the Aid of Citizens)

AUCC   Association of Universities and Colleges of Canada

CAUT   Canadian Association of University Teachers

CCPA   Canadian Centre for Policy Alternatives

CE   Conseil d'établissement

Cégep   Collège d'enseignement général et professionnel

CEQ   Centrale de l'enseignement du Québec (now CSQ)

CMEC   Council of Ministers of Education, Canada

CRIRES	Centre de recherche et d'intervention sur la réussite scolaire
CSDM	Commission scolaire de Montréal
CSE	Conseil supérieur de l'éducation
CSQ	Centrale des syndicats du Québec
CTF	Canadian Teachers Federation
DEC	Diplôme d'études collégiales
DEP	Diplôme d'études professionnelles
DES	Diplôme d'études secondaires
DI	Direct Instruction
EFA	Education for All
EI	Education International
EMO	Educational Management Organization
FSE	Fédération des syndicats de l'enseignement (CSQ)
FSU	Fédération syndicale unitaire (France)
FTAA	Free Trade Area of the Americas
GATS	General Agreement on Trade in Services
GATT	General Agreement on Tariffs and Trade
GED	General Education Diploma
GGE	Greenhouse Gas Emissions
GMO	Genetically Modified Organism
HEC	École des hautes études commerciales
HIV	Human Immunodeficiency Virus
ICEA	Institut de coopération pour l'éducation des adultes
ICFTU	International Confederation of Free Trade Unions
ILO	International Labour Organization
IMF	International Monetary Fund

INAC	Indian and Northern Affairs Canada
IREDU	Institut de recherche sur l'éducation (Université de Bourgogne)
LEA	Local Education Authority
MAI	Multilateral Agreement on Investment
MEI	Montreal Economic Institute
MELS	Ministère de l'Éducation, du Loisir et du Sport
MEQ	Ministère de l'Éducation du Québec
MITI	Ministry of International Trade and Industry
NAEP	National Assessment of Educational Progress
NAFTA	North American Free Trade Agreement
NCLB	No Child Left Behind
OECD	Organisation for Economic Co-operation and Development
Ofsted	Office for Standards in Education
PELO	Programme d'enseignement des langues d'origine
PISA	Program for International Student Assessment
PPP	Public-private Partership
QFL	Quebec Federation of Labour
SAIP	School Achievement Indicators Program
TRIPS	Agreement on Trade-Related Aspects of Intellectual Property Rights
UN	United Nations
Unesco	United Nations Educational, Scientific and Cultural Organization
UQAM	Université du Québec à Montréal
UQAR	Université du Québec à Rimouski
WCL	World Confederation of Labour

WHO   World Health Organization

WSF   World Social Forum

WTO   World Trade Organization

YNN   Youth News Network